CRISIS AND CONTINUITY

THE STATE OF MILAN IN THE SEVENTEENTH CENTURY

SWISS

CANTONS

St. Gotthard
Pass

GRISONS

ENGADINE

Simplon
Pass

Maloja
Pass

Domodossola

Bellinzona

VALTELLINE

STATE

Lake
Maggiore

Lugano

Lake
Como

VALSASSINA

VENETIAN

Varese

Asso

Lécco

DUCHY

Arona

COMO

BERGAMO

Lake
Garda

REPUBLIC

Gallarate

Busto Arsizio

Monza

BRESCIA

OF

Sesia River

Naviglio

Magenta

Martesana

Caravaggio

NOVARA

Grande

MILAN

Soncino

OF

VERCELLI

Abbiategrasso

Ticino River

Adda

CREMA

VIGEVANO

LODI

River

MANTUA

TURIN

Casale

PAVIA

Codogno

CREMONA

MONFERRATO

Valenza

Po River

MILAN

PIACENZA

Po River

Casalmaggiore

SAVOY

ALLESSANDRIA

TORTONA

DUCHY

PARMA

Cherasco

Novi

OF

DUCHY OF

REPUBLIC

GENOA

OF

GENOA

PARMA

MODENA

TYRRHENIAN   SEA

0   20   40

Km

CRISIS AND CONTINUITY

*The Economy of Spanish Lombardy
in the Seventeenth Century*

DOMENICO SELLA

HARVARD UNIVERSITY PRESS
CAMBRIDGE, MASSACHUSETTS
LONDON, ENGLAND
1979

Library of Congress Cataloging in Publication Data

Sella, Domenico.
  Crisis and continuity: the economy of Spanish Lombardy in the seventeenth century.

    Bibliography: p.
    Includes index.
    1. Lombardy—Economic conditions. 2. Lombardy—
History—17th century. I. Title.
HC307.L8S42   330.9′45′207   78-27184
ISBN 0-674-17675-8

To the memory of Piero

Preface

Despite its diminutive size, Spanish Lombardy has been the subject of an unusually large literature. The economic crisis that swept it in the seventeenth century has, in particular, attracted the attention of scores of writers, from contemporaries who suffered its consequences and searched for remedies and scapegoats to later scholars puzzled by the seeming failure of its economy to sustain the astonishing level of prosperity it had known since the late Middle Ages and to effect a transition into the age of modern capitalism, on whose threshold it had apparently stood at the close of the sixteenth century.

Adding yet another book to an already rich bibliography calls, therefore, for a word of explanation if not of apology. The present book has its roots not only in the fascination I have long felt for the Italian seicento, but also in my dissatisfaction with some features of the existing literature. One is its strong urban bias: the economic and social vicissitudes of the Lombard cities have attracted far greater attention than those of the surrounding countryside, despite the fact that the latter provided by far the largest employment, as well as being the largest source of income. To a considerable extent, then, what follows is an attempt at doing justice to the neglected world of fields and farms, villages and market towns, peasants and rural craftsmen.

A second reason for my dissatisfaction is the penumbra of uncertainty and conjecture that has surrounded the causes of Lombardy's crisis in the seventeenth century: from the very time of the crisis itself down to our own time a multiplicity, not to say a surfeit, of quite plausible causes—ranging from Spanish misrule to the devastations of war, from foreign competition to the ravages of the plague, from taxation to the so-called defection of the native bourgeoisie—have been proposed. Yet, all too often these causes have been accepted on grounds of plausibility rather than on the strength of clear evidence, and too little effort has been made to assess the relative weight of individual causes.

Lastly, in the course of my own research I developed serious misgivings about the generally accepted view of the seventeenth-century crisis as an irreparable break in the economic and social texture of Lombard history. Except for an occasional discordant voice, the consensus on this point has been that, as a result of that crisis, little was left of a glorious and promising past and that by 1700 Lombardy had sunk to the condition of a stagnant backwater largely cut off from the mainstream of European economic life. Given this grim view of the seventeenth century, Lombardy's rebounding vitality in the late eighteenth century and the fact that in the nineteenth century it became the stage for the earliest and most successful upsurge of industrialization in the Italian peninsula have generally and inevitably been regarded as entirely new developments totally unconnected with past achievements. The further my research proceeded, however, the stronger I felt that this view had been unduly colored by the urban bias in the historiography; I also came to realize that a close study of conditions and developments in the countryside could provide the missing links between the Lombardy of the Renaissance and that of the Risorgimento.

I was first drawn to my subject many years ago when I was engaged in a study of wages and labor conditions in seventeenth-century Lombardy, a study funded by the Rockefeller Foundation and since published. It was then that I began to gather some of the source material that eventually found its way into these pages. In 1967 a grant from the Italian National Research Council (CNR) enabled me to pursue further research in Milan; and to that city I was able to return for shorter periods of time thanks to grants from the Graduate School of the University of Wisconsin in Madison. A year spent at the Institute for Advanced Study in Princeton as a member of the School of Historical Studies, during which I was jointly funded by the Institute itself and by the University of Wisconsin Graduate School, provided me with time and an ideal environment, intellectually and physically, for working on a first draft of my book. To all these institutions I wish to express here again my sincere appreciation.

I feel, of course, deeply indebted to all those scholars whose published work I have so often drawn upon in the course of my research and without which my own contribution to the subject would have been all the poorer. I owe, however, a very special debt of gratitude to those colleagues who have graciously and repeatedly given me their time and advice. Over the years my friend and former mentor Professor Carlo M. Cipolla of the University of California at Berkeley has been a constant source of encouragement and advice; he read the entire manuscript and I have greatly benefited from his suggestions and criticisms. Professor Giovanni Vigo of the University of Pavia has also been a gracious reader and a stimulating critic. If, despite their efforts, errors of fact or of judgment still mar these pages, the responsibility and the blame are, needless to say, wholly mine: occasionally I have chosen to disregard their advice and I have done so at my own peril. Since I began doing research for this book, professors Aldo De Maddalena of Bocconi University in Milan and Dante E. Zanetti of the University of Pavia have kindly answered my innumerable queries and have freely shared with me their expertise in the economic and social history of seventeenth-century Lombardy. My colleague Maureen F. Mazzaoui read Chapter 1 and offered some very useful comments and suggestions on the textile industries. During my stay at the Institute for Advanced Study I was fortunate in being able to discuss aspects of my work with professors Felix Gilbert of that institute, Pierre Deyon of the University of Lille, and Stanley J. Chojnacki of Michigan State University and to benefit from their comments and insights.

Lastly, I wish to express my thanks to the directors and staffs of the Archivio di Stato, Archivio Storico Civico, and Archivio della Curia Arcivescovile in Milan, as well as of the Memorial Library of the University of Wisconsin in Madison, for their unstinted cooperation; to Signor Enrico Gavazzeni for his help in identifying some of the most recondite riches of the Archivio di Stato; to the cartographic laboratory of the University of Wisconsin in Madison for their expert assistance in preparing the figures; and to the secretarial staff of the University of Wisconsin history department for typing most of the manuscript.

Contents

CRISIS AND CONTINUITY

CHAPTER I

THE PARADISE OF CHRISTENDOME

To the end of the sixteenth century, Lombardy, particularly its western portion then known as the State of Milan, enjoyed a reputation as one of the most prosperous corners of Europe. Small in size, even by the standards of a notoriously fragmented peninsula, and much reduced, by a series of territorial losses, from the ephemeral grandeur it had attained under the Visconti and Sforza dukes, the State of Milan continued to elicit lavish praise for the opulence of its landscape, the size of its cities, the skill of its craftsmen. In his survey of the world's "most famous kingdomes and commonwealths," Giovanni Botero, writing toward the end of the century, waxed ecstatic when he broached the subject of a land where he had long served and which he knew well: "What shall we say," he wrote, "of the State of Milan? Is there a duchy more abundant in victuals, grain, rice, livestock, cheeses, wines, and flax, more replete with artificers and traffic, more densely populated, or more conveniently located?" And he concluded that here was "the richest and most civil part of Italy, a fact borne out by the splendor of its cities."[1] Nor was he alone in his enthusiastic appraisal of the small Italian province which, long coveted and bitterly fought over by the Valois and the Hapsburgs, in 1535 had finally fallen under the latter's rule and become the capstone of Charles V's hegemony in Italy. Writing in 1549, an English visitor used terms not unlike those Botero was to adopt forty years later: "As for the richnesse and the beauty of the country, I am afeard to speak of, lest to him that never saw it I should seem overlarge in the due praising of it . . . Nevertheless . . . this much I will say: that such another piece of ground for beautiful cities and townes, fields, and pastures, and for plenty of flesh, fowl, fresh water fish, grain, wine and fruites is not to be found again in all our familiar regions."[2] Milan, the capital of the state, impressed visitors with its size, which they invariably overestimated, and its wealth, which seemed dazzling. "Not without reason," wrote a diplomatic envoy in the 1590s," it has earned the title of great [for] it is commonly reckoned that the souls of Milan number 350,000."[3] Michel de Montaigne, who had been there in 1580, mistakenly asserted that Milan "is the largest city in Italy," but was basically correct when he added that "it is large, full of all sorts of artisans and merchants."[4] And, in the words of a Venetian diplomatic agent, Milan "can be called a nursery of manual arts and the fountain-head of pomp and luxury."[5]

What travelers could see just outside the city walls, in the luscious plain that stretches south of Milan all the way to the banks of the Po, evoked equally strong expressions of admiration. Philippe de Commines has recorded for us the enormous impression the Lombard plain made on him when he first sighted it in 1495, as he accompanied the French king Charles VIII on his first Italian campaign: "Coming down from the mountains we discovered the spacious countryside of Lombardy, the fairest and finest and most bountiful in the world." And, familiar as he was with the Low Countries, he had noticed at once two features of Lombard agriculture that reminded him of his homeland. "There are canals everywhere as in Flanders," he wrote and, with a clear reference to intensive farming and the disappearance of the fallow, he added, "the soil here never rests."[6] A century later, a German traveler noted that: "here pasture is ever plentiful thanks to the abundance of irrigation, for in this territory one can see three or four canals built with great ingenuity one above the other, something surely wonderful and very convenient. Whereby three or four times a year and even five is hay mowed in the said meadows. And this is why milk is produced to make cheese in such quantity as to seem unbelievable to those who have not seen it."[7]

In those same years, Sir Thomas Sherley, as he passed through Lombardy on his homeward journey from Constantinople, compared the Lodi district, "low and full of ditches," to the Low Countries, but went on to notice a distinctive feature of the Lombard landscape, namely the rows of trees festooned with vines that lined the arable fields: "The fields are full of trees planted by man his hande, in sutche order that they hinder not the growth of corne under them, and the vines growe agaynst them so that a man has his breade, wyne, and fewell in one field."[8] Intensive land use, the careful layout of fields, irrigation, density of population, rich towns—all this was summed up in a literary flourish by another English traveler when he dubbed Lombardy "the very Paradise and Canaan of Christendome."[9]

The eulogies that celebrated sixteenth-century Lombardy as an exceptionally populous land studded with thriving cities and enjoying an enviable level of economic well-being are confirmed by a good deal of independent evidence. To begin with, recent research on population, while rejecting some of the extravagant figures so popular among contemporaries, has shown that at the close of the sixteenth century the State of Milan, after several decades of sustained demographic expansion—temporarily interrupted but not reversed by the plague in 1576—numbered about 1,200,000 souls. This was an impressive figure indeed at a time when the population of the entire Italian peninsula stood at about 13 million, that of France close to 18 million and that of the British Isles probably still under the 7 million mark.[10] It meant, in fact, that with a surface of but 16,000 square kilometers, the State of Milan had a density of seventy-five people per square kilometer, or nearly twice that of Italy as a whole. This rather exceptional density, which was unparalleled in Europe outside the Low Countries, was matched by a high level of urbanization. There is, of course, considerable uncertainty as to which communities should be considered urban rather than rural centers, the more so as agricultural activities in those days often penetrated the life even of sizable towns, thus making a hard and fast distinction based on economic functions rather artificial.[11] However, we can confidently label as urban those communities that contemporaries called *città* as opposed to *borghi* (market towns) and *terre* (villages). Although the term *città* originally applied to episcopal sees and continued to have strong legal and administrative overtones,[12] by the sixteenth century it covered Lombardy's nine largest population centers. First among them, of course, was Milan, with a population of about 120,000; next came four cities (Cremona, Pavia, Como, and Lodi) ranging in size between 30,000 and 10,000; lastly there were four smaller cities (Novara, Tortona, Alessandria, and Vigevano) with less (and

generally much less) than 10,000 people.[13] Altogether, the population
of those nine cities can be estimated at about 240,000, or one-fifth of
the state's entire population. To this unmistakably urban core should
be added the population of a score of market towns, such as
Caravaggio, Casalmaggiore, Domodossola, Gallarate, Monza, and
Soncino, whose size was comparable to that of the lesser città and
whose residents, as will be seen, were primarily engaged in
commercial and manufacturing activities typical of urban centers. All
told, it seems safe to set the urban population of the State of Milan at
about 300,000, or 25 percent of the total—a percentage that can be
considered high by the standards of sixteenth-century Europe.

It is much harder to assess with any degree of accuracy the validity
of contemporary comments about the prosperity and indeed the
opulence of Lombard agriculture—all the more so in that what
travelers generally described in glowing terms was that portion of the
Lombard countryside that lies south of Milan and extends to the banks
of the Po river; this is the low plain, known as la bassa, which formed
then, as it does now, the pride and jewel of rural Lombardy. Within
that region, the travelers comment mostly on the area between Milan,
Lodi, and Cremona, where by 1600 irrigation had made the greatest
progress. The low plain, however, covered but 40 percent of the total
surface of the state and not all of it was irrigated. Therefore, if we are
to avoid a lopsided and overly optimistic picture of rural Lombardy,
we must broaden our purview to include the entire state in its
sixteenth-century borders and attempt to do justice to the astonishing
diversity of its landscape.[14]

A cross-section of Lombardy reveals, from north to south, a
succession of four main zones, each with distinctive soil conditions,
vegetation, and types of settlement. Starting at the extreme north, one
first encounters the mountain zone, with elevations above 700 meters,
which covers about 30 percent of the total surface of the State of
Milan. With its rugged terrain and interminable winters—which make
arable farming virtually impossible except on narrow terraces carved
out with incredible patience and labor from the lower flanks of the
mountains—the mountain zone had then but two main resources,
besides mineral deposits in a few select areas, namely, coniferous
forests and natural pastures. The former, however, were then of

limited economic value, owing to the difficulty of hauling the timber down to the plain. In the words of a sixteenth-century source, "from the woods located in the mountains, unless they be near a river or a lake, virtually no timber is supplied and it is hardly ever cut except for the use of local people."[15] Mountain pastures, on the other hand, offered far better prospects and were commonly utilized to graze cattle during the short, cool summers, at the end of which the cattle were driven to the plain or fed in stalls.

The basically pastoral economy of the mountain zone gives way, between 700 and 300 meters of altitude, to the more diversified economy of the hill zone. Covering about 20 percent of the territory, it was, until the massive deforestations of the late nineteenth and early twentieth centuries, the natural habitat of the deciduous forest and the man-made habitat of two important crops, the chestnut and the grape vine, with only a fraction of the land being devoted to arable crops such as rye and millet or, exceptionally in the vicinity of Lakes Como and Maggiore, to olive groves.

To the south of the indented pattern of morainic hills, between 300 and 150 meters of altitude, lies the high plain, a band 20 to 30 kilometers wide covering about one-tenth of Lombardy and characterized by coarse, porous soils (gravels and alluvial sands), low water tables, and deeply incised rivers and streams. As such, it is naturally dry and ill-suited for irrigation; its western portion, which has especially acid and coarse soils, consists primarily of heaths interspersed with woodlands and poor arable fields; its eastern portion is more suitable to farming and has, traditionally and typically, been the home of interculture (*coltura promiscua*), in which fields sown with cereals also host fruit trees, mulberry trees, and vines. But despite such intensive and ingenious utilization of the soil, farming in the high dry plain remained caught, to the end of the sixteenth century and beyond, in the vicious circle all too common in the past: low yields could only have been corrected with the generous use of fertilizers; yet dry conditions and the lack of adequate irrigation prevented the development of stock raising and thus restricted the availability of manure and perpetuated low yields. "The land badly needs manuring," it was pointed out in the sixteenth century, "and yet no hay is produced, no cattle is raised, and manure is therefore scarce."[16]

Further south, in the low plain with its celebrated, almost legendary fertility, the vicious circle was broken and replaced by a "virtuous circle."[17] There the permeable coarse gravels and sands give way to finer alluvial sediments; not only does the soil retain its moisture, but the slow-running, meandering rivers and natural springs (*fontanili* or *risorgive*) have provided ideal conditions for the creation of a network of irrigation canals and the development of a system of convertible husbandry in which arable farming and stock raising are closely integrated, thus ensuring high yields per unit of land. The systematic harnessing of water for irrigation purposes and the transformation of the low plain from a land of swamps and marshes to one of intensive, highly complex farming got under way as early as the twelfth century, albeit on a limited scale, at the initiative of the Cistercian monks; it was massively pursued first by the medieval communes (Milan, Lodi, Cremona) and later by the Visconti and Sforza dukes, only to be fully completed in the nineteenth century. By the sixteenth century, at any rate, over large portions of the low plain, notably in the triangle between Milan, Lodi and Cremona, an elaborate irrigation system was in operation, and the farming methods that were practiced bore a striking resemblance to the convertible husbandry of the Low Countries. Sixteenth-century land surveys indicate that little land lay uncultivated and swamps had virtually disappeared; on cultivated land, cereal crops alternated periodically with artificial grasses and industrial crops such as flax, thus dispensing with the need for periodic fallowing. Lastly, stall feeding had largely replaced the grazing of cattle on open, natural pastureland, and a flourishing dairy industry had become firmly established.[18]

The farming that was practiced in the dry plain and hill zone stood in sharp contrast with the convertible husbandry of the irrigated plain. On the dry soils just south of the Po River, for instance, "the land that is used to raise crops must rest every year"; on the hills near Alessandria, in the words of a local farmer, "the soil is dry and poor . . . and we have no choice but to let it rest every other year—and if we did not do so, we would get nothing out of it"; and another farmer pointed out that "the soil is barren . . . and must lie fallow one year and be under crop the next."[19] Much the same could have been said of the dry plain and the foothills north of Milan.[20]

The sharp differences in climate, vegetation, and farming methods that characterize the four main agricultural zones of Lombardy have traditionally been reflected in equally sharp differences in the density of settlement, the size of holdings, and the forms of land tenure. Concerning population density, the earliest precise evidence dates only from 1723, when density ranged from 37 inhabitants per square kilometer in the mountains, to 82 in the hills, 89 in the high plain, and 103 in the low plain,[21] but it is unlikely that the pattern had been radically different a century or so earlier, when the total population of the State of Milan was roughly the same as in 1723. As for the size of holdings and the forms of tenure, the spectrum ran from peasant ownership of small plots in the mountains and the hills to large capitalistic estates, usually leased out to tenants, in the low plain; in the high plain, too, most land was owned by absentee landlords, but estates did not quite attain the size of those in the irrigated plain and contracts combining sharecropping arrangements and the payment of a fixed rent in kind were far more common than the leaseholds of the low plain.[22]

The four main zones that make up the mosaic of the Lombard rural landscape did not, of course, form as many separate worlds. Their very differences made for a measure of complementarity and thus encouraged specialization and trade between zones. Information on this point is scant and fragmentary, and an attempt at estimating, let alone measuring, the size or value of commodity flows between zones would be unrealistic. Nonetheless, it is still possible to say that the purely self-sufficient rural community, if it ever existed outside the textbooks, is certainly hard to find in Lombardy in early modern times. What one does find over and over again are villages and hamlets that, while largely geared for subsistence, have at least a foothold in the market economy.

In the mountain zone such a foothold was established mainly in order to secure a minimal supply of cereals from the plain, to compensate for a notoriously inadequate local production. In return, the mountain people could offer, first of all, the marketable surplus of their pastoral economies, notably cattle and cheese; in a few select districts simple metal goods or bar iron manufactured out of local ores could help offset grain purchases; almost invariably, however, the grain-consuming mountain zone showed a deficit in its trade with the grain-producing plain; the deficit was made good by invisible exports, in the form of cash earned by migrant workers from the mountains who spent long periods away from home working as herdsmen, farmhands, stonecutters, masons, or common laborers in the plain or in the cities.[23]

"Our wretched land is by nature very barren," explained a spokesman for the communities of Val Formazza at the northernmost edge of the State of Milan," and yields nothing but some hay and enough grain to last us one month of the year . . . We have no other occupation but herding cattle."[24] What he did not explain was how those communities managed to make up for the shortfall in cereal food, which their spokesman so forcefully lamented and may have slightly exaggerated. But we know from another source that Val Formazza and adjacent valleys to the north and west of Lake Maggiore sold to the city of Milan meat, veal, butter, and diverse cheeses.[25] More rarely, the sale of charcoal "carried by men on their back" to the nearest town, could help too.[26] Another glimpse of the ties that linked the mountain economy to the outside world is provided by a petition filed in 1572 on behalf of the mountain community of Valtorta.[27] "By ancient custom," the petition reads, "it has been granted to us to fetch four loads of bread in Lecco every week for our own use. This has been done in recognition of the benefits which the community brings to this realm by abundantly supplying it with nails and other iron ware." In nearby Vedeseta, where, we are told, "there is nothing but hay and wood . . . and no grain is grown nor are there vineyards or other fruit trees," basic foodstuffs had to be purchased in either Lecco or Bergamo. To pay for them, however, Vedeseta counted not on the sale of manufactured goods, but rather on the earnings of its emigrants: "nearly all our men are away from home, some of them as far as Rome, some elsewhere."[28]

The number of persons temporarily absent from a village could reach astonishing proportions indeed. A census taken in the mountain parish of Olmo, not far from Valtorta, in 1606 lists a total population of 375; of these, 131 (or 35 percent) were reported as being "absent," in Milan or Venice for the most part.[29] The case of Olmo may have been exceptional, but migration, whether temporary or permanent, was a widespread phenomenon throughout the Lombard Alps: of Valdossola it was said that "the men here are generally peasants most of whom are forced to go out into the world [*in giro per il mondo*] trying to make a living, for this land is very barren." Of the Bergamasque mountains (in the Venetian portion of Lombardy) it was reported that "no grain is grown here and the majority of the people go out into the world and throughout Italy, mostly to Rome and Venice, earning their keep as peddlers, innkeepers, cauldroners, and in sundry other trades; they come home every two or three years and spend six months there."[30] What Fernand Braudel has said of the Mediterranean mountains in general—that they were "a reservoir of men for other people's use"[31]—certainly holds true of the Lombard mountains at the turn of the sixteenth century.

In the hills some of the features typical of the mountain zone still obtained: scarcity of cereals, availability of timber and, more rarely, of mineral resources, and population pressure resulting in out-migration. What were missing were the great alpine pastures and the pastoral economy that depended on them. On the other hand, the gap between grain production and consumption, although not as wide as in the mountains, was still very real, but it was bridged by the export of wine to the towns.

As portrayed in documents of the late sixteenth and early seventeenth centuries, Valtravaglia provides a good illustration of the working of the hill economy and of its links with the outside world. The valley itself extends eastward from Lake Maggiore and reaches elevations of nearly 600 meters. "The terrain is nearly all rugged," we are told, "and only one-third of the land is under crop, the rest being all wooded and yielding little else but chestnuts and timber." Peasant property, not surprisingly, was widespread ("nearly everyone owns at least some land") and the chief agricultural resources were the vineyards: "barring foul weather, more wine is produced than is locally needed and what is left over is sold to wine merchants who ship it to Milan by the way of Lake Maggiore."[32] The sale of wine probably helped pay for much of the grain the valley needed and secured from the markets of Intra and Pallanza across the lake, but other things helped too. Valtravaglia was renowned for its limestone, and lime kilns or furnaces were common there; in addition, an obviously redundant labor force found an outlet, much as its counterpart in the mountains did, in emigration, sometimes to cities as far as Naples.[33] On the hills of the Brianza as well, vineyards loomed large in those days, as they no longer do. Besides "all sorts of grains," which, however, had to be supplemented by purchases in Milan and Como, the area around Incino in the Brianza was reported in 1620 as producing "plenty of wine which, when it is in excess, is sold in Milan to pay for other necessities."[34]

In the high plain, conditions varied considerably from place to place. In some districts the production of cereals (and notably of rye) apparently exceeded local needs and afforded a surplus for sale in nearby urban centers.[35] In others, such as the districts of Busto Arsizio and Gallarate, the local crop was clearly inadequate because of both the lack of water and the heathlike nature of the soil; it was mainly through the development of handicraft industries producing for the market that the rural population managed to compensate for the natural deficiencies of their land.[36] Throughout the high plain, however, a new vital element was injected in the course of the fifteenth century, one that fitted particularly well the pattern of interculture typical of that region: this was the mulberry tree and its concomitant, the raising of silkworms. Although the history of silk growing in Lombardy is still imperfectly known, there is little doubt that by 1600 raw silk represented a major crop in the State of Milan[37] and that in certain areas it had become the main link between the peasant household and the market.[38]

While not even the remotest hamlet of the Lombard Alps seems to have been totally cut off from commercial contacts, it is, of course, only in the rich low plain that the agrarian economy, undoubtedly under the influence of the urban demand for foodstuffs, appears to have been fully commercialized and monetized. With most of the work force consisting of day laborers (*brazanti* or *pigionanti*), with long leases paid in money rather than in kind, with large estates geared to specialized cash crops covering much of the best land, by 1600 (and, in fact, at an even earlier date) commercialization had become the dominant influence on the agriculture of the low plain.

Vestiges of an older and different economy had, of course, survived. One such vestige was the presence of occasional pockets of small peasant property in districts which, in course of time, were to be characterized by large farms and intensive irrigation. Around Vigevano, for instance, in the sixteenth century, as much as 80 percent of the land still consisted of small holdings, a majority of them measuring but one-third of a hectare (less than one acre) in size; at Olevano Lomellina some sizable estates owned by gentlemen coexisted with small peasant property.[39] It is more surprising, however, to find small peasant holdings in the very heartland of Lombardy's irrigated agriculture, the Lodi province: in Maleo Lodigiano, as late as 1644, we find them side by side with the large commercial estates typical of that area.[40] Equally surprising is the presence of the vine in the low plain, in a habitat that is notoriously ill-suited to that plant.[41] The anomaly, which presumably reflected the peasant's desire to ensure a supply of wine for his household, did not escape Fynes Moryson's perceptive eye: after noticing that, in contrast to the hills, "the fields of Lombardy are lesse happy in yielding fruites, but give excellent pasture and corne," and that "in the furrows the husbandman plants Elme trees . . . and likewise plants vines which shoote up in height upon the bodies of those trees," he concluded by saying that "these vines yeeld but a small wine by reason they grow so high and in plaine country."[42]

For all this, there is little doubt that commercial farming on a grand scale was the keynote in the southern half of the State of Milan. It was from there, of course, that in normal years large quantities of grain and other farm products were shipped abroad; the chief customer was probably the Swiss Confederacy, whose heavy dependence on Lombard grain loomed large in their diplomatic relations with the rulers of Milan and provided the latter with considerable leverage whenever the Swiss threatened to interrupt communications over the Alpine passes.[43] But of greater consequence to the economy of the low plain was trade in agricultural commodities within the State of Milan itself, where considerable disparity in resource endowment between zones, combined with a high level of urbanization, inevitably made for massive sales of foodstuffs. We know little about the volume or the value of internal trade in agricultural commodities, but we may gain some rough idea of the order of magnitude when we reflect that the city of Milan alone, with its 120,000 souls, may have absorbed something like 28,000 metric tons of grain a year and that this represented the yield of approximately as many hectares (or about 70,000 acres) of good farmland.[44] And the city's appetite for grain was apparently paralleled by that for meat and cheese: in 1593 the Milan butchers had reportedly slaughtered 27,486 heads of cattle, while the city's consumption of pork in that year was said to have been 450,000 kilograms and that of cheese about 52,000 kilograms.[45]

Predictably enough, the villages of the low plain thrived on the sale of victuals to the cities, the more easily so the closer they happened to be to the cities themselves. Thus, Lachiarella, halfway between Milan and Pavia, was described in 1607 as a community made up of people "much given to trading" (*gente mercantile*), as they "deal in all sorts of merchandise and attend particularly to carrying victuals to Milan and Pavia." The surrounding countryside was said to be "fertile and plentiful" and the villagers themselves to live "in some comfort and civility" (*stanno assai commodi et vivono civilmente*). Nearby Melegnano (better known as Marignano in the annals of Renaissance warfare) was described in 1600 as a village in which "everyone engages in some business [*ciascuno si traffica in qualche cosa*], some men serving as tenants, others dealing in cheese, cattle, and other commodities . . . and all the produce is sold partly in the village itself, partly in Milan, Pavia, and Lodi." Further south, in Santa Cristina on the left bank of the Po, grain, rice, wine, and cheese were reportedly not only "sufficient to support the local people," but also available for sale on the nearby markets of Sant'Angelo and San Colombano. A survey of San Fiorano, some 10 kilometers north of the Po in the luscious Lodi province, is more informative and vividly illustrates the remarkable degree to which commercialization had penetrated the rural economy. In San Fiorano convertible husbandry, with its pattern of rotation in which artificial meadows were periodically sown with grain, yielded an abundance of hay, wheat, millet, beans, and flax, with only a little wine being produced on the side. "Most of the wheat [was] brought to Lodi for sale" and so was flax, while, predictably enough, "wine and millet were consumed *in loco*." The villagers, we are further told, went to Codogno, a much larger village a few miles from there, "to fetch the things they do not themselves make such as clothes, cheese, medicines, and other things."[46] Practicing much the same farming systems and growing similar crops, the village of San Vito in the province of Cremona seems to have been a step behind San Fiorano, for in the former the local crop of wheat, rye, millet, flax, and a little wine was said "to suffice in one year and to fall short in another, depending on how the harvest goes." There was, however, one exception to that somewhat precarious condition of self-sufficiency: flax was "sold to outsiders" and one of the chief occupations in the village was "the working of flax into thread."[47]

In the southeastern corner of the State of Milan, the district of Casalmaggiore formed a unique enclave in the broad lowland belt that runs from Lomellina eastward along the left bank of the Po. Despite its low elevation (a mere 30 meters above sea level) and the proximity of the large, meandering river, the district had no land under irrigation and its soil—of recent alluvial formation—was definitely inferior to that of the Lombard plain. Stock raising had apparently been attempted in the area, but by the early seventeenth century was reported as declining, while cereal crops fell far short of local needs. The Casalmaggiore district, however, had developed a strongly market-oriented economy of its own: its dry, porous soil had been converted to vineyards and by the early seventeenth century its wines were shipped "throughout the State in large amounts." By that time Casalmaggiore itself, then a market town with a population of over 5,000, was a bustling river port and trading center, featuring a weekly market and an annual fair; its residents were described as being "very industrious and much given to trade," one of their main lines of business being the shipping of locally produced wine as well as of flax and linen from the Cremona province "down the Po as far as Venice."[48]

Casalmaggiore was but one among the numerous trading centers that dotted the Lombard countryside and formed foci in the intricate web of commercial exchanges through which even small and remote rural settlements kept in touch with the outside world and the market economy.[49] One such trading center was Domodossola at the foot of the Alps near the Swiss border; at its weekly market "grain, cattle, cheese, linen, woolens, notions, shoes, and sundry other goods" were actively traded—partly, one can assume, for the benefit of the surrounding valleys and partly for the benefit of more distant areas, because, located as it was at the point where the great highway (*strada reale*) from Milan, by way of Gallarate and Arona, started its climb toward the Simplon Pass, Domodossola played a role as a stopping place and a clearinghouse for trans-Alpine trade. Local residents took an active part in and benefited from that trade: besides engaging in service activities connected with the storage and haulage of goods in transit, they also shipped their own wine over the Simplon into the Vallais and availed themselves of a variety of commodities brought there from considerable distances—"cloth from Germany, Bergamo, and Como, spices and metal goods from Milan, grain from the Novara privince, and cheese from the canton of Bern"; in short, as our source puts it, "all the things they themselves do not make."[50]

The twofold role played by Domodossola, with its weekly market—ensuring contacts between the rugged, inhospitable hinterland and the outside world as well as linking the trans-Alpine trade—Gallarate played further south, vis-à-vis the western portion of the high plain. A 1578 document, after asserting that the people of Gallarate "are nearly all artificers . . . and most of them hold their wealth in the form of merchandise, for this is a place of traffic," gives the following description of the weekly market: "A great market is held there every Saturday to which are brought commodities from divers parts, and cattle, and other things . . . and those commodities come from Milan, Monza, the provinces of Vercelli and Novara as well as from towns and villages of the territory of Lugano and of the Bergamasque."[51] Likewise, Caravaggio, in the easternmost district of the state, had its weekly market featuring "all sorts of goods, but particularly linen and thread, with great concourse of foreign merchants, and notably from Brescia and Crema." Its role as trading center was matched by that as service center for the surrounding countryside: "There are divers artificers here, such as blacksmiths, tailors, linen weavers, and carpenters, who cater not only to the people of the town itself, but also to those of nearby villages."[52]

Predictably, information on smaller trading centers is hard to come by, and it is only in the later seventeenth century that we can identify a number of such centers scattered throughout the Lombard countryside. It is, therefore, all the more instructive to be able to catch a glimpse of one small center, the village of San Fiorano in the Lodi province. At the opening of the seventeenth century San Fiorano, with a population of 450, or less than one-tenth that of Casalmaggiore or Caravaggio, held a weekly market where trinkets, footwear, cheese, and cattle were traded; as such, it reportedly attracted people from nearby communities.[53] As later evidence will show, small markets such as that of San Fiorano must have been common throughout Lombardy; nor can their role be underestimated, for it was there that the peasants could find an outlet for their surplus crops and even indulge in the purchase of a few articles from what must have seemed distant and exotic places.

Contacts between peasant consumers and distant producers were also assured, on a minuscule scale but in a capillary form, by itinerant craftsmen and peddlers. Not surprisingly, their passage has left precious little trace in the records of the past, but an occasional document is there to alert us to their ubiquitous presence. At one point we come across three peddlers freshly arrived in Codogno: one is from Piedmont and is said "to earn his living by carrying around boxes of goods"; another is originally from Chiavenna, but has now a permanent residence in Milan, from which he has just emerged "to do business in the Lodi province carrying with him boxes and baskets"; the third man is a native of Velletri in central Italy and "sells clothes and devotional pictures, but also begs along the way." In Vigevano, a French peddler is arrested one day and his box of merchandise is opened for inspection: its contents include some twenty scissors, a dozen jackknives [*colteli desnodati*], twenty-five combs of various sizes, over two hundred buttons, and "one sword with a French hilt." It is doubtful that the last item in the peddler's box would have easily found an eager customer among the peasantry, but the other articles (most likely originating from the Forez or from Dauphiny, two districts with a long-standing reputation for their *quinquaillerie*) probably give us a realistic idea of the kinds of goods that reached peasant households through the services of petty itinerant merchants. The latter often combined trade with some kind of manual skill. Thus, an itinerant craftsman from Bergamo is described as "making spindles and earning a living by peddling them," and another is mentioned in a document as one who "makes and sells scoops [*pallotti*] and other wooden utensils." Tinkers, too, were frequent visitors in the village, and so were sawyers, often from Dauphiny, "who do not have a permanent residence and are poor and hire themselves out by the day."[54]

The market economy intruded upon the countryside in yet another way, namely, through the presence of a small but not negligible industrial sector. Although information on this sector is scant and fragmented, there is enough to assure us that the Lombard countryside, while overwhelmingly agrarian (and, as such, dependent either on simple homemade artifacts or on outside purchases for its nonnutritional needs), did harbor, here and there, small-scale industries producing for the market.

Extractive industries and some downstream activities connected with them are, of course, an obvious example, and the Valsassina offers the single most notable instance of a rural district whose economy included an important nonagricultural element. Since late medieval times, and possibly earlier, the mining and smelting of iron had been a major activity in that valley and a vital ingredient, along with stock-raising and emigration, in the economy of a rugged, inhospitable region. By the late sixteenth century, the Valsassina could boast an annual output of about 1,000 metric tons of pig iron—a trifle by the standards of our time, but a respectable figure in an age when total iron production in Europe may have been in the neighborhood of 100,000 tons.[55] The iron mined in the upper reaches of the valley was smelted in seven blast furnaces and from there found its way down to Lecco, where in many small forges it was turned into bars, sheets, wire, tools, and cannonballs; metal goods of higher quality and more elaborate design were produced, as will be seen, in the workshops of Milan, but even in the countryside iron metallurgy seems to have attained a considerable degree of specialization. The small village of Valtorta, perched in relative isolation in the Bergamo mountains, specialized in nail-making[56]—and it was by selling nails in Lecco or Bergamo that the community secured the grain necessary for its survival. In Concorezzo, a small village of the high plain just north of Milan, the manufacture of needles occupied a large portion of the population in the sixteenth century,[57] while Busto Arsizio had an established reputation, among other things, as a center of the wire-drawing industry, with some of its wire being exported as far as the Levant.[58]

Another group of extractive industries firmly rooted in a rural setting were those connected with building materials—marble, stone, bricks, and lime. The construction of rural dwellings depended, of course, on whatever materials happened to be available in the immediate vicinity. Urban construction, on the other hand, requiring as it did the concentration of vast quantities of materials in a limited area, had to draw on more distant sources of supply. The location of the latter was determined not only by geology, but also, given the prohibitive cost of overland transportation for bulky, low-value goods, by the presence of navigable waters. Not surprisingly, therefore, the marble selected for the Milan cathedral came from the quarries of Candoglia, located on the western shores of Lake Maggiore, whence the marble could be shipped to Milan down the Ticino River and the Naviglio Grande. The Valtravaglia, on the opposite side of the lake, used the same water route to supply Milan with lime produced by calcination from local limestone quarries.[59] Bricks, so far as we can tell, came mainly from the plain, where suitable clays and argil were in large supply; and the brickyards of which trace has been found in the documents were all near a navigable river or canal: Vermezzo and Abbiategrasso on the Naviglio Grande, Gorgonzola, Melzo, and Crescenzago on the Martesana, Cassano on the Adda, Soncino near the Oglio River.[60]

While a rural rather than an urban location was a practical necessity for extractive industries, no such constraint applied to handicraft industries—and, in fact, most of them were found in the cities. Nonetheless, handicraft industries were not totally absent from Lombard villages and hamlets. In addition to such simple manufacturing work as no doubt was done in the peasant household to meet some elemental needs for clothing and common utensils, rural communities did occasionally harbor industrial activities aimed at a larger constituency. When we read, for instance, that in the village of Boffalora there lived three papermakers (*folladori da carta*),[61] we must assume

that they worked for a clientele that extended well beyond the village
limits; and the same applies when we find as many as twelve tanners
all living in the village of Abbiategrasso.[62]

How common it was for handicraft industries to be located in rural
communities is impossible to say, for the evidence on the subject is too
scant and sporadic. A few localities are on record, at any rate, as harboring handicraft, and notably textile, industries. The best-known
example is Torno, a village of one thousand souls on the shore of Lake
Como. An important center of the wool industry and an economic
and political rival of nearby Como in the late Middle Ages, by the
sixteenth century Torno had been outdistanced by its powerful neigh-
bor, but had managed somehow to survive as a modestly successful
textile center with an annual output of a few hundred cloths.[63] In the
province of Milan around 1540, Monza and several villages nearby
harbored a goodly number of weavers, while in the early seventeenth
century, if we are to believe sources dating from the 1640s, cloth had
until recently been woven in considerable quantities in the hill zone
and notably in the Brianza and the Valassina.[64] How large production
may have been we cannot tell. We do know, however, that it consisted entirely of "shortcloths [panni bassi] of inferior quality and low-
price goods for the poor," in sharp contrast to "cloth manufactured in
Milan which is of very high quality and is priced accordingly,"[65] the
implication being that the rural wool industry did not really compete
with that of the city. When it did, the urban guilds were likely to com-
plain loudly and to fill pages with denunciations and petitions to the
government, thereby providing posterity with some information
about industrial activity in the countryside. It is precisely thanks to a
protest filed at the opening of the seventeenth century by the weavers
of Milan that we learn about the presence, in a number of villages just
north of the city, of substantial clusters of weavers.[66]

Needless to say, no broad generalization can be based on the few
fragments of evidence that research has been able to turn up so far.
But it is clear, on the one hand, that in villages such as Torno production far exceeded local needs; and the same applies to the village of
Lissone, with its 110 looms, or to Erba in the Brianza, of which it was
said that "cloth made here is sold outside the village."[67] On the other
hand, the paucity of evidence bearing on clothmaking in the country-

side strongly suggests the limited scope and significance of that industry in the Lombard economy at large.

Much the same probably holds true of another branch of the textile industry, for which at least one Lombard city, Cremona, had, as will be seen, an enviable reputation—namely, the making of cotton fabrics (*fustagni*) and of fabrics mixed of cotton and flax (*bombasine*).[68] Little trace has been found of these two manufactures in the countryside, with at least one notable exception: in the course of the sixteenth century, the making of *fustagni* and *bombasine* had vigorously developed in the large village of Busto Arsizio, and by the opening of the seventeenth century the new industry was reported as a major source of employment there, second only to the drawing of wire.[69]

In the flax-growing low plain, and notably in the provinces of Lodi and Cremona, an important source of rural employment, at least on a part-time basis, was the making of linen both for local use and for export. This may have been true as early as the fourteenth century, when Lombard linen was listed among imported commodities in Genoa and when the making and wearing of linen apparently became widespread in the countryside.[70] It was still true at the opening of the seventeenth century, when an English traveler could write, after journeying from Milan to Lodi: "In this space I observed nothing memorable, but only the drawing of *lino* in many places of their ground, of which *lino* they make their flaxe and with their flaxe fine linnen for sheets, shirts, bands, curtaines for their beds, etc. and some linnen they make of a courser sort, of which kinde the apparel of most of their country people is made."[71] At that time flax was also an important crop in the Cremona province, and we have every reason to suppose that the making of linen or of linen thread was as common there or in the nearby district of Caravaggio as it reportedly was in the Lodi province. Of Caravaggio it was said in 1607 that many of its men were linen weavers and that the spinning of flax was a common occupation among women. Caravaggio, however, also served as a clearinghouse where "many people from distant places . . . come and buy great quantities of fine thread and flax," most of which ended up in Venetian territory, in the district of Salò on the eastern shores of Lake Garda, which was then and was long to remain the home of a reowned bleaching industry.[72]

Whatever may have been the importance and size of industrial production in the Lombard countryside, it was certainly dwarfed by that of the cities. The manufactures for which the State of Milan had an undisputed reputation throughout Europe at the close of the sixteenth century were primarily urban, and it was from the cities that large amounts of manufactured goods were shipped to virtually every corner of Europe to satisfy the tastes and whims of a wealthy and sophisticated clientele.

In the industrial spectrum of sixteenth-century Lombardy, pride of place belonged unquestionably to the silk industry of Milan and to the closely allied manufacture of the gold thread that went into the making of richly embroidered silk fabrics. While we cannot accept the self-serving claim made by the guild of the silk merchants of Milan in 1596 that their industry "ensured the livelihood of more than fifty thousand poor in this city,"[73] the towering position of the Milan silk industry in the Lombard economy is beyond doubt and is unmistakenly borne out by a detailed census of all manufacturing and commercial activities (*estimo del mercimonio*) taken in 1580 for purposes of taxation:[74] in that census the value of silk goods produced in Milan represented 15 percent of the value of all manufactured goods produced in the entire state and 22 percent of those from the city of Milan itself.[75] In that same year 5 million lire worth of silk goods cleared the city gates, and a decade later a knowledgeable source estimated the value of silk goods made in Milan at twice that amount. In 1606 it was claimed that 300,000 pounds of native silk and 100,000 pounds of imported raw silk was annually fed to the 3,000 looms then reportedly at work in Milan.[76] None of the above figures can, of course, be accepted as fully accurate, but they do bear witness to the size and prosperity of what must have been by far the single largest manufacturing industry in the State of Milan.

The industry's prosperity heavily depended on its long-standing reputation abroad. When Thomas Coryate wrote that the Milan embroiderers "are very singular workmen" and that "silkmen do abound here which are esteemed so good that they are not inferior to any of the Christian world,"[77] he was echoing a widely held opinion, for the rich fabrics spun of silk and gold thread and the expensive velvets exported from Milan had as yet little to fear from foreign imitators; they found a ready market in Poland and Hungary no less than in the Low Countries, Germany, and England.[78] But by far the largest outlet was probably France, where—since the Italian wars of the early sixteenth century—an insatiable appetite had developed for the luxuries of the peninsula, and notably for its silks.[79] Commercial and customs records in Lyons, the chief clearinghouse in the trade between France and Italy in the sixteenth century, clearly bear out the importance of that trade and the leading place held in it by Milanese goods. In 1569 at least one-third of all Italian goods brought to Lyons were from Milan, and that third consisted overwhelmingly of silk fabrics, ribbons, tassels, embroidered handbags, gloves, and gold thread—in return for which Italian merchants purchased cheap English kerseys and French or Flemish linen.[80]

The wool industry of Milan, with an annual output of 4,500 pieces or bolts of high-grade, expensive broadcloth (*panno alto*),[81] ranked second in the tax assessment of 1580, but it lagged considerably behind its richer and more celebrated sister, the silk industry.[82] Wool, on the other hand, formed in those days the backbone of the economy of Como, a city which, with a population less than one-tenth that of the capital, could boast a production of fine cloth comparable to Milan's, while in the even smaller city of Vigevano cloth making, albeit on a smaller scale, provided the chief source of livelihood.[83] Cremona, for its part, was the largest center for the production of fustians, bombazine, and *mezzelane*,[84] nor was its position seriously threatened, it would seem, by the younger and growing, but still small, industry in Busto Arsizio. Cremona's reputation was of course, of medieval vintage and may have reached its highest point in the late fourteenth or early fifteenth century, when as many as 40,000 bolts of fustian had been annually shipped to Venice alone and an unspecified number to other Italian cities and to France, Germany, and the Low Countries.[85] In 1565, at any rate, Cremona, with an output of 62,000 pieces was still a textile center of international stature.[86]

While silk, wool, and cotton can be confidently viewed as the leading urban manufactures in late sixteenth-century Lombardy, they did not exhaust the industrial spectrum, for the latter also encompassed the making of fine linen both in Lodi and Cremona, the bleaching of imported German linen in Como,. ceramics in Lodi, paper and soap making in Pavia and Cremona.[87] In varying degrees, virtually all of these activities were also found in Milan, the "nursery of manual arts" and the epitome of the rich and diverse industrial texture of the Lombard economy. Two industries, however, seem to have been peculiar to Milan and to have contributed considerably to its reputation— namely, leathermaking and the manufacture of arms and armor. Although information on the leather industry is very scant, its importance can be inferred from the large numbers of cattle driven to Milan's slaughterhouses. Municipal law prohibited, under severe pecuniary penalties, the sale outside the city of the hides of cattle slaughtered within its walls, thus ensuring an abundant supply of hides and leather to its craftsmen. From this policy, it was contended, "very great benefits accrue to the City, for out of those hides many useful articles are made, such as scabbards, belts, hoods for carriages, footwear for the poor, harness for horses, pouches, shoe laces, covers for chests, boots, and shoes."[88] The city itself, with its large population and a heavy traffic of horse-drawn carriages, no doubt was an excellent market for all kinds of leather goods, but the latter were also exported and much admired abroad.[89]

In the manufacture of arms, Milan could not quite match the leading Italian center of gunmaking—Brescia, in the Venetian portion of Lombardy.[90] Nonetheless, until the close of the sixteenth century, heavy ordnance and small firearms were produced in Milan both for local use and for export, and the gunmakers' guild was by no means one of the least in the Ambrosian capital. It was, however, in the making of armor (whether ordinary helmets, breastplates or corselets for the infantry, or heavy suits of armor for the mounted soldier) that Milan had long ago achieved a position of unquestionable distinction. Actually, in the fifteenth century the supremacy of Milan in the field had been unchallenged. In the subsequent century German competition, as well as changes in methods of warfare, had brought fresh challenges and had deprived Milan of its absolute edge over the rest of Europe. Nonetheless, the city's armorers had managed to hold their own by improving the quality and resistance of the steel they used in common-service armor, as well as by developing new designs of finely chiseled, inlaid armor for use, if not in battle, at least in parades and tournaments.[91]

"The greatness of Milan rests on its manufactures," reads a 1566 document.[92] "The city," wrote a Venetian envoy in 1583, "has an infinite number of craftsmen versed in all the mechanical arts, so that it can be called the nursery of manual skills."[93] "No City of Italy," echoed Coryate at the beginning of the seventeenth century, "is furnished with more manuary arts than this, which it yeeldeth with as much excellency as any City of all Christendome."[94] The evidence presented in the preceding pages, incomplete though it is, lends support to the consensus of contemporary opinion. There is little reason to doubt that, just as the agriculture of the low plain of Lombardy had few parallels in sixteenth-century Europe, so Milan and, to a lesser extent, the other cities of the state had few equals as industrial centers. It is only by looking very closely at other and less conspicuous aspects of the economy and the society of the State of Milan that one can detect some ominous, if still barely noticeable, signs that all was not well in "the Canaan of Christendome."

CHAPTER II

OLD CONSTRAINTS AND NEW PRESSURES

The economic prosperity of Lombardy, which contemporary observers admired so much, ultimately reflected the precocious technological advances and the pervasive market orientation that had been attained in that area since the late Middle Ages. This is most certainly true of agriculture: whether one looks at the interculture of the high plain or at the convertible husbandry and continuous cropping of the irrigated plain, it is clear that the application of ingenious systems of intensive farming—as well as the high degree of specialization fostered by regional and international trade—represented major achievements; thanks to them Lombardy could sustain a population density and a level of urbanization that had few parallels in early modern Europe, while, at the same time, exporting sizable quantities of farm commodities. In the case of manufactures, contemporary opinion—supported by what evidence we have about exports—unmistakably points to the superiority Lombard craftsmen had attained in the production of a wide variety of goods, from silks to cotton fabrics, from fine woolens to gold thread, from armor to ceramics. Together, the progress achieved in agriculture, the clear lead Lombardy possessed in a number of manufactures, and the strong commercial orientation of both its agricultural and industrial sectors convey the definite impression of an economy and a society that, at an unusually early date, had developed many of the traits we normally associate with an advanced stage of modernization.

And yet, while the impression is to a large extent justified, in the sense that the State of Milan, like much of northern Italy, had moved further along the road of modernization than most other European nations, this impression should not make us lose sight of the fact that much in its economic and social makeup was still archaic and typical of premodern, preindustrial times. This recognition is important, not only in order to form as realistic a picture as possible of Lombardy at the close of the sixteenth century, but also in order to avoid the anachronism of viewing it as an example of full-grown capitalism *ante litteram* or even as an economy that, having severed its medieval moorings, was now poised on the brink of modern industrialization.

For all their reputation and undeniable achievements, the manufacturers of the Lombard cities were certainly closer to their medieval predecessors than to their counterparts of the factory age. Not only did production rely on the muscular strength and manual skill of the craftsman far more than on inanimate energy and machinery; not only was it carried out, for the most part, in diminutive shops rather than in large industrial plants; but, by and large, the goods produced (whether silks, suits of armor, or high-grade cloth), intended as they were for a select clientele rather than for a mass market, owed their success more to superior workmanship, exquisite design, and even individual styling than to low prices and an ability to satisfy the ordinary needs of large numbers of consumers. In other words, urban manufactures, despite the fact that they came to employ thousands of workers, retained all the features of medieval crafts. Not surprisingly, the labor force, although paid wages by the merchant-manufacturer under the putting-out system, continued to be organized in such typically medieval institutions as the craft guilds and to find in them the best safeguard of those attitudes that for centuries had been the hallmark of the urban artisan class—namely, adherence to traditional standards of workmanship, a determination to monitor closely and, if necessary, to restrict new admissions to one's trade, and punctilious defense of a guild's privileges and exclusiveness.[1]

The Lombard economy, of course, also shared other traits with preindustrial Europe. One was the recurrence of severe, at times catastrophic, and always unsettling "subsistence crises" triggered by a crop failure and aggravated both by the lack of adequate food reserves and by the difficulty of bringing in emergency supplies from distant sources.[2] The existence of such crises is clearly attested by a number of exceptionally sharp fluctuations in the price of food during both the sixteenth and the seventeenth centuries: around 1530 and 1540, in the 1590s, in 1628-29, and again in the late 1640s grain prices jumped twofold and even threefold.[3] Although the available evidence is still too scant to enable us to analyze all the complex consequences of such crises, we have every reason to assume that in Lombardy, as elsewhere in Europe, they brought in their wake higher mortality levels, a sharp decline in fertility, the temporary disruption of trade, and in some instances serious social disturbances.

An even more serious, if less frequent, source of instability was represented by outbreaks of epidemic disease of such proportions as to cause significant losses of lives and, exceptionally, to wipe out in a few months the demographic gains achieved over several generations. The plague of 1576-1578, for example, inflicted major losses without reversing the upward trend under way since the mid-sixteenth century; the plague of 1630-31, on the other hand, did result in a severe reduction in population, which it took two generations to make good.[4] In either case, although to a different degree, the plague had unsettling effects on the economy: not only could it create temporary labor shortages and trade interruptions, but by abruptly reducing the number of mouths to feed it also brought about sharp drops in food prices, thus destabilizing the largest sector of the economy—agriculture.

The premodern character of the Lombard economy is further illustrated by the relatively high proportion of the labor force employed in agriculture. Admittedly, no precise data are available on this point. The best one can do is to attempt some crude estimates; let us start from the fact, previously alluded to, that 75 percent of the Lombard population was rural. This in itself unmistakably points to the predominance of agriculture in the economy, but should not be taken to mean that three-fourths of the labor force consisted of farmers or peasants. The percentage must have been somewhat lower, for allowance must be made for the weavers, miners, stonecutters, brickmakers, smiths, wheelwrights, carters, and shopkeepers who lived in so many of Lombardy's villages. Taking those nonfarm workers into account, we can assume that in Hapsburg Lombardy as a whole the percentage of the labor force predominantly engaged in agriculture fell somewhere between 60 and 70 percent. Low by the standards of sixteenth-century Europe, such a percentage is high by the standards of Western countries in our own time; it clearly indicates that agriculture and particularly food production absorbed then, as it does now in underdeveloped countries, by far the largest share of the labor force. This is tantamount to saying that the average productivity of labor, or output per man-hour, in the primary sector of the Lombard economy was still relatively low.

To speak of low output per man-hour may seem to contradict all that has been said in the preceding chapter about the prosperity of Lombard agriculture at the close of the sixteenth century. But the level of productivity should not be confused with the level of yield.[5] Before the coming of modern farm machinery and industrially produced fertilizer, relatively high yields per unit of land could be secured, in the main, only by intensive methods of cultivation (such as shorter fallowing, interculture, or continuous cropping), involving large inputs of human labor. Under these conditions, as Ester Boserup has reminded us,[6] each step taken toward intensification is bound to result in lower average output per man-hour, and such seems to have been the case in sixteenth-century Lombardy. Thanks to local specialization of crops and to the adoption of intensive methods of cultivation, Lombardy, as we have seen, had no doubt succeeded in achieving yields per hectare that were above average—sufficient to support a densely settled population, to feed sizable urban centers, and to generate a surplus for export. All this, however, had ultimately been made possible by the massive use of relatively cheap labor: interculture in the higher, dry zone called for relentless work both with the hoe and with the plough as well as for meticulous care of the vines and mulberry trees; in the irrigated plain, continuous cropping and its concomitant, convertible husbandry, absorbed prodigious amount of labor, not only for such normal operations as ploughing, sowing, and harvesting, but also for the upkeep of a capillary network of irrigation canals, for the frequent mowing of water meadows, and for the time-consuming care of the rice fields. Under the circumstances, it is not surprising that high yields were accompanied by low levels of output per man-hour and that the latter were reflected in low rates of pay.

As regards yields, one should not, of course, lose a sense of historical perspective and judge the conditions obtaining in the sixteenth
century with a yardstick appropriate to the twentieth century. Information on yields is very meager and spotty until the early eighteenth century, when average wheat yields per hectare in Lombardy
ranged from about 0.65 metric tons in the high, dry plain to one ton in
the low, irrigated plain—or less than half of what they would be two
centuries later.[7] No average figures are available for the sixteenth and
seventeenth centuries, but a few scattered data would seem to indicate
that yields were under half a ton in the hills and the high plain; in the
irrigated plain, on the other hand, yields of 1.5 tons per hectare are on
record.[8] While the available evidence is still too scant to warrant de-
finitive conclusions, it seems plain enough that wheat yields in Lombardy in the early modern period were much closer to those prevailing
in today's backward countries than to those now current in Lombardy itself. But, of course, those same yields, and notably those of
the irrigated plain, were quite respectable by early modern standards.[9]

At any rate, early modern levels of yield, coupled with the low
productivity of farm labor, certainly help account for another trait
that the State of Milan shared with much of Europe in early modern
times, namely, the basic poverty of its rural population. Here again
we should not use present-day criteria to gauge the past. What is crucial is that contemporaries were impressed by the sharp contrast between the state of destitution of the peasantry and the opulence of the
farmland on which they lived. Speaking of northern Italy in general,
Fynes Moryson observed that "the husbandmen and country people
live poorly and basely."[10] How true this was of Lombardy is hard to
say, but at the close of the seventeenth century a French visitor described the plight of the Lombard peasantry in equally bleak terms.
Lombardy, he wrote, "Is unquestionably one of the finest countries
one can behold, for the land here is level, well irrigated, and neatly
divided into parcels of about two acres planted with trees all around
. . . In short, we can consider this country as flowing milk and honey,
and yet in the countryside one sees nothing but poverty and misery,
and these are caused by the harshness of Spanish rule."[11] Leaving
aside, for the time being, the responsibility of the Spanish government, we have reason to believe that the blunt fact of rural poverty—

and the glaring contrast between a luscious landscape and the wretched conditions of the people who lived in it—was as true around 1600 as it was a century later. Not only was the level of productivity as low then as later, but what is known about the wage rates paid to farm laborers at the turn of the sixteenth century shows that they did not substantially differ, in real terms, from those paid at the turn of the next. In both instances they were half those received by urban construction workers, except for short periods at harvest time; moreover, there is enough evidence to indicate that the annual income a rural laborer could earn from such wages would have been insufficient, without some such additional income as might be secured from subsistence farming, to ensure even a biological minimum of calories to a family of four.[12] No wonder, then, that in a village in the very heart of the rich Lodi province, most peasants could only afford "huts made of straw" for their dwellings, and that in the hills and mountains chestnuts formed the mainstay in the peasants' diet.[13]

Granted that at the root of rural poverty lay the stark reality of high population density and low output per man-hour, we have good reason to believe that peasant conditions were made worse by other circumstances and pressures as well. The heavy demands placed by the Spanish rulers on Lombardy in general, and on rural Lombardy in particular, no doubt must bear, as we shall see, some of the blame. But of greater and more pervasive importance in depressing peasant incomes (and swelling urban ones) was the form of government under which the State of Milan had been ruled since long before the coming of the Spaniards, and which was to survive long after the Spaniards were forced to surrender Lombardy to Austria in 1706.

That enduring form of government can best be labeled "the city-state system," for, even though formally the city-state had long since been replaced by the territorial-dynastic state of the Visconti and Sforza dukes and, after a short French interlude, of the Hapsburg monarchs, much of its substance had survived virtually intact throughout all the changes and vicissitudes and was to survive until the great reforms of Maria Theresa and Joseph II.[14] In essence, what survived was a system of government predicated on the domination of

town over country, of *città* over *contado*.[15] In practice this meant
that: (a) virtually all high administrative and judicial offices in the
State of Milan were monopolized by city residents and more precisely
by members of the restricted patrician oligarchy; (b) a sharp distinction was maintained in legal and fiscal matters between townsmen
(*cittadini*) and country residents (*rurali*); and (c) the cities enjoyed
substantial economic privileges vis-à-vis the countryside, the latter
being regarded in many ways as a kind of colonial dependency, whose
main function it was to supply revenue, victuals, and industrial raw
materials to the cities.

The city-state system of government is epitomized by the position
of Milan relative to its own *contado* (technically known as the
"duchy" or *ducato*). Although the other eight cities, too, enjoyed a
role of preeminence and dominance over their respective provinces,
none could quite compare with Milan in this respect, since the latter,
as capital of the entire state, had achieved a position of supremacy
over its lesser sisters. In Milan, an exclusive patrician oligarchy (some
two hundred burgher families who owed their prestigious rank to
generations of residence in the city as much as to wealth and a long
tradition of public service) had a monopoly on municipal offices, and
notably on all seats in the city council (the *Decurioni*) and its executive
offshoot, the powerful *Tribunale di Provvisione*, whose authority
extended over the duchy as well. That same oligarchy, however, also
held most key positions in the government of the State of Milan as a
whole. Although the highest two officers (the governor-captain general and the chancellor) were, as a rule, Spaniards, Milanese patricians
filled a clear majority of the seats in the various agencies that controlled the day-to-day administration of the state.

Chief among those agencies was the Senate, a body of fifteen magistrates, three of them Spaniards and the rest Milanese patricians.[16]
Originally established by Louis XII on the model of the French *parle-
ments* to replace two preexisting ducal councils, the Senate of Milan
was first and foremost a high court of justice, with appellate and final
jurisdiction over all lower courts (both royal and feudal) throughout
the state. The Senate, however, was also charged with reviewing all
new legislation before it became operative in the whole of Lombardy
and was entrusted with supervising, in an administrative capacity,

such matters as higher education (the University of Pavia), heresy, and feudal tenures. Outside the Senate, Milanese patricians also filled five of the seven seats in the two chief finance departments of the State of Milan, the *Magistrato delle entrate ordinarie* and the *Magistrato delle entrate straordinarie*, within whose purview fell not only taxation, but also the regulation of trade, manufactures, and waterways. Patricians also held most key positions in the Treasury General and in the offices of Provisions (*Annona*) and of Health (*Sanità*), and one of them was appointed to the high position of *Capitano di Giustizia*, a state officer who combined broad police powers with some of the duties of a public prosecutor.

What is remarkable in all this is the firm hold the Milanese patriciate was able to maintain over the machinery of government through the centuries and under different political regimes. As far as the Spanish monarchy is concerned, the decision to retain virtually unaltered the traditional structure of the State of Milan was made at the outset by Charles V. As Federico Chabod has pointed out,[17] the successor of the last Sforza duke had no intention of bringing any measure of institutional uniformity to the many scattered territories that came under his rule; on the contrary, he prided himself on respecting the traditions and the identity of each, and he used this policy as an argument against those who accused him of aiming at a "universal monarchy." But other considerations, too, entered into the policy pursued by Charles V and his Spanish successors: their reliance on the patriciate of Milan and their insistence on the continuity of their own rule with the glorious ducal past were dictated by a desire to win and to keep the loyalty of the local ruling elite, to draw on their administrative and judicial expertise, and, ironically enough, to use them as a check against the ambitions of the Spanish governors themselves, the very governors whom the crown sent from Spain to oversee its Lombard possessions.

As for the patricians themselves, their hold on high offices was grounded more in tradition than in any clear legislative provision. Traditionally, only patricians were eligible for membership in four corporate bodies of great antiquity that represented as many pinnacles of social prestige and political influence in the city of Milan: these were the four "colleges" (or professional guilds) of jurists, notaries, physicians, and architects, each with a membership of between thirty and fifty. Although high-ranking officials and magistrates were, as a rule, appointed by the Spanish monarch, the latter invariably chose from among the members of the four great colleges, and especially of the most highly respected of all, the College of Jurists. From it came the Milanese members of the Senate and a majority of the questors who headed the finance ministries. Members of the Senate, in turn, sat in the offices of Provisions and of Health, alongside fellow patricians drawn from the College of Physicians, while lawyers, notaries, and architects of patrician extraction or trained in the patrician-dominated colleges filled lesser positions throughout the administration. In short, it is no exaggeration to say that the patrician oligarchy held in its hands virtually all the levers of power in the State of Milan, besides, of course, those in the administration of the city of Milan and its *ducato*.

Predictably, this awesome concentration of power in the hands of an urban elite had long been used to promote the city's interests. City residents enjoyed substantial privileges, both in fiscal and legal matters, over the less fortunate *rurali*. Throughout the state, city residents (patricians as well as commoners) were immune from the jurisdiction of local (and notably feudal) courts and could be tried only by city magistrates, and the privilege (*privilegium civilitatis*) extended to those they employed as servants, tenants, or day laborers.[18] Townsmen were also exempt from some of the direct taxes which weighed so heavily on rustics (the cavalry tax, the salt tax, the levy on crops known as *imbottato*) as well as from the obnoxious obligation of providing quarters and provisions to the soldiery in transit (*alloggiamenti*).[19] Farmland owned by townsmen, moreover, was assessed separately from, and was taxed more lightly than, land owned by villagers. When Charles V introduced a new direct tax (the infamous *mensuale*) that was to be levied uniformly throughout the state on all assets, movable as well as unmovable, the cities fought tooth and nail to be exempted from an imposition that they viewed as an intolerable infringement on their ancient privileges. To be sure, their opposition was eventually overcome, but the two separate tax rolls, one for farmland owned by townsmen (*pertiche civili*) and another for that owned by country residents (*pertiche rurali*), were preserved, with two important results: first, city authorities retained a measure of control over the assessment and collection of taxes levied on the country estates of townsmen; second, townsmen could not be made to contribute to military billets, as these continued to be viewed as a rural responsibility.[20]

Urban policies were also consistently aimed at the welfare of the city populace. Grain shipments from one province to another were closely monitored, and so were exports abroad. The intent here was to ensure as plentiful a supply of grain to the cities as possible. To that end, all landowners and tenants with a surplus to sell were traditionally obligated to bring one-third or even half of their crop to the city and to put it up for sale there in the chief market square; only such grain as found no buyer in the city could later find its way to lesser towns or to foreign countries.[21] Even more stringent restrictions applied to the trade in raw silk: its export was, as a rule, prohibited, or was allowed only after the needs of the Milan silk manufacturers had been met.[22] Milan itself had succeeded not only in preempting the supply of raw silk, but also in asserting its exclusive right to harbor a silk industry. As for other manufactures (fustians and woolens, metals, leather, and paper), each Lombard city had long claimed them as an exclusive prerogative to be jealously guarded by the city's guilds, while in the countryside only the manufacture of ordinary, inferior goods for local use was tolerated.

The countryside, of course, did not accept the claims and the privileges of the city without protest, nor were efforts lacking in the sixteenth century to modify or circumvent inequities. In the second half of the century, such efforts seem to have been especially vigorous and, in small part, successful. The introduction of the new levy known as *mensuale*, for instance, gave rise, as suggested before, to considerable tension between town and country, one issue being whether or not land owned by townsmen ought to be subject to the new tax. The outcome, as will be recalled, while still favoring the city, had at least prevented the entire burden of the *mensuale* from impinging on rural property. Another, and in the long run more important, by-product of the *mensuale* was the creation of a new body, the *Congregazione del Ducato*, consisting or representatives (*sindaci*) of the rural districts (*pievi rurali*) and serving both as an agency for the apportionment of the land tax among individual communities and as a forum in which the grievances of the countryside could be aired. Although largely advisory in nature, the new body gave the *contado*, for the first time, a voice in public affairs. Interestingly enough, it was under its prodding that legislation was enacted in 1614 to the effect that all land purchased by townsmen after 1572 would be considered on a par with all other land and thus would no longer be eligible for preferential tax treatment.[23]

Under the pressure of the overburdened rural taxpayers and through the voice of their newly founded Congregation, another step in the direction of greater, but by no means complete, fiscal equality between town and country was taken in the second half of the sixteenth century. Once again, the process was triggered by the *mensuale*, as the countryside claimed that the tax ought to be levied not merely on landed property (*perticato*), but on movable property, and notably on merchants' assets (*mercimonio*) as well.[24] Urban, and especially guild, opposition to this was, predictably, dogged and it was only after nearly fifty years of legal maneuvering and chicanery that the *mercimonio* was made to contribute its share of the *mensuale*.[25]

As for the traditional restrictions on the grain and silk trades, we can legitimately suspect that they found little more favor in the countryside than did tax inequities. We can also suspect that here the best defense was smuggling, although evidence for this is not readily available. Evasions of the prohibition against setting up certain manufactures outside the city walls and away from the supervision of the guilds are, on the other hand, attested to during the late sixteenth century. This was the time, as will be recalled, when the fustian industry, nearly extinct in Milan, had found a new home in Busto Arsizio and Gallarate, and when inroads were even being made into the one manufacture that Milan had always jealously kept to itself, namely, silk making. Pavia, which had earlier been denied the privilege of harboring silk weavers, somehow managed to have a sizable number of them in the second half of the century.[26] Hat making, another traditionally Milanese craft, had by 1600 begun to develop in the small town of Monza, much to the displeasure of the city's guild.[27]

But despite occasional breaches in the old city-state structure, the fact remains that to the end of the sixteenth century and beyond, the archaic dispensation that the State of Milan had inherited from the days of the medieval commune continued to persist. What distorting effects this lopsided structure had on the Lombard economy as a whole is not hard to imagine, although it may be impossible to measure. Clearly, inequality of taxation subsidized the cities (and particularly Milan, with its high concentration of officials and military personnel) at the expense of the countryside, thus tending to depress incomes in the latter. Restrictions on the location of industry and on trade in agricultural commodities worked in the same direction and tended to heighten the disparities between city and countryside and between townsman and peasant. Even more dangerously, by forcing manufactures to be located in the cities—behind the shield of protective legislation and under the watchful eye of guilds dedicated to the preservation of traditional privileges and to the suppression of competition from low paid, poverty stricken husbandmen—the traditional policies of the city-state may well have resulted in a less-than-optimal allocation of capital and manpower, in higher production costs in the city, and in depressed incomes in the countryside.

To the existing constraints created by high population density, low productivity, and a lopsided institutional framework, new strains were added in the late sixteenth century.

There were, first of all, alarming signs that the food supply, even in a land generally regarded as a cornucopia, was lagging behind demand. Largely as a result of the demographic upsurge that characterized the second half of the century, but possibly also as a result of deteriorating climatic conditions, food prices climbed rapidly throughout western Europe and especially in the Mediterranean regions. As the danger of food shortages made itself increasingly felt, cities began to take precautionary measures, the most common being the storage of grain reserves controlled by municipal authorities for use in time of famine.[28] In 1572 a public granary was built in Milan and more stringent regulations on the export of grain were enacted throughout the state.[29] In the early 1590s the long feared threat of famine became a reality throughout the Mediterranean world, and Lombardy, for all its legendary abundance, was not entirely spared. A

petition submitted in 1591 by the community of Codogno located
north of the Po River in the opulent low plain vividly describes the
repercussions that widespread and persistent scarcity could have even
on a rich farming area:

> The village of Codogno lies so conveniently close to the terri-
> tory of Piacenza that it serves almost as an open door to those
> who come from there, and actually such is the crowd of wretched
> beggars who driven by hunger daily descend from their moun-
> tains and find refuge in this village that it looks as if in a short
> time the village itself will overflow with people. This state of
> affairs has become the more alarming in that, since last year, the
> boatmen of the Po readily ferry all those wretches across the river
> to our shore, but refuse to take anyone back, claiming that such
> are the orders issued by their prince. As Piacenza thus tries to
> divert this flood onto us, before long we will be submerged . . . We
> therefore plead that instructions and authority be given to our
> local magistrate [*podestà*] and to the community itself to the
> effect that with the greatest possible dispatch they may clear this
> land of all those foreigners who are notoriously useless and
> harmful.[30]

We do not know whether the petition was accepted and what
measures, if any, were taken to cope with the problem of the refugees
from the Duchy of Parma and Piacenza. What we do know is that the
problem of food scarcity lingered throughout the 1590s and into the
early years of the next century, when Milan itself had to import large
amounts of rye (possibly of Baltic origin) via Genoa "as a remedy
against dearth."[31]

The food crisis of the 1590s had repercussions beyond sheer human
suffering and the social tensions that developed—such as those in
Codogno between villagers and refugees. Productive activity in the
cities was apparently affected too. In 1598, representatives of the city
of Milan argued before the central government that the intolerably
high cost of living was a major source of difficulties for the city's
manufacturers; the latter, it was claimed, "are now totally destroyed
and have moved elsewhere," and notably to the countryside, in order
to avoid heavy taxes and the "dearth of necessities" (*il vivere
carestioso*); the making of cotton fabrics, it was pointed out, had
shifted to Busto Arsizio, the manufacture of arms and armor to
Brescia, and that of woolen cloth to the Bergamasque.[32] The claim was

no doubt as exaggerated as it was self-serving, for we know that the industries of Milan were far from being "totally destroyed" at the time. Nonetheless, it probably contained a kernel of truth: steep food prices may well have exerted an upward pressure on wages, thus eroding profits and discouraging enterprise in the cities.

By the end of the century the cities that formed the heart and the pride of the Lombard (and north Italian) economy were confronted with serious difficulties—a fact that a few contemporary writers began to sense, however dimly. Writing in the 1590s, an anonymous English visitor to Italy mused over the paradox of a country where on the one hand, "fertilitie of the soile, temperature of aire and singularitie of wittes" combined to produce "such singular abundance," and where, on the other hand, he had "found so deare lyvinge." The latter fact he ascribed, rather simplistically, although not entirely without reason, to the division of the peninsula into so many separate states, each burdened by "the intolerable exaccions and pillages of their princes," but his comment is interesting primarily because of his emphasis on the high cost of living, and particularly on high food prices.[33] A similar concern was very much on Giovanni Botero's mind as he speculated on the causes of "the greatness of cities." Having noticed that the population of Venice and Milan, after a prolonged upswing, seemed to have leveled off as the sixteenth century drew to a close, Botero wondered "how it doth come to pass that the multiplication [of people] goes not onward accordingly." "Some answer," he went on to argue, "the cause thereof is the plagues, the wars, the dearths and such other causes. But this gives no satisfaction. For plagues have ever been and wars have been more common and more bloody in former times than now." In his view, the ultimate reason why urban population had stabilized lay in "the defect of nutriment and sustenance sufficient for it."[34] What we know about rising food prices in the late sixteenth century and widespread anxiety about scarce food supplies to the cities bears out Botero's insight.

The difficulties facing the cities as a result of population pressure and food shortages were compounded by the increasing competition urban manufactures encountered on both the domestic and foreign markets. The upward pressure exerted by soaring food prices on the artisans' wages may have undermined, as has been suggested before, the competitiveness of goods produced in the cities versus those made in the countryside, for in the latter living costs were presumably lower and, more importantly, the labor force, consisting of peasants who were only partially dependent on wages for their living, could afford to work for less pay.[35] But the most serious threat to the dominant position long held by the Lombard cities in manufacturing came from quite a different source, and notably from some of those very countries that had traditionally been among Lombardy's best customers.

Traditionally, the success of the Lombard manufactures on international markets had depended not on Lombardy enjoying any overwhelming natural advantage in the supply of raw materials, but primarily on the precocious development of superior techniques and skills that were hard to imitate and harder to emulate, and which gave its industries a comfortable edge over less-developed nations. Actually, most industrial raw materials used in the Lombard cities had to be imported: the fine wool that went into the high-grade fabrics of Como and Milan was secured from England, Spain, or Germany;[36] the cotton used in the Cremona fustian industry came from the Levant, via Genoa, Leghorn, or Venice; the making of gold thread (possibly the most admired achievement of the Milanese craftsmen) depended on the importation of precious metals, mainly from Germany. Only in the case of silk, flax, and iron could Lombard manufacturers rely on native sources of supply.

Even for these products, however, technology and know-how counted far more than the availability of native raw materials. Consider, for example, iron metallurgy: the ores found in the Lombard Prealpi (and notably in Valsassina) were low in iron content and definitely inferior to those found elsewhere in Italy;[37] nor was charcoal, the fuel then indispensable for smelting iron, especially plentiful in a heavily settled region such as Lombardy—the wood needed to make it was often enough not easily accessible. The strength of Lombard metallurgy rather lay in the relatively advanced methods used in smelting. This point is borne out by the fact that well before the close of the sixteenth century the indirect process of smelting in the blast furnace had become firmly established in the Valsassina, and this at a time when in other parts of Italy and of Europe the older direct process, using open hearth or shaft furnaces, was still widely practiced and would give way to the new, more sophisticated technology only at a later date.[38] To an area poorly endowed in iron ores and fuel, the early adoption of the blast furnace was of crucial importance: on the one hand, it made possible and economical, as the direct process did not, the smelting of low-grade ores; on the other, by reducing the input of fuel per unit of output, the indirect process helped save a scarce and expensive resource.

Further downstream, too, advanced technology helped to ensure the profitability and reputation of Lombard metallurgy. The armorers of Milan had made a name for themselves, thanks to their ability to produce ornate suits of armor, finely chiseled and exquisitely inlaid articles that were avidly sought in the courts and tournaments, if no longer on the battlefields, of Europe.[39] Similarly, the gold thread made in Milan owed its reputation to an ingenious and jealously guarded technique whereby the thread itself was made of gold-plated silver rather than solid gold, a technique that considerably reduced costs without apparently sacrificing the appearance and durability of the product.[40]

Even in the silk industry, skills and techniques contributed far more than an abundant supply of raw material to ensuring the success of the industry itself. In this connection, it is worth recalling that Milan became a major center of the silk industry long before the mulberry tree was introduced into Lombardy.[41] Moreover, it must be borne in mind that, unlike other raw materials, silk, because of its high value relative to weight or bulk, could be transported over long distances even in an age when transportation was notoriously expensive; accordingly, the proximity of a silk-growing area—such as the Lombard countryside had become since the late fifteenth century—was not of decisive importance in determining the location and the success of silk manufacturers. It is revealing, in this connection, that the Milan silk makers made use of but a portion of the locally grown silk and, for select articles, relied on imported varieties.[42] The point that needs stressing here, however, is that Lombardy's international reputation for silk fabrics and other manufactures at the close of the sixteenth century ultimately rested on the superior skills and techniques of its craftsmen, on their ability to turn out goods the like of which could not easily be found elsewhere. In the words of a French nobleman who visited Milan around 1600, "He who wishes to have the finest arms, fabrics, harness, embroidered works of all kinds and, in short, any of the things one can dream of, should avoid the trouble of looking for them elsewhere if he cannot find them in Milan."[43]

And yet, even before the end of the sixteenth century, ominous signs are discernible that Lombardy's industrial supremacy was being slowly eroded as other nations and other cities that had traditionally been among its customers were beginning to take bold strides along the road of import substitution, emulating their former purveyors and progressively narrowing the gap that had ensured the Lombard cities a comfortable lead until then.

Some of the earliest threats had come from Germany and had affected, interestingly enough, the manufacture of common, inexpensive textiles. Once the largest outlet for Italian (and mostly Lombard) cotton fabrics, Germany had developed, since the late fourteenth century, a cotton industry of its own, with Ulm, Ravensburg, Constance, and Augsburg as its chief centers. German merchants in Italy had gradually replaced their purchases of Italian fustians with those of raw cotton imported from the Levant through Venice. The loss of the German market and the increasingly stiff competition of German *barchent* on third markets signaled the end of Lombard supremacy in one important field, but by no means did they spell the ruin of the Lombard cotton industry. As has been seen, Cremona remained a major center of the cotton industry throughout the sixteenth century, and a fresh start was made in Busto Arsizio. What saved the industry in Lombardy from total decay may have been a certain superiority in dyeing techniques, the development of mixed fabrics (*bombasine*), the protection of the domestic market behind stiff tariffs, and, lastly, the retention of a sizable outlet in the Levant, where shorter distances and long-standing trade connections favored the Italian, rather than the German, merchant.[44] For all this, the fact remains that the rise of the German cotton industry inflicted an early blow on Lombardy: it may be regarded as the opening act of a long play in which the gap that had separated the Lombard economy from its more backward neighbors was progressively narrowed.

A second step in that same direction was taken by Germany, too, and it challenged, although it did not destroy, the armor manufacture of Milan. The latter had held pride of place in Europe until the end of the fifteenth century. In the next century the armorers of Augsburg, Innsbruck, and Landshut began to vie with those of Milan in the manufacture of both common-service articles and expensive, custom-made suits of armor. Predictably, the line of defense adopted by the Milanese craftsmen was to upgrade the quality of their steel and to improve the design and elegance of their product; the result here, too, was that the industry held its own well beyond 1600, but the halcyon days of untrammeled supremacy were definitely over.[45]

In the case of the woolen industry, one cannot speak of the erosion of Lombardy's lead in quite the same sense as one can for cotton and the making of armor, for cloth making had long been a ubiquitous industry, widely spread throughout Europe and northern Italy. At best, one can speak of a Lombard superiority in certain types of high-grade cloth during the late medieval period. That superiority had no doubt been seriously compromised in the early sixteenth century, when the devastations caused by the Italian wars had resulted in the virtual paralysis of a number of manufacturing centers in the Po valley.[46] After normality had been restored, however, both Como and Milan staged a remarkable recovery, and the cloth industry in both cities managed to reassert itself, in the face of increasing competition, by specializing in the production of certain varieties of fine, expensive cloth.[47] In the last two decades of the century, however, even this modest share of a highly competitive market was threatened by other Italian cities, such as Venice and Florence, as well as by other nations. In Como, output began to fall after 1580 and, if we are to judge from the declining number of merchant-manufacturers admitted to the wool guild, a similar trend developed in Milan in the last decades of the century. Nor did smaller centers of the wool industry, such as Vigevano and Alessandria, fare much better at the time.[48]

The silk industry does not seem to have been subjected to any comparable threat from new rivals before the close of the sixteenth century: the skill and know-how of the Milanese craftsmen were hard to imitate, let alone to surpass. Even then, however, there were signs that the clear edge they had traditionally enjoyed was about to be eroded—or so it seems from hindsight. At the very end of the century,

King Henry IV resumed the rather unsuccessful efforts of his royal
predecessors to establish a silk manufacture in Lyons, and to that end
he brought in skilled workers from Milan and erected protective
barriers to shield the infant industry from the competition of Milan
silk goods.[49] Not long afterward the English were experimenting with
the manufacture of "Milan gold thread" in a deliberate attempt to
reduce imports that were viewed as detrimental to their country's
balance of trade.[50] Neither attempt to undermine Milan's supremacy
was to have any serious result until later in the seventeenth century,
but they are noteworthy as indications that the gap between
Lombardy and the rest of Europe was gradually closing and that a new
age of stiff, unprecedented competition was at hand. For an economy
largely geared to the export of high-grade manufactures, this trend
could be nothing but alarming, the more so as the new developments
abroad coincided with a period in which domestic demand for
foodstuffs was placing heavy strains on the agricultural resources of
Lombardy and, presumably, forcing a reduction in the size of the
exportable surplus.

Economic conditions and prospects were likely to be affected by
diplomatic and military developments as much as by changes in
international trade, because, since the days of the Sforza dukes, the
State of Milan had had the unenviable distinction of being the single
Italian state most frequently involved in international disputes and
most susceptible to be turned into an armed camp or an actual
battleground. Its vulnerability had to do, of course, with its strategic
location at the center of the Po valley and at the intersection of most
of the routes connecting the peninsula with Europe north of the
Alps.[51] Appropriately enough, in diplomatic quarters the State of
Milan had been known, at least since the close of the fifteenth century,
as "la clef d'Italie" or "le faubourg de Naples," for any outside power
with ambitions over the entire peninsula had to be able to seize and
hold Milan.[52] And while its strategic value was bound to turn the area
into a hotly contested prize in international conflicts, the area itself
was notoriously vulnerable and hard to defend: to the north the
boundaries of the State of Milan extended to just short of the Alpine

watershed, which was controlled by the Swiss Confederates and the Grison Leagues; on the remaining three sides the only natural protection was afforded by rivers such as the Sesia, the Adda, and the Po, and military events were to prove over and over again how easy it would be for an invading army to cross them.[53]

During the days of Charles VIII and Lodovico il Moro and for the next half century the unique importance of the State of Milan as the key to Italy had turned it into an arena where French, Imperial, Spanish, and Swiss troops had clashed in the great battles of Marignano, Lodi, Pavia, and Mortara, until, at the Peace of Cateau Cambresis in 1559, France had finally agreed that the Hapsburgs should be the undisputed successors of the Sforza dukes. The next fifty years or so were a long parenthesis in the tumultuous and war-ridden history of what was then and was long to remain Spanish Lombardy, and it is no mere coincidence that in that long interval of peace the country experienced a demographic and economic expansion, as a result of which it stood once again, despite some disquieting symptoms of change, as an object of admiration and envy.

This happy parenthesis came to a close in the early seventeenth century, when international developments placed Lombardy again in the eye of the storm and brought to it new woes and renewed losses. To these we shall return later. What needs emphasizing at this point is that even in the peaceful and prosperous half century after the Italian wars, the State of Milan did not become a political or military backwater, but continued to play a prominent role in Spanish strategy. Not only did Philip II continue to view his Lombard possessions as essential to the preservation of Hapsburg hegemony over the Italian peninsula, but Lombardy also acquired a new role as a result of the outbreak of revolt in the Low Countries in the 1560s. As seaborne communications between Spain and the rebellious provinces grew more and more hazardous, supplies, manpower, and cash increasingly had to be rerouted through Genoa and from there overland across Lombardy, Piedmont-Savoy, Franche-Comté, and Lorraine all the way to Brussels and Antwerp.[54] Accordingly, to safeguard and preserve the southern links of this strategic lifeline—and notably to ensure that neither the Republic of Genoa nor the Duke of Savoy would stray from their loyalty to Spain—it became all the more imperative for Philip II to hold the State of Milan and to keep it militarily strong. As a Venetian diplomatic envoy put it, "The State of Milan . . . is one of the most valuable possessions of the Spanish king, for it stands in the way of any French intrusion into Italy and protects the Kingdom of Naples . . . It is also conveniently located to assist [Spanish interests] in Flanders, for here are assembled the Spanish troops who, by way of Savoy and Lorraine and across Burgundy, safely reach Flanders."[55]

Whether as an actual battleground or as a strategic outpost ensuring Spain's hegemony in Italy and vital supply routes, Lombardy had thus to be kept in a constant state of preparedness, and this meant not only that in normal times it hosted and supported substantial garrisons, but also that a ring of fortified places had to be built and kept in readiness all around the State.[56] Under these circumstances, it is not surprising that government spending, which had risen fivefold under the rule of Charles V, remained high under his successor even though Lombardy itself was not directly involved in war.[57]

One should like, of course, to be able to gauge the effect of all that spending on the Lombard economy, but precise information on this point has so far eluded the grasp of those who have studied the problem, the chief hurdle being, of course, our inability to estimate, let alone measure, the size of Spanish Lombardy's gross national product and hence to determine what share of it was absorbed by military expenditures. One point, however, is clear enough: most of what the Milan treasury spent was spent in Lombardy itself and went to defray the cost of fortifications, military supplies, and soldiers' pay. The high expectations nourished by Charles V and his advisors in the 1530s—to the effect that the newly acquired State of Milan, with its legendary wealth, would prove a rich source of revenue for the whole empire—had been disappointed from the start: not only had the defense of Lombardy absorbed all the revenue raised locally, but over and over again additional monies had had to be sent either from Spain or from the Spanish-ruled Kingdom of Naples to bail out a beleaguered governor faced with an empty treasury and a mutinous army.[58] Nor were conditions substantially different under Philip II. So far as is known, the State of Milan contributed no revenue to other parts of Philip's dominions. On the contrary, despite a high level of taxation, government spending there (mainly for military purposes) continued to outstrip local tax revenue, the shortfall being made up by large-scale borrowing and possibly by unilateral transfers from the central treasury.[59]

As to the impact that a high level of government spending may have had on the Lombard economy, one general observation seems warranted. To the extent that such spending was financed out of local revenue it obviously effected a shift of resources and manpower from civilian to military uses, from butter to guns. The magnitude of the shift itself cannot be measured with the limited information available to us, but that it was large enough to be sorely felt at the time is suggested by the complaints, however exaggerated these may have been, that the merchants of Milan voiced in the 1590s against the crippling effect heavy taxation was having on the city's textile manufactures.[60] A foreign observer, for his part, confirmed that the demands of the military were eating deeply into private incomes when he wrote that "the billeting of Spanish soldiers causes a great deal of ill feelings in the country . . . for they prey, harass, steal, plunder, and devour the substance of these wretched people; they come here ragged and hungry and depart well clad and better fed."[61]

That heavy sacrifices were imposed on the Lombard populace not only by arrogant quartermasters and rapacious soldiers but by the tax collector as well is also brought out by a 1594 document that discusses in considerable detail the pay of farm laborers in the countryside near Pavia. We learn that a farm laborer could earn about 200 lire a year by working for wages; we are also told that he had to pay between 20 and 30 lire in direct taxes, or between 10 and 15 percent of his total earnings. Since the latter were barely sufficient to ensure the worker's subsistence, it is clear that direct taxation alone took a very large bite out of the laboring poor's income.[62]

There was, however, another side to this grim picture, for while taxes no doubt imposed heavy sacrifices on the majority, large military spending benefited a number of people connected with the war effort—soldiers and camp followers, army contractors and armorers, iron merchants and gunsmiths. At the same time, to the extent that government spending in excess of tax revenue was financed with funds borrowed in Lombardy, a redistribution of income was effected from the mass of the taxpayers to the small elite of financiers, patricians, government officials, and churchmen who were in a position to lend money to the crown. The risk here was that of a hard-pressed government suspending interest payments—and Philip II's government was certainly not above resorting to such drastic measures. But in the 1590s the risk was greatly reduced in the State of Milan—and the position of government creditors was accordingly made more secure—following the creation of the Banco di Sant' Ambrogio, a well-run public corporation whose purpose was to raise funds from private creditors for investment in government loans and whose solvency was de facto guaranteed by the tax revenue of the city of Milan.[63]

Writing around 1590, a foreign diplomat observed that the Milanese "are not entirely dissatisfied with the Spanish king's rule, although with individual Spaniards brawls and quarrels are frequent."[64] We have no way of verifying the second part of this statement, and yet no difficulty in accepting it at face value. As for the first part, it is quite likely that it accurately portrays the feelings, if not of the heavily taxed populace, at least of large segments of the middle and upper classes, for as the sixteenth century drew to a close the State of Milan, despite some difficulties, a high cost of living, and considerable retrenchment, still enjoyed internal and external peace, financial stability, and an enviable degree of economic prosperity.[65]

CHAPTER III

WAR, DISEASE, AND DISLOCATIONS

The long period of peace and prosperity that Spanish Lombardy had enjoyed since the middle of the sixteenth century came to an end in the second decade of the following century; for the next fifty years the State of Milan served almost uninterruptedly either as a springboard for military campaigns against neighboring states or, and more often, as the actual battleground where the Bourbons and the Hapsburgs were locked in combat for the control of northern Italy.

The long, grim story began in 1613, in connection with the disputed succession of the Duchy of Mantua and Monferrato.[1] The small, prosperous state, under the rule of the Gonzaga family, lay in the heart of the Po valley and consisted of two separate segments located on each side of the State of Milan—Mantua proper to the southeast and Monferrato to the southwest. For Spain it was clearly essential that the Gonzaga state remain firmly in the Hapsburg sphere of influence, as it had been since the days of Emperor Charles V, for any hostile influence or interference in the affairs of the Duchy would pose a direct threat to the security and integrity of the Spanish dominions in Lombardy. Such a threat actually materialized in 1613, when Duke Francesco Gonzaga died without male issue, leaving two younger brothers, Ferdinand and Vincenzo, as heirs apparent. The brothers' right to succeed was at once challenged by Charles Emmanuel, the ambitious duke of Savoy and an ally of France, who claimed, if not the whole inheritance, at least that portion of it that was adjacent to his own lands, namely, Monferrato. Actual warfare erupted in 1613 when a Savoyard army invaded defenseless Monferrato and easily seized some of its key towns, thus posing a direct threat to the southwestern flank of the State of Milan and moving dangerously close to Genoa, a satellite of Spain and the gateway through which Spanish soldiers and supplies entered northern Italy. In response,

Spanish forces attacked from the State of Milan and for nearly five years war raged all along its western border and notably in Monferrato (1613), in Vercelli, which the Spaniards besieged and eventually captured (1617), and around Novara, whose territory was devastated by a Savoyard counteroffensive. In June 1618 an uneasy peace was finally arranged, which restored the status quo: while Vercelli was handed back to Charles Emmanuel, the latter was forced to withdraw from Monferrato and the rights of the brothers of the late Gonzaga duke were vindicated.

In 1627, however, the death of the last Gonzaga—without issue— re-opened the whole succession problem, but in a different and more ominous form. This time the major challenge came from France, as the latter supported the claim to the whole Mantuan inheritance set forth by the Gonzaga-Nevers, a collateral branch of the Gonzaga dynasty that had long become established in France and was fully committed to France. If their claim was intolerable to Spain, it was hardly more palatable to the Duke of Savoy. Confronted by a common menace, the two erstwhile foes closed ranks and agreed to a partition of the disputed inheritance, with its Mantuan portion going to a Spanish protegé (Gonzaga-Guastalla) and Monferrato to Savoy. For the next three years the second war of the Mantuan succession unfolded in an intricate pattern of shifting alliances, savage battles, and long-drawn sieges. What made this second war so much more devastating and destructive than the first was the active participation of two new combatants: the French, 34,000 strong, sent by Richelieu to defeat the Duke of Savoy and to seize Monferrato, and the Austrians (or Imperials) who descended with nearly as many men from the Tyrol and through the Valtelline to assist their Spanish cousins and keep Mantua in the Hapsburg camp. The outcome of the war was a compromise (the Treaty of Cherasco, 1631); the Duke of Nevers received most of the inheritance while paying lip service to the Hapsburg emperor as his liege lord; the Duke of Savoy made some limited territorial gains in Monferrato, while France secured a bridgehead, Pinerolo, on the Italian side of the Alps.

In the long run, however, the most important stipulation of the Treaty of Cherasco was to be the one that dealt with the touchy issue of the Valtelline: the valley was to be cleared of all foreign garrisons and the Alpine routes running through it were to remain open. In practice, this meant the withdrawal of Hapsburg forces from the area and paved the way to future French interventions in northern Italy; it also meant that the last corridor between Spanish Lombardy and northern Europe would be closed.[2]

To understand the importance of the Valtelline it may be well to recall that the "Spanish road"—which had ensured communications between the Mediterranean and the Netherlands, via Genoa, Lombardy, Piedmont-Savoy, Franche-Comté, and Lorraine, in the second half of the sixteenth century—had been closed in 1601 as a result of a rapprochement between France and the Duke of Savoy. Accordingly, Spain had been forced to look for alternative supply roads and had found two which, while longer and less convenient than the old road, at least ensured a continuous flow of supplies and manpower to the army of Flanders. By pledging large cash subsidies to the Swiss Catholic cantons, as well as to the Grisons, the Spanish monarchy managed to secure the right of passage to the Rhineland through Swiss territory—either over the Simplon pass or by way of the Valtelline and the Engadine. The Simplon road proved a valuable alternative for over a decade, but in 1613 it was closed to the Spaniards as France managed to win the Swiss cantons over to its side. There remained the Valtelline road: this became now the jugular vein of Hapsburg strategy, and all efforts were concentrated on keeping it open. Those efforts had actually gotten under way as early as 1603, when the large fort of Fuentes had been built at the northernmost tip of Lake Como, at the doorstep, as it were, of the Valtelline itself. In 1620, using as a pretext the outbreak of bloody feuds between Catholics and Protestants in the Valtelline, the Spanish government resorted to full-scale intervention in the valley itself: Spanish forces invaded the Valtelline and placed a permanent garrison there to protect its troops in transit. For the next decade the new, roundabout road functioned well both as a link with the Low Countries and as a corridor through which the Austrian Hapsburgs could easily dispatch an army to the Po valley—as they did in 1627 at the time of the second war of the Mantuan succession.

After 1631, however, conditions deteriorated rapidly for the two Hapsburg governments. Not only were they forced by the terms of the

Treaty of Cherasco to evacuate the Valtelline, but on the north side of the Alps both Alsace (in 1631) and Lorraine (in 1633) fell into French hands. Accordingly, all overland communications between northern Italy and the Netherlands were severed. Moreover, in 1634 a French army led by the Duke of Rohan marched into Grison territory, descended into the Valtelline, and brought war to the State of Milan itself: in the spring of 1635 Rohan, after devastating the Valsassina, appeared at the gates of Lecco. Shortly after, the maverick Duke of Savoy, once again an ally of France, attacked the western border of the State of Milan, first in Lomellina and then further north in the Novarese, and crossed the Ticino River in an attempt to link up with Rohan's forces and to cut Spanish Lombardy in two.

What saved the State of Milan from this two-pronged attack was both the spirited resistance staged by the hastily mobilized militia and the outbreak of civil war in Piedmont-Savoy following the death of Duke Vittorio Amedeo in 1637. As his son and heir was but a child, the regency was at once bitterly disputed between his widow, Madama Cristina, and his two brothers, the widow relying on French support to validate her claims and the brothers turning to Spain for help. The ensuing civil war not only relieved pressure on Lombardy's western border, but provided the Spanish governor of Milan with an opportunity for recapturing Vercelli (1638), for marching at the head of an army of Spanish and rebel Savoyard troops all the way to the outskirts of Turin (1639), and for laying siege to the stronghold of Casale Monferrato, then held by French and loyal Savoyard troops (1640). After nearly two more years of inconclusive warfare across Piedmont, however, Madama Cristina and her brothers-in-law patched up their differences, joined forces with the French, and turned against Spain—bringing war into Lombard territory, capturing (1643) and then losing (1646) Tortona and Vigevano, and laying waste the countryside around Alessandria, Novara, and Pavia. To make a critical situation even worse, in 1647 a new threat developed against the southern corner of the State of Milan, as the Duke of Modena, prodded by France, staged a surprise attack against and laid siege to Cremona and Casalmaggiore (1648).

The Westphalia settlement of 1648 did not bring the Franco-Spanish conflict to an end and for another decade war continued to rage in and around the State of Milan. After a relative lull in military operations from 1649 to 1653, when the French military effort was crippled as a result of the Fronde, hostilities resumed in full and reached a dramatic climax in 1655, when Milan itself was threatened from the west by an advancing Franco-Savoyard army, Pavia was besieged, and the surrounding countryside was systematically devastated by the Franco-Modenese soldiery. In 1658 another combined force of French and Modenese units renewed its attack further north, crossed the Adda River at Cassano, came within a few miles of Milan, and marched the whole width of the state as far as Lake Maggiore, leaving behind a broad swath of destruction. This, however, was the last grim act in the long futile drama that had unfolded for decades: before the end of 1659 France and Spain had concluded the Treaty of the Pyrenees and peace, at last, returned to a devastated Lombardy.

Warfare, prolonged though it was, may not have been the worst scourge visited on Lombardy in the first half of the seventeenth century, for although it had, as will be seen, unsettling and far-reaching effects on economic life, it did not possess the devastating force of its modern counterpart: seventeenth-century weapons were incomparably less destructive than their modern equivalents, the armies involved were vastly smaller, and the damages inflicted tended to be circumscribed to limited areas. As far as the loss of human lives was concerned, the chief offenders at the time were famine and, above all, epidemic disease rather than war—and Lombardy suffered heavily from both in the troubled period we are discussing.

There were three major occurrences of famine, in 1629, 1635, and 1649. In each instance a crop failure, caused by adverse weather conditions and aggravated by trade stoppages resulting from the war as well as from misguided or inadequate government policies, sent prices soaring and brought intolerable suffering and high mortality in its wake.[3] The intensity of the suffering is illustrated by the tragic sequence of events in the fall of 1629, culminating in the revolt of Martinmas in Milan;[4] the deadly impact of what have been called "crises de subsistance" is embalmed in the surviving burial registers of the time.[5]

But by far the worst killer to visit the State of Milan (as well as most of northern Italy) in those days was the great plague of 1630. Probably introduced into the area by German troops who had descended from the Valtelline on their way to Mantua in the latter part of 1629,[6] the disease broke on a country where starvation had been rampant for nearly two years and had already taken a heavy toll of lives.[7] During the spring and summer of 1630 the plague spread throughout the Po valley, mowing down human lives at a rate that had few precedents in the annals of the area.[8] What the demographic losses may have been cannot be ascertained with any degree of precision. As far as the major cities are concerned, fairly accurate data are available and, while they do not support some of the extravagant, apocalyptic estimates made by contemporaries, they clearly indicate that this last visitation of the plague took a frightening toll of lives, comparable, in fact, to that of the Black Death.[9] The population of Milan was nearly halved; in Pavia losses were on the order of 40 percent; Cremona saw its population reduced from 37,000 to 17,000; Como suffered a 30 percent loss.[10] It is hard to know what impact the plague had on the lesser towns and on the countryside as a whole. According to a 1641 memorandum a number of small market towns in northern Lombardy suffered death rates of about 50 percent.[11] The figures provided in that document, however, are but rough estimates and, intended as they were to support a plea for a tax reduction, may have been intentionally inflated. What the memorandum does suggest, however, is that the plague spared the market towns no more than the larger cities. As for the countryside, the scant evidence available suggests that the villages affected by the plague far outnumbered those that were spared, but we are in the dark concerning actual losses of lives. It is likely, however, that in the villages these were significantly lower, on the average, than in the overcrowded urban centers,[12] and there seems to be no reason for disputing the cautious estimate according to which the whole State of Milan lost about a third of its population, dropping, that is, from about 1,200,000 to something like 800,000 souls.[13]

The troubled decades during which Spanish Lombardy fell prey to war, famine, and disease were also a time of severe dislocation and prolonged difficulties for its economy.

This is true, first of all, of the largest sector of the economy at the time, namely, agriculture. Although any estimate of farm output and its fluctuations is wholly beyond our grasp, the marks of deep malaise, however scattered, are unmistakable. One such mark is provided by the desertion of farms. In the rich Lodi province between 1630 and 1647, as many as 70,000 *pertiche* (or about 5,000 hectares) of farmland, representing 7 percent of total acreage had reportedly reverted to waste. Around Caravaggio, east of the Adda River, one-fourth of the land—so it was claimed in 1643—had been abandoned in recent years due to a shortage of labor. Similar conditions prevailed in the Soncino district nearby: while at the beginning of the century only 1 percent of the soil was reported as being untilled, a survey made in 1668 revealed that 18 percent lay idle.[14] In the southwestern parts of the state, in the 1630s and 40s, large stretches of land were said to lie uncropped, "because the landowners cannot plough them." Further north in the province of Novara, according to one document, "two-thirds of the land have reverted to heath"; in Lomellina "a great deal of land" was said to lie idle as the local farmers confined their efforts to "the better soils only"; and in the embattled province of Cremona a survey made in 1634 indicated that tillage had been discontinued on as much as 31 percent of all farmland.[15] Other signs of a dramatic contraction in farming operations included sharp cutbacks in the size of herds, and a fall in the revenues accruing to feudal lords.[16]

But possibly the most telling evidence of the troubles then afflicting the rural economy is the drastic drop in agrarian income and land values. A great landed family, the D'Adda, with vast holdings scattered east and west throughout the State of Milan, had earned as much as L.15,000 a year from its properties in the first two decades of the seventeenth century; in the next twenty years, however, its annual income averaged a mere L.1,000.[17] Nor was their case unique. Just outside the Milan city walls, a large block of public farmland had been leased at an annual rent of L.42,300 between 1607 and 1634; the last tenant, however, had defaulted on his rent and when, in 1634, a new one was found, his rent was set, after prolonged negotiations, at a mere L.29,250.[18] On a noble estate located near Belgiojoso in the low plain, rents had climbed from mid-sixteeenth century until about 1620; thereafter, the trend was downward: L.10,000 in 1637, 7,000 in 1658, and 6,500 in 1671.[19] The Collegio Borromeo in Pavia, whose endowment included four large country estates, saw its income severely reduced between 1630 and 1670, as did the administration of the Milan Cathedral: in one of its estates just west of Milan the rent per *pertica* dropped from 60 soldi in 1615 to 41 soldi in 1645.[20] In Busto Arsizio it was remarked in 1631 that in recent years land rents had dropped by as much as 50 percent.[21]

Against this somber backdrop it is not hard to give credence to contemporary complaints about falling land values and the low profitability of landownership. "Land values have sunk so low," reads a memorandum for 1635, "that buyers and even people willing to accept land in gift are hard to come by."[22] "Nowadays there is little inclination to invest in land," asserted an official in 1647 as he tried to find a buyer for some public land.[23] "Money is scarce," complained a farmer in 1631, "and what land I own I would gladly give away if I only could find someone willing to pay my taxes."[24] And one noble landowner expressed feelings that must have been common in an age of agrarian depression when he confided: "I am a gentleman who lives off his property, but in these evil days of ours land is worth very little and I would be better off if I earned a living at some kind of trade."[25]

Nor was the picture any brighter outside agriculture: after 1620 some of the key manufactures that over the centuries had earned the State of Milan a solid reputation as a leading industrial region experienced serious and often irreversible setbacks.[26] One of them was the wool industry. In Como, cloth output fell dramatically in the early part of the century and by 1650 a once celebrated manufacture had virtually ceased to exist.[27] In Milan, if we are to judge from the dwindling numbers of new admissions to the drapers' guild, the malaise of the wool industry, which had manifested itself as early as the 1580s, turned into unequivocal decline in the 1630s or, at the latest, the 1640s.[28] In Cremona the wool industry was virtually obliterated in the third and fourth decades of the century, and a similar, if less precipitous, trend affected the making of fustians, linens, and silks in that city.[29] Outside the major cities, where some textiles, and notably coarse woolens, had been manufactured at the beginning of the century, production seems to have contracted, too. According to a 1647 report, in the Brianza district north of Milan the traditional manufacture of "inferior, cheap cloth intended for the poor" had been "almost wholly discontinued" in recent years; in Monza, cloth making had completely ceased between 1620 and 1640.[30]

Silk making, by far the largest manufacture in Milan at the opening of the century and the backbone of Lombardy's export trade, was losing ground as well. The number of silk looms in the city, which in 1606 had been reported at over 3,000, was down to 600 by 1635; fifty years later their number was up to 809, but by the close of the century only 461 were left.[31] These figures are admittedly sporadic, and the first two look very much like rough estimates; yet the reality of the decline in Milan is fully confirmed by the plummeting numbers of new members admitted to the silk merchants' guild—the guild of the merchant-entrepreneurs who commissioned work to the weavers: by the last decade of the seventeenth century new admissions were one-fifth what they had been in the second decade (Table 1).

The downturn of the Lombard economy in the third decade of the seventeenth century severely affected the construction industry, and here, too, the new developments contrasted sharply with the prosperity of an earlier, less-troubled age. The industry itself had no doubt been spurred, in the second half of the sixteenth century, by the needs of reconstruction after the Italian wars, by the general demographic expansion, and by urban expansion in particular. A further stimulus to civilian construction was the impressive spurt in conspicuous investment, in the form of private palaces, stately public buildings, and the grandiose churches of the Counter Reformation. The late sixteenth and early seventeenth centuries were the time when old and newly enriched families (Visconti, Medici di Marignano, and Odescalchi, as well as D'Adda, Marino, Annoni, Durini, and Arese) had handsome new residences erected for themselves in Milan, while the churches of San Vittore, Santo Stefano in Brolo, and San Fedele, the Palazzo dei Giureconsulti and the palazzo of the Capitano di Giustizia added new

Table 1. Admissions to the Milan Guild of Silk, Gold, and Ribbon Merchants, 1611-1700

Years	Gold and silk merchants	Ribbon merchants	Total
1611-1620	136	79	215
1621-1630	94	31	125
1631-1640	61	93	154
1641-1650	45	39	84
1651-1660	42	29	71
1661-1670	59	48	107
1671-1680	47	56	103
1681-1690	34	19	53
1691-1700	27	17	44

Source: ACM, *Codice C. 3,* "Matricula in qua descripta sunt nomina et cognomina mercatorum auri argenti ac serici ac mercatorum bindelle et frixarie." The existence of this register was first made known by Santoro, *La Matricola,* p. xvi n. The original contains the names of all individuals admitted to the guild and the date of admission of each; this table shows only total admissions by decade.

splendor to the Lombard capital; this was also the time when Pavia received the two impressive new buildings that hosted the Borromeo and Ghislieri colleges; and in Cremona such local magnates as the Affaitadi, Stanga, Schinchinelli, and Zaccaria led the way, with their newly built palaces, in renovating the medieval look of the second largest city in the state.[32] By the 1630s, however, the great wave of civilian construction had definitely receded as a result of economic depression and of the depopulation caused by the plague. The history of Lombard architecture presents at this point, and for the next three or four decades, if not a complete blank, certainly a very meager record.[33] More importantly, for the economy as a whole, the construction of ordinary houses came to a virtual stop: as late as 1656 the Milan College of Architects bemoaned the paralysis of the housing industry; home rentals, they added, had dropped by 25 percent "as a result of the plague."[34] In Como conditions in the housing market were so bad that in 1640 the municipal government was forced to take upon itself the burden of keeping vacant houses in a minimal state of repair;[35] in Pavia the situation was nearly as critical;[36] and throughout the state of Milan in the 1630s, a local chronicler writes, "houses and landed property fetched but ludicrous prices and were indeed viewed with contempt."[37]

There was, however, another side to this picture of seemingly unrelieved gloom. A few luxury industries seem to have weathered the storm rather well: art historians assure us that in Lodi the making of exquisitely decorated ceramics prospered throughout the seventeenth century,[38] and there is some evidence to suggest that the manufactures of cut crystal and of ribbons and trimmings held their own in Milan.[39] But, predictably enough, it is when we turn to industries connected with the war effort that we find the strongest evidence of sustained and even expanding activity.

In the first sixty years of the seventeenth century the Spanish government spent on a stupendous scale for the construction of new fortifications or the modernization of existing ones. Early in the century a redoubtable stronghold was erected at the entrance of the Valtelline, and the renovation of the defensive system of Milan got underway according to the latest principles of military engineering. It was, however, between 1630 and 1660 that work on fortifications reached its peak: Lodi was ringed with new walls and bastions to replace its outmoded medieval defences; Novara was turned into a formidable fortress "with ten bastions, crownworks, moats, and covered roads"; new fortifications were built near the borders of the state at Pizzighettone, Tortona, Mortara, Frascarolo, Arona, and Soncino, while existing ones at Pavia and Cremona were totally renovated.[40]

Expenditures on fortifications were, of course, paralleled in a war-ridden age by those on arms, ammunitions, and all sorts of equipment for the Spanish forces that either passed through Lombardy on their way to the Low Countries or stayed in Lombardy itself to fight. Although the needs for military supplies were partly met by imports,[41] there is little doubt that native manufacturers, too, were called upon to contribute to the war effort. Predictably, foremost among them were the gunmakers of Milan and the Valsassina: for

both, the war years were a time of considerable prosperity.⁴²
Likewise, the old and celebrated armor industry found fresh and
lucrative opportunities supplying common-service helmets, breastplates, shoulderpieces, and gorgets to the Spanish forces—a welcome
compensation at a time when the industry itself was rapidly
abandoning the production of expensive, custom-made suits of armor
in the face of changing styles in military attire.⁴³

Whether or not production for military uses was of sufficient
magnitude to offset the dramatic slump in the civilian sector
of the economy is a question to which we shall turn in the next
chapter. What needs stressing here is the fact that the available
evidence, fragmentary though it is, clearly points to a sharp, general
downturn in civilian production around 1620 and to a prolonged,
unrelieved depression in the next four decades.

The sweeping nature and the duration of the crises are
unmistakably borne out by the rents at which the excise tax (*Dazio
della Mercanzia*) was farmed out to private entrepreneurs between
1613 and 1663 (Table 2). The excise itself had been introduced in 1317
and was levied on most commodities "as they enter or leave the Cities
of the State of Milan," regardless of their origin and ultimate
destination. Thus, when Spanish wool was imported through Genoa
for the manufacture of high-quality cloth in Milan, the excise tax had
to be paid first in Tortona, the first town encountered on the way,
then in Pavia, and finally at the gates of Milan; when the finished
cloth left Milan the excise had to be paid again. Clearly, this rather
cumbersome fiscal mechanism reflected the notion (more realistic in
the fourteenth than in the seventeenth century) that commodity trade
(*mercanzia*) was essentially an urban affair. The rates charged had
originally been set at 2.5 percent of the market valuations of the
individual commodities in the early fourteenth century. In course of
time, those valuations had become rather meaningless as price levels
had dramatically changed over the centuries, but rather than
periodically revise the valuations, the government had modified the
rates charged: this had been done as early as 1329, and again at the
beginning of the fifteenth century and at mid-sixteenth century; the

Table 2. Annual rents of the farm of the Dazio della Mercanzia, 1613-1663[a]

Years	Rent (in lire)
1613-1615	1,919,471
1616-1618	2,014,993
1619-1621	2,102,620
1622-1624	1,798,199
1625-1627	1,647,654
1628-1630	1,660,216
1631-1633	1,157,952
1634-1636	1,297,739
1637-1639	1,225,511
1640-1642	1,094,100
1643-1645	1,190,000
1646-1648	949,291
1659	1,005,000
1663	1,315,162

Source: Tridi, Informatione, pp. 24-25, for the years 1613-1639; Carlo Girolamo Cavazzi della Somaglia, Alleggiamento dello Stato di Milano (Milan, 1653), p. 684, for the years 1640-1648; ASM, Censo p. a., 310/5, documents of 18 Aug. 1659 and 20 Apr. 1663, for data on these two years.

a. I have ignored the data prior to 1613 supplied by Tridi, because excise rates were altered in that year; they remained unchanged thereafter.

last increase came in 1613, when, despite vehement protests, rates were raised by one-third across the board.[44]

Because of the way the excise was levied, it is obvious that during the long periods when rates remained unchanged its annual yield reflected changes in the actual volume of commodities cleared through the gates of the cities and the major market towns of the State of Milan. As such, our data can be taken as a rough index of the level of economic activity, subject, however, to three important qualifications. First, the figures we possess, representing as they do not actual amounts collected, but the annual rent paid out in advance by the tax farmers (impresari della Mercanzia) to the Treasury, reflect the volume of trade expected in the coming triennium—and those expectations could, at times, prove disappointingly inaccurate. We cannot therefore, take them as precise measures of short-term fluctuations in trade, but merely as rough indicators of major trends. Second, since the excise was levied in the cities and towns only, trade flows that remained strictly confined within rural areas were inevitably left out of account: accordingly, our figures tell us about conditions in urban centers rather than in the countryside, although, given the close links between the two, it is reasonable to assume that significant changes in the one would have repercussions in the other.[45] Lastly, it must be borne in mind that all goods belonging to or intended for church and government agencies were exempt: the excise figures, therefore, take no account of those goods.[46] The omission of commodities intended for ecclesiastical institutions does not necessarily introduce any serious distortion in the overall trend, for the proportion of total trade represented by those commodities is unlikely to have changed substantially over time. On the other hand, the omission of goods purchased by government agencies is a far more serious problem, since those purchases increased sharply as a result of rising military expenditures during the time between the outbreak of the first War of the Mantuan Succession in 1613 and the Peace of the Pyrenees in 1659.

Even with the three qualifications just mentioned, however, the excise figures are instructive and can help us form a more accurate idea of some broad trends in the economy. They show that, beginning around 1620, the economy went into a prolonged downswing, that lasted until about the middle of the century and was followed by a mild recovery in the 1660s. The sharp drop around 1620 clearly reflected the crisis that swept over much of Europe in 1619, in the wake of the outbreak of the Thirty Years' War, and which persisted through 1624. The crisis, as is well known, did not spare Lombardy,[47] and the data on the excise faithfully, albeit with a slight delay, mirror the situation: the record high rent for the 1619-1621 triennium had been negotiated in 1618, before, that is, the onset of the depression; not surprisingly, the tax farmers found themselves in deep trouble as soon as their optimistic forecasts proved wrong, and they loudly complained to the government, pleading for a measure of relief.[48] Whether relief was in fact granted we do not know. What is clear, at any rate, is that the farm for the following triennium (1622-1624) reflected the persistence of the crisis as well as lesser confidence in the future. The second major downturn, around 1630, obviously coincided with the plague of that year,[49] and it is interesting to note that the first farm to be awarded after the plague was about 30 percent below that of the preceding triennium—a drop roughly equal to the estimated death rate of the plague. After the plague, despite some temporary recoveries, the trend continued to be downward and may have been at its lowest in the late 1640s or 50s, at a time when Spanish Lombardy was torn by war. Once again, the tax farmers found it difficult to recover the sums they had advanced or pledged to the Treasury: the reason for this being, as they put it, that "the trade of merchandise has come to a stop" or, rather, that what trade there was increasingly involved military supplies enjoying total exemption from taxation.[50]

CHAPTER IV

CAUSES AND SCAPEGOATS

The long depression so dramatically illustrated by the plummeting yield of the excise tax coincided with a period of nearly uninterrupted warfare, strongly suggesting, at first sight, a close connection between Lombardy's economic woes and her involvement in the long, drawn-out struggle between the Hapsburgs and the Bourbons. Even granting, as indeed we must, that population losses resulting from the plague of 1630 substantially contributed to a lowering of the level of civilian consumption and production, one is still inclined to ascribe to the disruptions and devastations caused by war a major responsibility for the sorry and deteriorating state of the economy.

Evidence for the hardships, destructions, and horrors caused by the warfare is certainly not lacking. The frequent references found in the sources to wretched peasants fleeing before an advancing army are proof enough that contemporaries had few illusions about the fate awaiting a defenseless civilian population that failed to seek safety in flight. What that fate might be is vividly described in an official report written in 1636, when a French army crossed the Ticino river and brought war to the very heart of the State of Milan: "The enemy now roams the countryside, destroying our crops, plundering defenseless villages, and putting to the fire and the sword any community that dares resist them . . . and what the wrath of the French fails to accomplish the fury of the German soldiery will achieve, for the latter, although they are supposed to defend us, do not hesitate to commit the same acts of savagery."[1] Much the same could have been said of the Lodi province in 1629, when it was devastated by the Imperial army on its way to the siege of Mantua, or of the Casalmaggiore district in 1647, when it was laid waste by the Modenese army.[2]

One should not, however, generalize from these and similar instances, real though they unquestionably were, and ascribe to seventeenth-century warfare a destructiveness it did not possess. Not only were weapons limited in their range and effectiveness and armies small in size by later standards, but military operations in general, consisting as they did of series of localized sallies, raids, and sieges, tended to affect only limited areas at any one time. One should also remember that the Lombard cities, sheltered behind their walls and bastions, proved far less vulnerable than the unprotected villages and market towns.

When contemporaries blamed war for the woes of the economy, they had in mind not so much the actual fighting and the devastations resulting from it, but rather the burden of taxation that the war effort placed on them. Taxation was repeatedly singled out as a chief cause of economic troubles and was variously held responsible for curtailing civilian demand, eroding the merchant's profits, or pricing Lombard goods out of the international market. As early as 1634 an official brief aimed at securing a tax reduction for the province of Cremona claimed that unrelenting fiscal pressure had "reduced the Gentry to utter poverty, exhausted the Merchants' resources, and brought desolation to both the city and the countryside, as people have been forced to pay out of their assets those taxes which they no longer can pay out of their income."[3] Twelve years later the Milan city council, in a rare expression of solidarity with the surrounding *contado*, pleaded with the Spanish governor for a measure of relief from the burden of taxation, which it blamed for the parlous state of the economy:

> If the destitution of all sorts of persons and the threat of impend-ing ruin did not suffice to prove under what kinds of burdens the Province and the City of Milan are now oppressed, conclusive evidence can be found in the very number and excessive nature of the taxes themselves. . . The land tax, the salt tax, the assess-ments [*estimi*], the excise on flour, wine, meat, poultry, charcoal, oil, leather, and sundry other things . . . and, lastly, the billeting of troops with the concomitant disruptions which of themselves would be enough to ruin even the richest realm, all of these have now forced laborers to flee, have reduced the landowners to poverty, and have caused the land to lie uncropped.[4]

In the eighteenth century, Pietro Verri, the economist and reformer, saw "the ultimate cause of the ruin" of the Lombard economy in the crushing contributions exacted from the State of Milan by its Spanish masters for the support of the troops stationed there.[5] In the mid-nineteenth century, Cesare Cantù, the author of a popular account of Lombard life in the seventeenth century, approvingly quoted Alessandro Manzoni's definition of Spanish taxation as "an unbearable burden imposed with a rapacity and a senselessness that knew no limits."[6] And in recent years, Bruno Caizzi, in his study of the Como province, has concluded that "the economic ruin of Lombardy . . . must be largely ascribed to Spain's huge war expenditures: to these her Italian dominions were made to contribute to such an extent as to be crippled in the process. . . And any attempt at recovery was to be in vain so long as that intolerable burden would not be lifted."[7]

These and similar indictments of Spanish taxation are plausible enough. In light of what is known both about Lombardy's involvement in warfare for over forty years and about the persistent outcry against the insatiable demands of the tax collector, it is quite likely that the war effort took larger and larger bites out of private incomes and assets and that the economy was increasingly made to sacrifice butter for guns and ploughshares for swords. It is possible and plausible, in other words, to portray the Lombard economy in those fateful decades as one in which civilian industries in general—from farming to textiles to trade—were forced to release resources, capital, and manpower to the military under the unrelenting and rising pressure of taxation.

Had this been the case, however, we would expect to see this massive shift of production factors from civilian to military uses reflected in the state budget, in the form of a rough parity between tax revenue and government expenditures. But, in fact, if we are to judge from the few budget figures available (see Table 3), conditions were dramatically different: far from revenue matching expenditures, every year brought stupendous shortfalls as receipts lagged behind expenditures. The chronic gap between the two was bridged, in part, by internal loans secured from the Banco di Sant'Ambrogio and by external loans obtained from Genoese financiers.[8] But it was also

Table 3. Treasury budgets (in *scudi*) between 1641 and 1658

Year	(1) Gross receipts	(2) Net receipts	(3) Expenses	(4) Gross shortfall	(5) Outside subsidies	(6) Net shortfall[a]
1641[b]	1,321,264	0[c]	2,948,026	2,948,026	827,266	2,120,760
1642	1,264,655	368,928	3,406,194	3,037,266	1,963,680	1,073,586
1643	1,250,242	373,881	3,059,107	2,685,226	1,130,957	1,554,269
1648	1,136,632	348,834	2,149,346	1,800,512	1,406,544	1,070,137[d]
1657	1,191,175	269,184	2,394,619	2,125,435	—	—
1658	1,263,142	295,079	2,279,881	1,984,802	—	—

Source: ASM, *Uffici regii p. a.*, 654, reg. 1, 9 Nov. 1641 (for the 1641 budget); ibid., 655, reg. 2, 4 Dec. 1649 (for the 1642 budget), 27 Jan. 1650 (for the 1643 budget); 20 Dec. 1647 (for the 1647 budget); and 14 Apr. 1650 (for the 1648 budget); ibid., 656, reg. 2, 11 Dec. 1657 (for the budget of that year); ibid., reg. 1, 18 Dec. 1658 (for the 1658 budget). All figures are in *scudi*, worth L.6 each. Fractions of *scudo* have been omitted. The documents used are official reports (*bilanzi*) commenting on the key elements in the budget. These elements include (1) gross receipts from taxation (*entrate*); (2) net receipts (*avanzo*)—what was available to the Milan Treasury for military purposes after existing commitments (*carichi*) in the form of officials' salaries and interest on debts outstanding had been paid out; (3) total expenditures for military purposes; (4) the gross shortfall (*mancamento*), equal to [3] minus [2]; (5) various subsidies (*soccorsi*) received from other parts of the Spanish monarchy as well as advances (*partiti*) made by tax farmers on future tax revenue; and (6) net shortfall (*mancamento effettivo*), equal to [4] minus [5]. The data for subsidies are not available for 1657 and 1658 in the original documents.

a. Nothing is said in the *bilanzi* as to how the net shortfall was ultimately bridged. No doubt, short- and long-term loans were resorted to, but the practice of delaying soldiers' pay must have been common. In the 1641 budget the comment is made that for lack of pay and adequate provisions "the soldiery are in such a state of want that many of them defect every day."

b. The 1641 budget seems to be an estimate rather than a final statement of income and expenditure.

c. The original text reads at this point: "Altogether net receipts ought to be 388,276 scudi which should accrue to the Treasury if the *Mensuale* and other taxes had been collected . . . This, however, has not been the case due to current hardships, despite all our efforts."

d. This last figure is clearly not the difference between gross shortfall and outside subsidies. Our source must contain one or more erroneous figures, but we have no way of identifying the error or errors.

bridged by huge unilateral transfers of money from other Spanish dominions, and notably from the Kingdom of Naples and from Sicily.[9] In the 1640s these roughly equaled total receipts from taxation.[10] One conclusion is, therefore, obvious enough: the war effort in the State of Milan was largely financed from outside sources (unilateral transfers plus foreign loans) and the Lombard economy in that period can be seen as one in which deficit spending loomed as large as taxation.

This being the case, the argument that blames taxation for Lombardy's economic woes loses much of its force and tends to obscure the far more important question of how massive deficit spending affected that economy. Here, two alternatives must be considered. One is that deficit spending impinged on an economy that was near full-employment levels, and that the necessary shift in the use of resources and manpower was achieved via the pricing mechanism, that is to say, by bidding factors away from civilian use at the cost of price inflation. The other is that deficit spending found an economy already suffering from severe unemployment—for reasons unrelated to the war—and could thus mobilize factors that would have been idle and harness them to the war effort at no additional real cost to the economy as a whole.

Between these two alternatives the choice is easily made, for we know that during most of the seventeenth century Lombardy knew no inflation: after about 1620, despite high levels of deficit spending, commodity prices either sagged or remained stable (except, of course, for the short-term fluctuations in farm prices) and so did wages.[11] The conclusion seems, therefore, inescapable that the war was visited on an economy that ran well below full-employment levels for reasons that had little to do with wartime taxation, and that the inflationary impact of government spending was effectively dampened by the slack of widespread unemployment. A corollary to this is that general economic conditions would have been even more depressed than they actually were had it not been for the additional employment and the fresh rounds of income generated by deficit spending.

It is, of course, still possible that an ill-designed and ill-distributed system of taxation did cripple some economic activities while leaving others relatively unscathed. But to imply, as has so often been done in the past, that civilian production in general would have experienced no dramatic downturn had it not been for the "senseless rapacity" of the tax collector is not warranted by the available evidence.

We must now consider the possibility, and indeed the likelihood, that an inequitable system of taxation may have caused irreparable harm, if not to the economy as a whole, at least to select sectors thereof. A first and obvious candidate in this respect would seem to be agriculture. Contemporaries had few doubts that most of the landowners' and the peasants' troubles in the 1630s and 1640s were to be ascribed to the growing, intolerable demands placed on the countryside in the form of taxes, requisitions, and the billeting of soldiers. In their view, those demands had forced many a peasant to quit, merely in order to escape the clutches of the tax collector or the insolence of the quartermaster; crippled by taxation and requisitions, tenants had defaulted on their rents; farms had been deserted and land values had collapsed. Referring to the Cremona province, a 1633 official report contended that peasants had fled in droves across the border into Venetian or Mantuan territory, because "Taxes and impositions are now so many and so burdensome . . . that what the wretched farmer can produce with his weary arms and the sweat of his brow no longer suffices to pay them; he and his family often have to go hungry in order to feed the soldiery, not to speak of all the inconveniences and indignities he has to endure time after time at the hands of licentious soldiers billeted on him." According to the same source, rural conditions were compounded by the landlord's financial straits: "The landlords, who in the past were wont to help and assist their tenants, are now reduced to such poverty that they can hardly meet their obligations toward the Fisc nor can they adequately provide for their families. And, in fact, a good deal of land now goes uncropped and is deserted, because the landlords are unable to supply the necessary implements and seed grain."[12]

The sweeping indictment of wartime taxation as the chief cause of the agrarian debacle is supported by what is known about the steady rise of the poll tax (*censo del sale*) levied on the rural population.[13] It is borne out, moreover, by vivid portrayals of the sorry plight of individual rural communities. In one such village near Milan tenants were so hard to recruit in 1630 that most landowners were forced to manage their estates themselves rather than leasing them out, as had been customary in the past. "Tenants are reluctant to take new leases," it was claimed, "because they do not want to have soldiers billeted on them."[14] An obscure chronicler of Busto Arsizio, writing in 1632, drew an equally grim picture of conditions in that part of Lombardy: "Many peasants have fled out of despair, abandoning their homes and their lands, because of the intolerable burden of the soldiery, and the price of both houses and holdings has dropped so low that [their owners] find it impossible not only to sell but even to lease them out."[15] In a locality of the low plain near the Ticino River, most tenants were said to have left by 1638, "as a result of exorbitant burdens," and in eight years rents had dropped by more than two-thirds.[16] In Caravaggio, a few years later, conditions must have been equally bad, for, according to one source, "There are many individuals who are willing to sell their holdings, but can find no buyers on account of the taxes the latter would have to pay; as is well known, those holdings (were they free of taxes) would yield a good return if properly farmed, but this is not the case owing to the dearth of people [per la carestia delle persone]."[17] At mid-century, taxation was said to have totally disrupted the land market on the right bank of the Po: "Before the war good and even mediocre land sold for two ducatoni each pertica, but with the war their value has been halved, and even so buyers are hard to come by because of the great burdens the land has to bear, so much so that one Signor Geromino Claverio has been forced to donate his land to some peasants at no charge."[18]

Despite all these grim tales and recriminations, however, wartime taxation cannot be viewed as the chief, let alone the sole, cause of the crisis that beset agriculture in Hapsburg Lombardy. For one thing, a rising level of direct taxation (whether in the form of a land tax such as the perticato or a poll tax such as the censo del sale) may well have had the effect, up to a point, of forcing many a farmer to work harder and to expand cultivation in order to meet his obligation as a taxpayer.[19] For another thing, while wartime taxation can plausibly account for the desertion of farms and falling land values, it can hardly explain the prolonged downswing in the price of basic foodstuffs, and particularly of cereals. The chief cause of the latter must rather be found in the changing balance between population and resources resulting from the reversal of the great demographic upsurge that had characterized western Europe in the sixteenth century. As demographic expansion gave way to sharply reduced populations in countries such as Spain, Germany, and Italy, and to a slight decline, or at best stability, elsewhere, the overall effect (possibly reinforced by more bountiful crops in the third quarter of the century) could not be but a drop in food prices followed by serious dislocations in the agrarian sector throughout Europe.[20]

Northern Italy was one of the first areas to feel the impact of the demographic downturn, and one of the most hard hit.[21] Following the plague of 1630, food (and notably cereal) prices fell abruptly and, except for occasional spurts caused by crop failures, long remained at levels 30 to 40 percent below those of the 1620s. Land values and rents followed prices on their downward course, while the plight of food producers was made worse by deteriorating terms of trade. In all this, taxation played no decisive role.[22] What taxation did do, was to compound the Lombard farmer's woes by adding substantially to his costs precisely at a time when receipts from the sale of his crops were dwindling.

The only detailed study available of a large estate administration in early seventeenth-century Lombardy bears this out very conclusively.[23] From the relatively high level maintained in the first three decades of the century, the estate's gross receipts dropped sharply around 1630 and continued to fall through the 1640s, in keeping with falling grain prices; on the other hand, outlays, and especially tax payments and other contributions in kind, followed a roughly contrary trend, their sharp rise in the 1630s and 1640s virtually wiping out all profit margins. In such a situation an outcry against taxation is perfectly understandable; it should not, however, obscure the fact that ultimately the agrarian depression had been triggered by forces that had little to do with the needs and the demands of the Spanish treasury.

In the eyes of contemporaries the textile industry was another and even more conspicuous example of an economic activity whose prosperity was being destroyed by the growing and intolerable demands of the tax collector. Possibly the earliest, and certainly the most articulate, spokesman for this view was a cloth merchant and manufacturer from Como, Giovanni Maria Tridi, who in June 1641 published a memorandum (*informatione*) in which he proposed to call the government's attention to "The damage caused to His Majesty [the King of Spain] and to the Cities of the State [of Milan] by the imposition of a tax on the trade of merchandise, by the increase of the Excise by one-third, and by the importation of foreign woolens and other goods."[24] In his tract Tridi saw the year 1616 as the turning point when the prosperity of trade in general and of the woolen industry in particular had given way to an unmitigated decline, and, as the chief cause of all subsequent ills, he unhesitatingly pointed to the government's decision of that year to raise the excise rates by one-third.[25] In his view the stiffer rates, falling as they did both on incoming raw materials and on outgoing finished goods, had resulted in higher prices, had made Lombard manufactures uncompetitive both at home and abroad, and had caused widespread unemployment and an exodus of skilled workers to other countries. Tridi further argued that even before 1616 the competitiveness of Lombard manufactures had been undermined by the decision to force the craft and merchant guilds to contribute fixed amounts to the infamous *mensuale*, the new tax that Charles V had imposed on his Lombard dominion and which he had originally conceived merely as a land tax. Not only had the introduction of a fixed assessment (*estimo*) to be paid by each guild added a fresh burden to its members, Tridi argued, but, as business had declined, the fewer and fewer guild members found their shares of the *estimo* proportionately increased.

To buttress his case against a system of taxation that he considered inequitable and punitive, Tridi produced data on the rent paid for the excise farm, showing that this had dropped sharply from about 1620; he also quoted a few data showing that the wool industry both in Como and in Milan had lost much ground after 1616.[26] Although some of his figures on cloth production were far from accurate,[27] Tridi certainly stood on firm ground when he spoke of the debacle of an industry that he knew so well. To other manufactures he paid but scant attention, but in pointing to the plummeting figures of the excise he clearly intimated that the depression was not confined to the wool industry alone.

As for remedies, he proposed mainly three, notably a reduction of the fiscal burden placed on manufactures, an outright ban on imported goods such as "woolen cloth, silk fabrics, hats, cotton textiles, and the like," and, lastly, an embargo on the export of industrial raw materials and particularly of silk. This combination of tax relief and protection, he concluded, would restore prosperity to a tottering economy: "At once shall we see poverty turn into prosperity . . . and our own people, reassured that our manufactures will have a market, will endeavor to increase production, while foreigners, finding no outlet for their own goods, will decrease it. Our artisans will then return to their homes lured by the prospect of greater earnings."[28] And two months later, replying to a critic, he summed up his diagnosis of Lombardy's economic malady in the following terms: "The cause of [our ills] lies in the scarcity of people; the scarcity of people is caused by the lack of business, and the lack of business is brought about by increased taxation; with the result that, as our commodities cannot sell within the state as cheaply as foreign commodities can, consumers buy from those countries where prices are lowest; accordingly, enterprise drifts to those countries where goods are vented, leaving our State stripped of both money and people."

Turning once again to his favorite remedy, he added: "It is clear that the higher tax rates rise the lower are the receipts thereof and that, if we wish to augment the latter, the only remedy is to lower the former, for if this be done, business will recover, the number of people will increase, and with a larger population revenue will be larger too."[29]

Tridi's indictment of the tax system and his plea for fiscal relief as a means of restoring health to the economy and, specifically, to the textile industries drew considerable attention both in government circles and among various economic groups, stirring a spirited debate, which is preserved in a number of memoranda, tracts, and proposals written during the 1640s. To the debate itself we shall return in a later chapter. For the time being it is important to note that the idea that taxation was the chief cause of industrial decay continued to loom large in all discussions of Lombardy's economic troubles. At mid-century the damage allegedly inflicted on manufacturing by what a contemporary called the "cursed serpent" of taxation[30] was acknowledged by no less an authority than the Ministry of Finance (*Magistrato delle Entrate Ordinarie*), which, however, broadened the indictment of taxation to include its evil effects on labor costs: "The causes of higher prices are well known: one is the excise charged on raw materials, the other are all the burdens and direct taxes paid by individuals. For in order to keep at a moderate level the price of commodities made by the artisan's hand two things are required: the ingredients must not cost too much and neither must the labor of those artisans who make those commodities."[31] In 1653 Count Gerolamo Cavazzi della Somaglia, auditor general of the city of Milan and the author of a large tome on fiscal reform, joined the growing chorus of protest against an insatiable fisc. The ruin of our manufactures, he wrote, has been brought about "neither by the war nor by the plague," but solely by the fact that "our merchants have given up in the face of the many burdens fastened on them."[32] The same view received its strongest, most articulate, and official formulation in 1732 at the hands of a committee (*Giunta per la rinnovazione del censimento*) especially appointed by the newly installed Austrian rulers and charged, among other things, with making recommendations as to whether the old and much criticized *estimo mercimoniale* ought to be retained and in what form. After rehearsing the history of the *estimo* from its creation by Charles V, the committee dealt extensively with the damage it had caused to Lombard manufactures, quoting Tridi as its chief authority on this point and basically endorsing the latter's views.[33]

The conclusions reached by the committee in 1732 were repeated by eighteenth-century writers to support their argument for sweeping fiscal reforms. Among them was Pietro Verri, who, much as Tridi had done a century earlier, singled out taxation in general and the *estimo* in particular as the chief villain in the bleak story of Lombardy's industrial decline.[34] In a similar vein, a less well known economic writer of the eighteenth century, Angelo Pavesi, wrote that "The trade of our cloths and silk goods . . . entered its notorious period of decline toward the end of the sixteenth century, a decline that grew exceedingly worse in the following century . . . Its fatal cause was the excessive fiscal burden . . . as a result of which our manufactures had to be discontinued for lack of customers and an infinite number of artisans were forced to emigrate."[35] Early in this century the chief authority on the administrative and financial history of eighteenth-century Lombardy summed up a long-standing consensus when he wrote that the increase of the excise rates in 1613, "coinciding as it did with the worst period of Lombardy's history, dealt trade and industry a mortal blow."[36]

Tridi's main argument—that the chief Lombard manufacturers were forced to raise their prices in order to meet their growing fiscal obligations and, in so doing, priced themselves out of the market—is plausible enough. It does assume, however, that Lombard manufacturers had a measure of control over prices. This is unlikely, especially in the textile industries, where production was diffused among numerous firms[37] and where international competition was notoriously stiff. A more realistic assumption would seem to be that prices were exogenously determined and that an increase in taxation could not simply be passed on to the consumer in the form of higher prices, but had to be absorbed by the producer in the form of lower profit margins. If this was so, then the argument about the adverse impact of taxation ought to be modified, but would still retain the same degree of plausibility.

But, however plausible, the argument itself has never been subjected to empirical verification, for the latter would require a close comparative analysis of prices, tax rates, and profits in both Lombard and foreign industries, and the data for such an analysis are simply not available. We are thus left, it would appear, with a reasonable hypothesis but no firm conclusion as to the cause of the decline of the wool industry. The crucial issue, of course, is not whether higher taxes did any harm to the industry, for they most certainly did, but rather whether they were the chief cause of its undoing. To put it differently, the issue is whether a bold and straightforward policy of tax relief could have saved it. There are serious reasons for concluding that it could not have done so.

For one thing, Tridi himself, in discussing the causes and the remedies of the troubles then besetting the cloth industry, betrayed considerable uncertainty as to exactly where the blame should fall, for while he extolled tax relief as the infallible cure for the industry's decay, he also advocated stringent protective measures and, in fact, a total ban on foreign-made cloth, thus implying that the industry's inability to compete had causes that ran deeper than a crippling system of taxation. Further, one must bear in mind that the decline of cloth making in Como got under way in the 1580s, some thirty years before the much maligned increase in excise rates. Thirdly, the fiscal system itself, ill designed and harmful though it may have been, was not as watertight as it first appeared, but contained an escape hatch, as it were, for merchant-manufacturers who felt harassed by a rapacious fisc. As the *estimo* was assessed on the urban guilds and as the excise was levied at the city gates, both burdens could have been evaded by setting up shop out in the villages. Admittedly, legislation had long been on the books that was intended to forbid the practice of certain trades and crafts outside the city walls, but by the seventeenth century enforcement must have been rather lax if Tridi himself denounced the threat rural industries posed to their ailing urban counterparts: "The *contado*, being free of the burden of the *estimo*," he wrote, "has drawn to itself most of the business, to the great disadvantage of the city."[38] The odd thing is, however, that few entrepreneurs took advantage of this convenient loophole: for all we know, the making of high-quality cloth and of silks failed to develop in the countryside on a large scale and never made up for the decline of urban manufactures.[39] One is forced to conclude that the advantages to be gained from avoiding urban taxation were not enough to lure enterprise to the countryside.

The alleged responsibility of taxation for the dismantling of Lombard manufactures is further open to question when one looks at the industrial record of other Italian cities which were not under Spanish rule, which enjoyed during most of the seventeenth century the blessings of neutrality and peace, and which presumably did not have to bear fiscal burdens in any way comparable to those fastened on Milan, Como, and Cremona as a result of a prolonged, massive war effort.

At the opening of the century the two largest centers of the wool industry in the Italian peninsula were Venice and Florence. Both enjoyed a redoubtable international reputation as producers and exporters of high-quality woolens. To both of them, however, the first half of the seventeenth century brought, as it did to Como and Milan, sharp, if less rapid, decline. In Florence, cloth production, which had stood at nearly 16,000 cloths in 1616, was down to less than 7,000 thirty years later;[40] in Venice annual output fell from a peak of over 20,000 pieces around 1600 to half that many by mid-century, and the downward trend continued to the end of the century, when but 2,000 pieces were produced.[41] The silk industry also suffered a decline similar to that in Milan. Production of silk fabrics in Venice decreased by about 60 percent between 1600 and 1660;[42] Genoa, which had long shared with Milan and Venice a prominent position as a center of silk making, saw the number of its silk looms tumble from over 4,000 at the beginning of the century to 2,500 by 1675.[43]

The trend of textile production in Milan and Como, then, was not unlike that in other major centers of north Italy, although its downward course was more abrupt in the Lombard cities than elsewhere. Interestingly enough, the similarity was not confined to the malady, but extended to the diagnosis as well: in Venice and in Genoa, much as in Milan and Como, excessive taxation was invariably singled out as the prime source of industrial decay.[44] There is, of course, no a priori reason why the hand of the tax collector should not have been as grasping in the Venetian and Genoese republics as it apparently was in the State of Milan, but this is highly improbable. Genoa, Venice (at least until the outbreak of the Candian war in 1645), and the Grand Duchy of Tuscany not only enjoyed uninterrupted peace, but because of their cautious, unambitious foreign policy were also spared the necessity of large-scale military preparations. Moreover, both the Republic of Saint Marc and that of Saint George reaped substantial economic benefits from their Lombard neighbors' very trials and tribulations, as the one found an ample outlet there for its arms, ammunitions, and sundry military supplies and the other served as a seemingly inexhaustible source of loans to the Milan treasury. The fact that the outcry against taxation was as loud in other Italian states as it was in Hapsburg Lombardy does not necessarily prove that they all suffered under similar burdens; it does prove that confronted with similarly depressed industrial conditions and dwindling profits, merchants and craftsmen everywhere found in the tax collector an obvious scapegoat and in tax relief a seemingly simply remedy to their problems.

A few among Tridi's contemporaries did realize that other causes may have been as important as, or even more important than, taxation in bringing down Lombardy's once flourishing manufactures. A memorandum written a month after Tridi had made his views known, and probably by Count Bartolomeo Arese, president of the Milan Senate, took a broader view of Lombardy's economic ills and, while not denying the adverse effects of taxation, pointed to several other causes of industrial decline.[45] The wars then raging in or around Lombardy were, in his view, one such cause, but, interestingly enough, they were not blamed for inflicting physical destruction and loss of lives on the country, but rather for luring "an infinite number of artisans" away from their shops and into military service with the prospect of "an easier life and glory." Arese also mentioned the adverse effects of the wars then being fought north of the Alps, for these, he argued, were causing trade stoppages and impairing the import capacity of countries that had traditionally been important outlets for Lombard goods: "France, Flanders, and Germany . . . having either been cut off from us as trade partners after the closing of their borders or torn asunder and devastated by war, can neither afford to buy the fabrics of gold and silk which in times past used to be shipped to them in large amounts from our city, nor can they send to us their own commodities in return."

On the question of the inflow of foreign-made goods, Arese's paper took a somewhat different position from Tridi's. Rather than ascribing the success of imported fabrics merely to the fact that the latter somehow avoided the payment of the excise and were not subject to the *estimo*, he argued that their lower prices reflected "their being lighter in texture and inferior in quality, yet capable of deceiving the consumer with their colors," while Lombard fabrics were made "with more material, better workmanship, and better dyes, although their finish and appearance [did] not match that of foreign fabrics." He went on to point out that, given the choice between better quality at higher prices and inferior quality at lower prices, Lombard consumers tended to prefer the latter: "In view of the scarcity of money that is caused nowadays by the burdens which our own people, and particularly the nobility, have to shoulder, cheaper articles are preferred."

Having thus diagnosed the crisis, Arese could not regard a reduction of the tax load or a ban on imports as adequate remedies. While cautiously endorsing a revision of the guilds' fiscal assessments, as well as strict restrictions on imports, he also advocated a number of other measures. One was the partial resumption of normal commercial relations with France (which had been severed in 1635), with the Dutch Republic, and with the German states that happened to be in the anti-Hapsburg camp: "As long as no victuals, war supplies, horses, manpower, or any other thing likely to increase their power and decrease our own are involved, I do not believe we ought to discourage trade in other commodities, and if France, Holland, and the Free [Imperial] Cities [in Germany] wish to send money hither and purchase our commodities, I do not forsee any harm resulting from such policy, but only great benefits." Other suggested remedies included barring craftsmen from enlisting in the army, exempting merchants from contributing to the billeting of troops, keeping the highways clear of undisciplined soldiers, and offering various inducements to attract artisans to the State of Milan. Arese also advocated, as Tridi had done, a ban on foreign-made textiles, but pragmatically cautioned against too sudden measures, suggesting gradual changes instead, so as to allow "sufficient time for the workshops to be put in working order, for old artisans to return, for new ones to be trained," and a selective approach whereby textiles made in France and England would be banned, but not those made in Spain nor the cheap cloth from Bergamo and other localities in Italy. Lastly, Arese proposed to restrict, but by no means totally suppress, the export of raw silk: "I suggest . . . that the Merchants, Shopkeepers, and Weavers of our State make an estimate of how much silk they are likely to need, taking into account the actual number of workers now available or expected to be available soon, in order that Your Excellency [the Governor] be in a position to regulate the extent of the embargo so that silk, whether wrought or raw, may find an outlet and not remain unsold in the State to the detriment of the King's subjects."

Arese's diagnosis, with its emphasis on the disturbed conditions prevailing on the European market, sounds convincing enough. It was weakened, however, by his own admission that foreign-made articles kept flooding the home market and by his endorsement, cautious though it may have been, of import restrictions. Clearly, he was as much worried by the troubled conditions of international trade as by the Lombard manufactures' inability to compete. And later developments would tend to prove that of the two problems, the latter was the more serious and intractable, for when peace and normal trade relations were restored in 1659, the manufactures of the Lombard cities, as will be seen, failed to recover their former prestige and prosperity.

Arese himself had, in fact, hinted at another possible cause of industrial decline when he stressed that imported fabrics, thanks to inferior quality and a more attractive, if deceiving, look, found a ready market in Lombardy: this suggests that, despite trade stoppages or slowdowns, foreign-made textiles successfully competed with Lombard ones, on account both of lower prices and of more attractive colors or designs. And if this was indeed the case, the troubles besetting Lombard manufactures could have been solved only by modifications in the quality and appearance of textiles to meet changing consumer tastes and the demand for lower-grade ordinary articles.

Confronted with so many conflicting recommendations, the government in Milan took only limited and half-hearted measures. A decree of 15 December 1646 placed a ban on all foreign-made textiles that might compete with native goods;[46] with this decree the government implicitly recognized the very serious threat posed by foreign manufactures and strove to preserve the internal market for native goods, whose competitiveness abroad was now openly written-off. The results of this policy were disappointing. A few years after the new decree had been in force an official candidly reported that, "Our efforts have not paid off . . . and, particularly in the case of woolen cloth, we have observed that, despite the ban on foreign fabrics and the rigorous enforcement thereof . . . we have failed to restore even a minimal fraction of a manufacture which in years past was so prosperous and supplied the whole of Italy and most nations beyond the Alps."[47]

As for the reason behind this failure, it was unequivocally found in the higher prices of native manufactures: "We believe," the official report went on to say, "that the principal reason why business has not recovered lies in the fact that our cloth sells at higher prices than cloth made elsewhere." Higher prices, in turn, were blamed on the excise duties levied on raw materials and finished products at the gates of the cities and to the high wages paid to urban artisans.

The same official report, however, concluded with a revealing observation: after pointing out that the Milan silk industry was "on the brink of extinction," it remarked that in France and England, "minds have greatly sharpened of late and our own products are now being imitated with immense skill."[48] It was a belated, painful recognition that the age when the Lombard cities could enjoy a comfortable edge over other less-advanced economies, thanks to superior skills and sophisticated techniques, had definitely come to an end.

The gap that had traditionally separated Lombardy (and other areas of northern Italy) from the rest of Europe had begun to narrow, as will be recalled, even before the close of the sixteenth century, as other nations had taken early steps to develop (often with the help of Italian mentors) their own manufactures, to produce goods they had traditionally imported from Italy, and to strike out in new directions. It was in the seventeenth century, however, that the trend gained full momentum.

The most dramatic example of a former customer closing the gap and eventually supplanting its former purveyor and mentor is that of France developing a silk industry of her own. To the end of the sixteenth century that country had been a major outlet for silk articles made in Lombardy and merchants from Milan had held a position of undisputed supremacy in Lyons, the great clearinghouse of French trade with Italy. A silk industry, it is true, had been founded there as early as 1536, but until the close of the century had remained confined to the manufacture of simple, plain fabrics and thus had not reduced French dependence on Lombard imports.[49] By 1635, however, Milanese sources unequivocally ascribed to the vigorous development of the silk industry in Lyons and Tours the decline of their own,[50] and by the end of the century Milan itself had become an important market for French silks.[51] A similar loss was experienced in the case of the so-called Milan gold thread, a commodity in which the Lombard capital had long had a virtual monopoly. Around 1600 attempts were being made abroad to emulate the Milanese in this field: Henry IV actually managed to lure some artisans from Milan to Paris to start a gold-thread manufacture in the French capital.[52] The new undertaking was probably not a complete success, for some sixty years later Colbert made renewed efforts to break the Milanese monopoly: once again skilled craftsmen were brought in from Milan, and by 1683 the new industry, based in Lyons and duly sheltered by protective legislation, employed 120 workers.[53] Similar efforts had been made elsewhere, too: gold and silver thread "after the manner of Milan" was being produced in England as early as 1624.[54]

The industrial lead of the Lombard cities was eroded in other fields as well: in the sixteenth century German armorers had made headway at the expense of the Milanese; in the heartland of French metallurgy, the Forez, hilts and other metal goods "à facon de Milan" were produced in the 1590s, while in Auvergne at that time hats were beginning to be produced that imitated Lombard styles and design.[55] In the case of the woolen industry the process of erosion is not so easily discernible, and yet it was no less real. To speak of a Lombard or even of a northern Italian monopoly in this area would, admittedly, be inaccurate, because cloth making had for centuries been widely diffused throughout Europe and some of its major centers had, in fact, been outside Italy, notably in the Low Countries and in England. Nonetheless, if we think in terms of specific fabrics rather than of woolen textiles in general, we can say that individual Italian cities had established a distinctive reputation for themselves on the European markets with certain kinds of heavy, high-grade broadcloth (*panno alto*) made of fine, carded wool, while Italy herself imported coarser and less expensive fabrics such as kerseys, bays, and says from England and the Low Countries. This situation radically changed in the course of the seventeenth century, as a result of a dramatic shift in consumer tastes away from traditional carded fabrics and toward new worsted textiles, the so-called "new draperies," that were being produced in a profusion of different colors and patterns in the Low Countries, in the Rhineland, and above all, in England.[56] All centers of the traditional industry were hurt: England saw the export of her own version of broadcloth to the Baltic countries drop from 22,000 to 2,000 units in the course of the century, and her exports of kersies to the Mediterranean did not fare much better;[57] in Beauvais and Amiens, too, a once-flourishing wool industry that produced cloth of good quality suffered serious setbacks,[58] as did those of Venice and Florence. The Lombard cities were thus no exceptions in witnessing the rapid decline of their own "old draperies."

What differentiated the wool industry in Como and Milan from its counterparts elsewhere was the irreversible and sweeping nature of its decline: cloth making virtually disappeared from those two cities. In Beauvais, Lille, and Amiens, on the other hand, losses were serious, but fell far short of total extinction;[59] in Venice and Florence cloth production, while dwindling, managed to survive at low levels;[60] in the Venetian portion of Lombardy, Bergamo held its own by marketing inexpensive, coarse woolens that were largely manufactured by peasant weavers in the mountainous hinterland;[61] in England the decline of the old draperies was largely offset by the vigorous expansion of the new, and the latter, ironically, found in the Italian peninsula one of their best markets;[62] Leiden, of course, represented an exception, as the seventeenth century witnessed the astonishing success of its wool industry, one that specialized in heavy, high-quality fabrics of the old drapery kind, but added to them, apparently thanks to a new pressing technique, a special shine and a unique, attractive look.[63]

To survive the challenges presented by the rapid progress of manufactures abroad and by changing consumer tastes the Lombard urban manufacturers should have pared their costs down to competitive levels in some cases, made changes in the quality of the goods produced in others, and found new markets for traditional goods. It is not unreasonable to assume that all these steps were seriously hampered by Lombardy's involvement in war for over four decades: taxation may not have been as crippling as it was said to be, but it obviously added to the merchant's and the craftsman's costs; enlistment or impressment in the Spanish army probably added considerably to the labor shortage created by the plague; government borrowing on a vast

scale raised interest rates and diverted funds away from normal investment channels; a general sense of insecurity, as well as temporary
interruptions in commercial relations, could only discourage new and
bold initiatives. It remains to be seen whether or not, once the scourge
of war had receded, the cities of the State of Milan, which, after all,
still possessed small nuclei of experienced craftsmen and merchants,
would prove capable of making the necessary changes and of mobilizing the resources, the skills, and the enterprise that were needed to
meet the challenge of a new age.

CHAPTER V

THE ATROPHY OF THE CITY

In 1659 the Treaty of the Pyrenees brought an end to decades of warfare between Spain and France; thereafter, Hapsburg Lombardy enjoyed thirty years of peace and, although in both the War of the League of Augsburg (1689-1697) and in the War of the Spanish Succession (1701-1713) it was turned again, for brief periods, into a battleground, neither of those wars brought a repetition—on quite the same scale and with the same intensity—of the devastations and the privations endured in the early part of the seventeenth century. The return to peace and normality in 1659 thus ushered in a new period in the economic history of the State of Milan, much as the Peace of Cateau Cambrésis had done a hundred years earlier.[1] It was a period of reconstruction and recovery, not unlike the second half of the sixteenth century, but, in sharp contrast with the latter, the late seventeenth century witnessed neither a rapid urban expansion nor the vigorous recovery of urban manufactures: this time, recovery largely bypassed the cities and their role in the economy was a marginal one—and such it was to remain, in fact, until the late nineteenth century.

To be sure, intimations of recovery were discernible in the Lombard cities after peace was restored to the State of Milan: a new mood of optimism and confidence pervaded them and efforts were soon afoot not only to heal the scars of war, but also to recover lost economic ground. A small but telling sign of the new mood was noted by a visitor in 1666 when he wrote that in Milan "a great many houses have been redecorated and day by day others are being repaired."[2] Other promising signs were also present: in 1670 a foreign merchant applied for permission to start in Milan the manufacture of cloth "according to the style of Flanders"; two years later a request came from a native of Como who had "spent several years in Amsterdam and other principal

towns of the States of Holland where at his own expense and with
great effort he [had] learnt cloth making and [had] plied that trade
with special care in order that one day he might be able to introduce it
into Italy."[3] The enterprising man had now returned, bringing with
him foreign artisans as well as the necessary tools, and was ready to
start in business provided the city of Como would grant him a ten-
year patent of monopoly and other privileges. In the 1680s new initiatives were reported in the Milan silk industry, and here, too, attempts were made to introduce foreign techniques and designs: in 1681
one silk maker began to produce fabrics "according to the English
style"; the following year another man set up a workshop "after the
manner of Venice"; and in 1687 it was the turn of two partners who
attempted to imitate silk fabrics "according to the style of Messina."[4]

A new outlook seems to have inspired policy makers as well in
those years. Comprehensive legislation was enacted in 1664 that was
aimed at revitalizing a dying wool industry in Milan.[5] It embodied
many of the measures that had been advocated, but only partially
implemented, in the 1640s and 50s: a 30 percent reduction of the excise
duty levied on fine Spanish wool and other ingredients; tax exemptions for six years for anyone who would start a new cloth manufacture in Milan; and stiff protective duties on imported fabrics, notably on high-grade ones.[6] At the same time, in an effort to lure fresh
capital and enterprise into trade and industry, the Senate recommended the reversal of the 1593 ruling that had forbidden nobles to
engage in business, and in 1682 a proclamation of King Carlos II
formally declared that the ownership and management of a textile
business involved no "derogation" from noble rank.[7]

But the government's chief concern in the postwar years continued
to be the parlous state of public finance. The huge military expenditures of the preceding forty years, financed as they had been largely
by increased government borrowing, had resulted in enormous interest charges absorbing the better portion of state and local revenue.
In the 1650s the demands of war had been so pressing, and public
finances so strained, as to impair the servicing of the public debt, and
even so solid and prestigious a financial institution as the Banco di
Sant'Ambrogio had met its obligations toward its own shareholders
only fitfully and partially: by 1658, when interest payments had to be
suspended, the shares of the Banco had dropped to a mere 35 percent

of their face value, thus making it virtually impossible for the government to borrow fresh money.[8] The return to peacetime conditions in 1659 eased the pressure on government finances and, insofar as the size of the army stationed in the State of Milan could now be reduced, taxpayers experienced a measure of relief. Nonetheless, decisive measures were urgently needed if a total repudiation of government debts was to be avoided. The government eventually settled for a partial repudiation: in 1671 all interest charges on outstanding short-term loans, which had been variously contracted over the years at interests as high as 8 percent, were reduced to a flat 2.5 percent[9]—a move that, in fact, amounted to taxing those financiers who, in the public's eyes, had profited handsomely from war conditions. As for the Banco di Sant'Ambrogio, its central place in the whole financial structure of the State of Milan, its close ties with the internatonal money market, and the prestige it had long enjoyed both at home and abroad made it imperative that it be salvaged at any cost. The authorities in Madrid were called upon to help, and while at first the beleaguered royal treasury resorted to vague promises and dilatory tactics "in the hope that, peace having returned, conditions will improve so as to make it possible for us to remit at the fairs and thus to still the outcry of those involved," eventually it authorized, and in fact imposed, a radical overhaul of the Banco itself. On the one hand, the board of directors was given authority to collect or farm out certain municipal taxes so as to ensure that the receipts thereof would accrue to the Banco regularly and in full; the shareholders, on their part, were assured of a modest, but fixed, 2 percent return on their investment—a measure that transformed the Banco from a partnership in which profits and losses were spread among shareholders into an agency that issued bonds and saw to it that interests were punctually paid. The results were, from a strictly financial standpoint, quite satisfactory: the securities of the Banco jumped from 35 to 60 percent of face value, thus yielding an actual return of 3.3 percent, a return comparable to that from alternative forms of investment. The Banco was now in a position where it could balance its own budget, meet without undue trouble its obligations towards the bondholders, and even set aside, after 1669, a small part of its profits for a gradual and limited repayment of the debts incurred by the Milan city government.[10]

Improvements in the aftermath of the war were not confined to a flurry of new initiatives, fresh legislation, and the reorganization of state finance. There is some evidence to suggest that the economy as a whole experienced a substantial, if still modest, upturn. The annual yield of the farm of the excise, which had dropped to less than one million lire in the late 1640s and may have sunk even lower in the next decade, netted L.1,300,000 in 1663, the only postwar year for which a figure is available.[11] More importantly, gold and silver issues in the Milan Mint, which had been more than halved between 1620 and 1660 largely, it would seem, as a result of dwindling exports, began to climb again and by the end of the century stood close to pre-1620 levels.[12] The exact causes of this upward trend in mint issues are not easy to determine, but there is a strong presumption (supported, as will be seen, by a good deal of circumstantial evidence) that the trend itself did reflect the recovery of the Lombard economy as a whole and the steady expansion of its exports from the low level attained in the war years.

The bulk of those exports, however, were not to be generated by the urban centers. The economic recovery of Lombardy after 1659, unlike that which had followed the end of the Italian wars a hundred years earlier, was not spearheaded by its cities. In fact, we have every reason to believe that in the late seventeenth century the cities played a negligible role in, and in some cases were actually by-passed by, the new upward trend.

The cities' atrophy, their inability to rebound, are illustrated by their demographic history after the plague of 1630 and up to the beginning of the eighteenth century. In a period in which the State of Milan as a whole saw its population rise by about 50 percent, back to preplague levels, only Milan and possibly Lodi experienced a comparable growth, while Pavia, Como, and Cremona conspicuously did not.[13] But it is when we turn to their economies that we clearly sense the inertia of the cities, for, despite the return to normal conditions, the legislation aimed at revitalizing their moribund manufactures, and a flurry of new, promising initiatives, the cities' industrial structure failed to respond to the new stimuli and, with but rare exceptions, continued on its downward course toward near-extinction.

This holds true, first of all, for the wool industry. As pointed out in an earlier chapter, Como, which had produced thousands of cloths a year at the beginning of the century and a mere 400 around 1650, produced none at all by 1700. In Milan, where approximately 3,000 cloths had been turned out as late as 1640, output was down to about 1,000 a year in the 1660s, and to little more than 100 by 1705.[14] The more modest wool industry in Cremona apparently fared not much better and by the eighteenth century was negligible. Cremona's chief losses, however, were in the field of fustians, those cotton fabrics that had formed the backbone of the city's economy until the late sixteenth century, when over 60,000 pieces had been produced annually, providing employment, so it was claimed, to 14,000 workers. The output of fustians plummeted inexorably during the seventeenth century, and by the mid-eighteenth century the industry employed but a few hundred workers.[15]

A similarly dismal record characterized the silk industry. This was true of Como, Pavia, and Cremona, where silk making had made its appearance, albeit on a very modest scale, in the late sixteenth century; in all three, by the end of the seventeenth century silk making had virtually disappeared.[16] But of course, it is in Milan that the decline of this once-celebrated manufacture is best observed. What few figures we have on the number of silk looms at work in the capital unmistakably point to an overall downward trend in production, a trend fully confirmed by the dwindling numbers of silk merchants admitted to the guild.[17] Nor was the going much better in another branch of the silk industry, namely the preparation (reeling and twisting) of the thread: the number of silk mills (*filatoi*) operating in Milan dropped from 388 in 1674 to 270 four years later and to a mere 100 by 1698.[18] And in those same years Milan also witnessed the virtual extinction of one of the few industries that had enjoyed considerable prosperity in wartime: before the close of the seventeenth century the making of small firearms, swords, and common service armor had died out altogether.[19]

To be sure, there were a few bright spots in this otherwise gloomy picture. The seventeenth century, after all, was the golden age of Cremona's violin makers,[20] as well as of Lodi's renowned ceramics.[21] For its part, Milan continued to enjoy a considerable reputation for its silk ribbons and above all for its gold thread;[22] the latter was used in the making of lavishly embroidered fabrics, and Milanese embroiderers continued to be so highly admired that silk fabrics made abroad were shipped to Milan to be perfected by the local artisans.[23] The knitting of silk stockings too seems to have fared rather well, if in the 1660s it reportedly employed some eight thousand women.[24]

For all this, there is no denying that the major Lombard cities had, by the end of the century, ceased to be the buoyant, prosperous, widely admired manufacturing centers they had once been. Clearly, the hopes and expectations expressed after 1659 had failed to materialize. The few luxury industries that did survive in that period were certainly not negligible, but their significance is greater for the history of music and the arts than for economic growth.

It is harder to be specific about the role of the cities as strictly commercial centers. In the case of Como we can safely assert that such a role became insignificant: stripped of its wool industry, it no longer attracted imported wool and dyes; and its earlier function as a center for the bleaching of German linens and as an entrepôt for the leather trade came to a complete halt as well.[25] Of Cremona it was said in the first half of the eighteenth century that "there are no longer any well-endowed merchants capable of doing business on a grand scale."[26] Milan, on the other hand, retained a significant role as a commercial center, on account not only of its size, which called for vast supplies of foodstuffs and other necessities, but also on account of the presence within its walls of a large class of government officials, high-ranking churchmen, and wealthy landowners. The conspicuous consumption generated by this concentration of wealth is illustrated by sporadic bits of information. In the 1660s it was reported that over 1,500 horse-drawn coaches were kept in the city by wealthy residents.[27] In 1691 a survey was made of all the silk shops in the city, in order to determine the amount of foreign-made silk articles actually in stock: the survey revealed the existence of an astonishing 60,000 meters of silk cloth and a roughly equal amount of ribbons in stock, with Florence, Turin, and, above all, Lyons looming as the main places of origin for the imported goods. A quarter of a century later, a similar survey, but one that included both imported and native silks, reported stocks of 280,000 meters scattered in 140 separate shops.[28] Even assuming that a good portion of those silks would eventually find their way into the hands of retailers in lesser towns and villages, rather than into the wardrobes of Milanese consumers, it is still undeniable that the city continued to provide a very attractive market for silk goods and we can easily agree with that visitor who, in 1666, remarked that in Milan "merchants are rich."[29] This is all the more plausible in that we know that in the late seventeenth century Milan continued to serve as a clearinghouse for the trade that linked Lombardy and Genoa with Geneva and Lyons, a trade that now involved rice, raw and wrought silk, and an assortment of luxuries in one direction, and linens, woolens, trinkets, and Lyons silk fabrics in the other. Milan's commercial role was probably enhanced in the late seventeenth century as a result of trans-Alpine trade being increasingly diverted from the Piedmontese route (via Turin, Susa, and Mont Genèvre) to the Swiss route over the Simplon pass. At any rate, middlemen, merchants, and carriers (*grands voituriers*) with international connections were present in Milan in that period and helped preserve a cosmopolitan flavor to a city which by then had no doubt lost its former towering position in the European economy.[30]

Nor did things really change in the course of the eighteenth (or, for that matter, for much of the nineteenth) century, either in Milan itself or in the other Lombard cities. Despite the sporadic appearance of new small-scale manufactures, in purely economic terms the urban scene generally remained quite barren.[31] For nearly two centuries those cities served mainly as centers of consumption, feeding on a flow of agrarian rents and government expenditures.[32] Between the urban economies of the late Middle Ages and the Renaissance and their industrial successors of the twentieth century there is, in other words, a gap, a striking discontinuity: the break had occurred in the fateful decades between 1620 and 1660 and nothing remained of the earlier greatness to foreshadow the resurgence of the Lombard cities under the impact of modern industrialization two centuries later.

The atrophy of the urban economies, so dramatically revealed by demographic stagnation, the dismantling of their manufactures, and the growing dependence of their populace on foreign-made goods, may well be one of the most distinctive aspects of Lombard (and, one might add, of northern Italian) history in the seventeenth century. It is unquestionably its most intriguing aspect, and one which contemporaries discussed in earnest and students of the period have assiduously analyzed and variously attempted to explain.

One of the most popular explanations has been to the effect that the economic decadence of the cities was the end product of a long process of social involution, whereby the vigorous spirit of enterprise that had presided over the rise of the Lombard cities to a position of European supremacy in the late Middle Ages gave way to new attitudes, values, and aspirations that were hostile to the practice of trade and manufacturing as socially demeaning and not consonant with the life of a gentleman. As a result of this changed outlook, so runs the argument, a once dynamic and aggressive bourgeoisie withdrew from business, sank its wealth into land and the trappings of nobility, and was ultimately transformed into a class of flaccid landowners and idle rentiers, while trade and industry were allowed to drift into decay for lack of capital and enterprise. This line of argument goes back at least to the late seventeenth century, for one of the measures enacted by the government of King Carlos II, in order to stimulate the economic recovery of the State of Milan, was to declare that active participation in business was in no way incompatible with gentility.[33] Eighteenth-century reformist writers, for their part, saw the roots of old and persisting economic ills in the changed attitudes and values allegedly injected into Lombard society by the Spaniards from the early sixteenth century, and notably their "prejudice according to which business of any kind is unbecoming to noblemen." Such a prejudice, it was contended, "has ruined Spain . . . and both there and here has caused trade to be forsaken . . . with the result that manufactures have decayed, craftsmen have migrated abroad, and great harm has befallen the whole State."[34]

It was for nineteenth-century historians and publicists, however, to give wide currency to the notion that under Spanish rule the moral fiber of the Lombard bourgeoisie had been irreparably corrupted, with disastrous consequences for the economy. Until the coming of the Spaniards, wrote Cesare Cantù, "Italians had been industrious and actively engaged in trade and industry . . . Then suddenly came those arrogant Spaniards and told us that to attend to business was shameful and defiling."[35] Carlo Cattaneo used even stronger language in denouncing the evils of Spanish influence:

> Those families which, in keeping with our native traditions, had continued to practice honest and noble trades even after they had achieved great wealth, now, finding themselves outranked by the least Spanish captain, began to despise the labors of their forefathers and strove to purify their blood by a life of sloth . . . Then the vast sums of capital that had been invested in business in Lyons, Paris, Antwerp, London, and Cologne were gradually withdrawn and were sunk in land and titles, in aristocratic ostentation, in alms which corrupted the industrious populace. Our wretched artisans, idled by the shortage of capital, died of plagues, famines, and daily despair; once celebrated manufactures wilted away; others moved to Zurich, Geneva, Lyons, and Paris, and in this way young nations rose in inverse ratio to our own decay.[36]

Twentieth-century scholars have avoided the shrill rhetoric and the nationalistic outrage of their predecessors, but a number of them have basically subscribed to these views, albeit in a revised form.[37] Rather than blaming the Spaniards, they have found in the humanistic concept of *otium* (leisure), in the Renaissance revival of the study of law, and in the resurgence, under French influence, of courtly pageantry and chivalrous "honor" the roots of a widespread attitude that, as early as the fifteenth century and possibly even earlier, frowned upon trade and manufacturing as being tainted and unworthy of a true gentleman. Hence there was a "rush to the land" (*corsa alla terra*)—a tendency on the part of rich merchants and financiers to invest their wealth in landed property, as the latter seemed capable of ensuring a safe economic return and, more importantly, of providing the indispensable means for a life of leisure and public serivce. In the words of the foremost authority on sixteenth-century Lombardy, "Landed property was not merely the place of rest, of leisure, the *villa* made fashionable by the humanists' ideal of *otium*, but also the most practical investment for anyone who wanted to serve in government, rise to high position, and achieve, along with economic security, honor and reputation . . . ; it was, in other words, the form of investment typical of an age in which the aspiration to the lawyer's gown and to public office was taking root in the minds of the elite causing them to feel contempt for the life of the merchant."[38]

The attraction exerted by landownership, together with a new-fangled "craving for gentility," thus marked "the end of the bourgeoisie which had characterized Italy in the age of the communes and the *signorie*."[39] "Little wonder, then," wrote another historian, "that, having adopted such attitudes, Italy was transformed from a country of towns throbbing with trade and manufactures into a country of rural markets in some of which a few luxury industries somehow managed to linger on."[40]

These views have been supported with literary texts dating from the fifteenth and sixteenth centuries, in which the life of the country gentleman is extolled at the expense of that of the merchant; with legal texts, and notably with the ruling issued in 1593 by the Milan College of Jurists stressing the incompatibility of base and sordid occupations such as manual labor and commerce with patrician status; and finally, and more importantly, with the history of individual Lombard families, which, in the course of the fifteenth and sixteenth centuries, invested in land an increasing share of the wealth they had accumulated in trade, manufacturing, or banking. The conclusion has been that this "rush to the land" or this "defection of the bourgeoisie" drained the cities of their lifeblood and ushered in an age of economic decay.

The argument, however attractive, is open to serious doubt. There is, first of all, the question of chronology: When did the alleged change in social values and the concomitant "rush to the land" actually start? On this question no consensus has emerged. Some scholars have stressed the early sixteenth century, while others have located the starting point a good two centuries earlier.[41] Faced with such widely different views, one is inclined to believe that Hans Baron's skeptical comment on the historiography of Renaissance Florence applies equally well to the State of Milan: "We cannot be cautious enough in our use of the often heard theory that there was a general "return to the country" and to agriculture among the urban-commercial classes during the Italian Renaissance. As for Florence, there is not a single generation from the thirteenth to the sixteenth century for which it has not been asserted by some student that such transformation occurred."[42]

What may account for this wide disagreement about chronology is that our knowlege of the whole process of land acquisition from the fourteenth to the seventeenth century is still woefully inadequate, and further that in any of those centuries one can find instances of successful merchants and financiers buying country estates and ultimately settling down for a life of leisure or of public service.[43] Nor does one have to invoke any far-reaching change in social values to account for the decision to abandon the countinghouse and the workshop for the emblazoned villa. The switch was not uncommon in late medieval and early modern times, nor was it confined to Italy; it has been observed, albeit at a somewhat later date, in countries such as England, Holland, and France, which did not fall prey, as Italy did, to economic decadence.[44] What H. J. Habakkuk has written of the reasons why wealthy merchants in seventeenth- and, to a lesser extent, eighteenth-century England were anxious to buy land seems basically applicable to their counterparts in sixteenth-century Lombardy: not only did a country estate bring with it social prestige and an aura of gentility, but it was also, and more importantly, the best available way of holding wealth in a permanent form for anyone who had accumulated a sizable fortune.[45] Alternative methods (besides the hoarding of bullion or plate, which earned no income), such as putting money out at loan, the farming of taxes, or dealing in bills of exchange or in government loans, were probably more readily available at an earlier date in Italy than in England, but they either involved high risks or required a good deal of personal attention and expertise on the investor's part. In the sixteenth century, moreover, with land values steadily climbing, the purchase of an estate held special attraction as a long-term investment for the rich upstart desirous to protect his assets against inflation, to enhance his reputation for financial solvency, and to secure his possessions against the whims of fortune and the ineptitude of his heirs.

Granted that it was commonplace for wealthy townsmen throughout Europe to turn to landownership and to aspire to gentility after attaining a certain level of affluence, it is hardly surprising to find that in Lombardy, where the cities had achieved commanding positions as commercial and manufacturing centers well before the close of the Middle Ages, the acquisition of land attained stupendous proportions: by the mid-sixteenth century, well over half of the best farmland in the fertile *bassa* was already in their hands.[46] The crucial question, then, is whether or not this outpouring of wealth into the countryside actually drained the cities of their economic vitality and had a stifling effect on the economy as a whole. The answer cannot but be a negative one. We have seen in an earlier chapter that in the second half of the sixteenth century—at a time, that is, when the return to the land had already brought vast amounts of land into urban hands—Milan, Cremona, Pavia, and Como experienced a vigorous commercial and industrial expansion and enjoyed a period of renewed prosperity that was to last into the first two decades of the next century. Clearly, neither capital nor enterprise was lacking in those cities at that time.

This would seem paradoxical only on the following assumptions: that investment in land did not contribute to overall economic growth, but represented, in fact, a flagrant misallocation of resources; and that the acquisition of land and promotion into the aristocracy seriously depleted the ranks of the urban-commercial classes, insofar as no new individuals came up to replace those who had moved to a different and more prestigious social level. Both assumptions seem unwarranted. We know that in the course of the fifteenth century, when a good deal of urban money flowed into the Lombard countryside, net capital formation—in the form of consolidation of holdings, new irrigation canals, the introduction of new crops, and the expansion of stockraising—gained momentum and contributed to making the Lombard lowlands a model of agricultural excellence.[47] A prosperous, highly productive countryside could, in turn, assist urban expansion by making available a more plentiful supply of food and industrial crops, by providing a growing market for manufactured goods, and even by generating fresh funds for trade and industry.[48] As for the second assumption, there is little evidence to support it and there are sound reasons for rejecting it. Of course, if one traces the history of those families (the Borromeo, the D'Adda, the Litta) which in the course of the sixteenth century rose to prominence in terms of landownership, public office, and noble rank, one invariably finds that their fortunes had originated generations earlier in banking, trade, or industry.[49] Yet, it would be a mistake to conclude from these and similar cases that the makeup of Lombardy's urban society and its economy was being radically altered. What was happening was that, as the most successful merchants withdrew from business into gentility, other individuals rose to take their places in the countinghouse and the guild.[50] To be sure, we know far less about the latter than we do about their more fortunate predecessors, but this is largely because historical records tend to be more hospitable to the few who make it to the top than to the many who are still striving to get there. That these existed in great numbers in the Lombard cities during the reign of Philip II is, however, beyond doubt: how else could we account for the recovery and prosperity of the metal trades, silk making, and the fustian and wool industries in that period?

Even the view implicit in so much of the rush-to-the-land literature—that the example set by the merchant turned patrician inevitably tended to discourage potential new recruits from taking up where their social superiors had left off and thus had, in the long run, an adverse effect on the supply of enterprise—is hardly convincing. It seems safer to assume that as long as the urban economies remained viable and vital and commercial opportunities looked bright (as, by and large, they did in the fifty years or so after 1559), the ranks of the commercial bourgeoisie were easily replenished from below by men spurred, if not by the capitalist ethos, at least by the prospect and the hope of joining some day the charmed circle of the landed aristocracy.[51] To do so a man must, of course, be able to command sufficient money for the purchase of a respectable country estate—and trade or manufacture, tainted and despised though they may have been, still represented in the sixteenth century one of the few avenues open to the ambitious and the lucky for doing just that, and doing it fast.

For all its shortcomings as an explanation of the troubles that were to befall the Lombard economy in the seventeenth century, the hypothesis of a "rush to the land" or of a "defection of the bourgeoisie" has served a valuable purpose in that it has highlighted a significant change in the political structure of the State of Milan, which could conceivably have had unfavorable repercussions on the urban economies. The change consisted in the progressive tightening of the qualifications for admission to the Milanese patriciate and hence for eligibility to high office in the city and the state administration: in the course of two centuries, long residence in the city, the reputation of one's family, formal training in the law, and evidence that one or more generations had not practiced "base and sordid trades" came to be required for acceptance into the patriciate; by 1593 the expression "base and sordid trades" was construed to include not only retail trade and all manual work, but wholesale trade as well, even when practiced through intermediaries.[52] In this way merchants and craftsmen were excluded from the patriciate, the latter consolidating itself as a closed oligarchy of professionals generally endowed with large landed incomes. Accordingly, the possibility, indeed the likelihood, that the economic and fiscal policies of the State of Milan would increasingly tend to favor the landed rather than the commercial and urban interests must have presented itself. To what extent such was, in fact, the case will be discussed later; at this point it will suffice to say that, if indeed the change in the composition of the ruling elite resulted in the enactment of policies unfavorable to the urban economies, their effects were not seriously felt until after 1620. Nor is it hard to see why they were not. On the one hand, in a period of general economic expansion such as the second half of the sixteenth century unquestionably was, the conflict between urban and agrarian interests was likely to be cushioned by the very fact that prosperity made enough room for both. On the other hand, even though the highest offices in the state came to be monopolized by the landed patriciate, there still existed in the cities a number of well-organized intermediate bodies, such as the guilds, capable of making their voices heard, all the way to Madrid if necessary, and of defending their corporate privileges.[53]

After about 1620 conditions certainly changed, both for the landed oligarchy and for the urban guilds. The latter lost much of their strength and influence in the wake of adversity at home and of stiffer competition abroad; if their voices remained loud and even strident, their effectiveness in protecting their own interests inevitably waned. As for the oligarchy, while their power increased in inverse proportion to that of the debilitated merchant and artisan community, their economic base underwent subtle changes. For one thing, the purely economic motives for buying land were weakened, as will be recalled, by the collapse of land values and rents; for another, alternative forms of investment became increasingly available which ensured safe, if low, returns. Writing in the 1670s, an Italian jurist observed that

"nowadays no one would think of letting his money lie idle and fruit-
less [for] opportunities to invest money are now at hand especially
after the recent and more frequent introduction of rent charges [*censi*]
and exchanges as well as of those public bonds . . . which in Rome are
known as *luoghi di monte.*"[54] Recent research has shown that in that
period the Genoese-controlled fairs of exchange developed into well-
oiled mechanisms for mobilizing private savings and for ensuring low
but solid returns.[55] As for state finance, we know that in Milan a re-
organized Banco di Sant'Ambrogio did represent, after 1660, a de-
pendable outlet for those who wished to hold part of their wealth in a
form that was secure and yet more liquid than land.

The seventeenth century brought another change too: the decline of
the cities as centers of trade and manufacture reduced the number of
nouveaux riches anxious and able to push their way into the ranks of
the nobility or to take the place of those who had already made the
transition. The upward mobility of the sixteenth century thus gave
way to a less dynamic social structure, and this fact, more than anything else, may account for the diminishing esteem in which merchants came to be held: it is conceivable that the practice of trade
came to be increasingly viewed as an unpromising dead-end rather
than a steppingstone between the condition of the lowly commoner
and the exalted position of the patrician.[56] Merchants, of course, did
not disappear altogether in the seventeenth century, nor did handsome estates for them to buy. A 1682 memorandum produced by the
guild of the Lodi merchants, intended to explain why some members
no longer appeared on the guild's roster and no longer contributed to
the common tax chest, spoke of "merchants [who], having grown
rich, have withdrawn from trade"—a clear intimation that their breed
was not extinct and that, as in the past, the most successful among
them continued to move into the ranks of the landowners.[57] Such was
certainly the case of that Milan merchant and financier who, in 1685,
purchased from a debt-ridden nobleman an estate and a fief at Brignano Tortonese.[58] Of this upstart we are told that "he formerly used
to deal in the exchange," that his newly accumulated wealth now enabled him "to live honorably and in comfort with a goodly number of
servants and a carriage," and that in recent years he had ceased to take
an active part in financial transactions. He was thus ready to move, if

not yet into the exclusive coterie of the patricians, at least into the looser ranks of the country nobility—and the financial woes of an established, but sinking, noble dynasty offered him the long-awaited opportunity for doing so.

If the failure of the urban economies to hold their own in the face of adversity and to recover lost ground once normality returned cannot be convincingly ascribed to an alleged extinction of the old bourgeois spirit, we have little choice but to assume that, in the course of the seventeenth century, capital and enterprise deserted the cities because the cities themselves no longer provided existing or potential entrepreneurs with conditions favorable to business and thus forced them to give up or to look elsewhere for more rewarding outlets.

That such was indeed the case is abundantly suggested, as will be recalled, by the incessant complaints that contemporaries voiced about urban manufactures being priced out of the market by rising costs and being displaced by goods produced either in the Lombard countryside or abroad—in their view their failure to compete reflected either a mounting burden of taxation or a wage level that was out of line with that obtaining elsewhere, or a combination of both factors.

As far as taxes are concerned, it bears repeating that the burden did increase very substantially under Spanish rule. One should also re-member that since the late sixteenth century the relative share of tax-ation borne by the cities grew larger as the cities were stripped of a number of fiscal privileges that they had traditionally enjoyed vis-à-vis the countryside. Before the end of the century, as mentioned, the unprecedented step was taken of extending to commercial assets (*mercimonio*) the direct tax (*mensuale*) originally levied on landed property only, each guild being now required to pay annually a fixed sum (*estimo*) roughly proportional to its economic importance. A further breach into the city's fiscal immunity occurred in 1597 with the institution of the *equalanza*, whereby the burden of military billets and victuals, formerly shouldered by such individual rural communi-ties as had the dubious honor of hosting His Majesty's troops, was to be spread over the entire state. This was a major blow to the cities, for until then they had been exempted not only from the onerous obligation of actually providing quarters to troops in transit, but also from contributing monies to help defray the cost thereof. Under the newly instituted system, any community in which troops had been stationed, housed, and fed in a given year could claim a refund; all such claims were then added up and the entire state, cities not excluded, were assessed their fair share of the total bill.[59] In 1604 the pressure on townsmen's wealth was stepped up as the Spanish government, at the request of the rural communities, authorized village treasurers to levy a tax (*mezza pertica*) on the acreage owned by city residents in the village itself and to use the revenue to help defray any expense incurred in connection with the quartering of troops. Lastly, in 1633 a final blow to urban privilege was dealt by a hard-pressed government: from then on troops in transit were to be quartered in the cities no less than in the countryside.[60]

And yet, even though the fiscal burden placed on the cities did increase both absolutely and relatively, the argument that primarily blames taxation for pricing urban manufactures out of the market is unsatisfactory. No one would deny that taxes hurt merchants and craftsmen in their struggle against their new rivals. What one must take issue with is the view that had it not been for the rapacity of the royal fisc Lombardy's urban manufactures would have weathered the storm or at least recovered their vitality once normal conditions were restored.

A memorandum submitted in the 1660s by the drapers' guild of Milan to protest the unfair competition of unlicensed cloth-makers operating in the village of Canzo and illegally producing cheap imitations of fine Milan cloth does indicate that at the time the worst problem was not of a fiscal nature. To buttress their case against their new rural rivals, the city drapers asserted that producing a cloth in Milan cost L.65 more than it did in Canzo and proceeded to show, item by item, where the additional expense came from. Interestingly enough, in their analysis the obnoxious *estimo del mercimonio* was said to claim only L.6 (or less than 10 percent) of those additional L.65 and the excise duties levied at the city gates another L.8 (or 12 percent). By far the largest discrepancies between urban and rural costs they ascribed to wage differentials and, secondly, to the strict specifications that the guild imposed on the urban craftsman in the preparation of the warp: of the total of L.65 in additional costs allegedly borne by the urban cloth-maker, wages absorbed L.30 (or 46 percent) and the preparation of the warp L.18 (or 28 percent). The thrust of the drapers' argument, then, was that cloth made in Milan, burdened as it was by higher labor costs and the stricter enforcement of standards, could not possibly compete with its rural counterpart.[61]

Although we have no way of verifying the accuracy of these figures, there is little reason to suspect that the drapers were grossly distorting the truth, since any blatantly false claim on their part could have been easily exposed by the city authorities. The reality of a wide gap between urban and rural wages in particular is quite plausible. In the first place, the urban labor force had been severely depleted by the plague of 1630 as well as by the enlistment or impressment of craftsmen into the army and the militia during the long war that had just come to an end,[62] and this must have created a condition of labor scarcity, which the craft guilds, with their strict admission policies, no doubt tended to perpetuate. Secondly, and more importantly, one can easily see why, even in normal times, labor costs would be lower in the countryside than in the city: rural workers typically combined subsistence farming with work at the loom or at the spinning wheel and, being thus only partially dependent on wages for their living, could afford to work for less pay than their urban counterpart.[63] Lastly, it must be remembered that at the time of the drapers' memorandum, Lombardy, like the rest of Europe, was witnessing a sharp downswing in cereal prices; in the marginal, less favored agricultural regions (and such no doubt was the hill zone where Canzo was located) this downward trend was bound to discourage the growing of grain crops, thus heightening those conditions of rural underemployment that made for a more plentiful and cheaper supply of labor in the countryside.[64]

Higher labor costs, then, do provide us with a plausible clue to the cities' industrial malady,[65] but our diagnosis cannot stop there, for even granting that in Lombardy urban wages were out of line with rural wages, it does not follow that every urban manufacture would thereby be doomed to extinction nor that they would all be equally affected. Much depended, of course, on the labor intensity of individual industries—and on this score there was anything but uniformity.[66] At one extreme stood the wool industry, where the wage bill claimed close to half of total production costs; at the other end of the range was the making of gold thread, where labor costs represented 12 percent of the total, and jewelry, with a labor content of but 2.5 percent; in between, and in descending order of labor intensity, one finds plain silk fabrics (30-40 percent), richly embroidered silks (20 percent), and silk throwing (17 percent).[67] Given this wide range of labor intensities, it is obvious that high labor costs would have a widely different impact on individual industries: one would expect the wool industry to prove especially vulnerable, while silk throwing or the making of gold thread would hardly be affected.

In actual fact the decline of Lombardy's urban industries conformed only in part to the expected pattern: cloth making, to be sure, did register irreparable losses, while the gold-thread industry managed to survive; on the other hand, silk throwing, despite its lower labor content, deserted its traditional urban setting and, as will be seen, set fresh roots in the countryside. There are, therefore, sound reasons for doubting, if not the reality of high labor costs in the city, their role as the sole cause of urban industrial decline. Clearly, other causes were at work too, and if we are to judge from contemporary complaints, a major one was that some Lombard manufactured goods compared unfavorably with foreign imports in terms of quality and appearance, rather than just price.

As early as 1641 the growing success of foreign-made fabrics on the domestic market was said to depend on the fact that, although "lighter in texture and inferior in workmanship," those fabrics could "deceive the customers on account of their color," while Lombard cloth, for all the excellence of its ingredients and workmanship, seemed "to lack the shine of foreign cloth."[68] Forty years later the Milan drapers ascribed the growing success of imported (and notably French) textiles to a superior finishing technique that imparted a special brilliance.[69] A similar concern about differences in quality was voiced with regard to the silk industry: at mid-century it was claimed that Genoese silks were preferred "on account of a certain shine" that those made in Milan did not quite match;[70] in 1678 it was unequivocally stated that imported textiles, both silk and wool, had won the hearts of Lombard consumers: "Owing to a new fashion which is so harmful to the common good, men, both in winter and in summer, dress in clothes made with imported material . . . and the ladies despise anything made here; whence it has come to pass that our silk manufacturers, seeing that their articles no longer sell well, have dismissed large number of workers."[71]

Urban manufacturers in seventeenth-century Lombardy were thus faced with two difficulties as they set about recovering lost ground: high labor costs and outmoded products. The first difficulty was in no way insuperable: the cities could (and to some extent did) concentrate on resource-intensive productions or, even more so, on the making of artistic goods in which individual styling and excellence of workmanship were far more important that price in determining consumer choices; labor-intensive industries, on the other hand, had little choice but to relocate to the countryside. The second problem, however, proved more intractable: its solution called for bold moves away from traditional designs and specifications; it called for the commitment of fresh merchant wealth and ingenuity to new lines of production and new techniques—but, as the dismal record of urban industrial production suggests, the response was sporadic at best and ultimately grossly deficient.

The failure to innovate or to emulate the new competitors was blamed on the craft guilds. After stating that, "Foreign cloth, while not better than our own in terms of intrinsic quality, looks better and more readily catches the customer's eye on account of its extrinsic beauty, and the latter mainly depends on the method used to press the cloth and to confer shine to it," the drapers of Milan, writing in 1680, went on to charge that, "If a foreign craftsman wishes to introduce [the new method] here (and there are many who are so inclined), they [the Milanese craftsmen] stand in his way demanding that he first be duly enrolled in their guild and that he pay the admission fee and other dues. As they [the foreign craftsmen] are poor and unable to pay, the new technique cannot be adopted."[72]

This indictment of the Milanese craftsmen by the drapers who put out work to them would be suspect were it not for two facts: one is that the guildsmen, each working in his own shop according to traditional methods, were precisely the men who stood to lose most by the intrusion of outsiders capable of producing next door, as it were, the very fabrics that were already driving their own from the market; the other fact is that the opposition of the cloth workers to innovation was in no way an isolated reaction to change. In 1663 the Milan hand-knitters succeeded in securing an injunction, not repealed until 1722, against the stocking frame imported from England; likewise, the attempted introduction in 1696 of a new mechanical device (*molinello*) for the manufacture of gold thread was frustrated by the protests of the Milan guild of goldleaf beaters (*battiloro*) on grounds that the new device would leave many of them unemployed.[73]

The craft guilds, to be sure, had long been in existence and there is no reason to assume, nor evidence to suggest, that before the seventeenth century they had been any more flexible and open-minded. But what had been of little consequence in the past became a serious handicap now. In their halcyon days the success of the Lombard manufacturers had been due not so much to their ability to produce articles that were better or less expensive than those produced elsewhere, but rather to their ability to produce them at all at a time when other nations still lagged far behind in skills, technology, and know-how.[74] This precocious lead had ensured the Lombard cities in the late Middle Ages, and well into the sixteenth century, a protective shield behind which their merchants and craftsmen could prosper without undue concern for costs, productivity, and innovation. From the late sixteenth century, however, the gap which had for so long separated Lombardy (and some other areas in norther Italy) from its more backward European clients rapidly narrowed as those clients caught up with, and eventually left behind, their former purveyors and mentors. At that point the pressure of competition posed new challenges and called for major adjustments which the old manufacturing centers, steeped in tradition and privilege, proved unable to accomplish.

Reflecting on a somewhat similar situation, an eighteenth-century Florentine writer and an advocate of economic reform analyzed the downfall of his native city's trade and manufactures in terms that could well fit the industrial history of Milan, Como, and Cremona in the seventeenth century: "Let us face it. Our economy rested on a monopoly. We waxed rich thanks to the barbarous ignorance and indolence of others. Now the other nations . . . have dispensed with our services as they can make themselves the things which they formerly allowed us to make for them . . . The very nature and the precarious base of our economy was bound to lead to this sooner or later."[75] More than a century earlier an obscure tax farmer in Milan had made much the same point, although in a rather cruder form. In lamenting the economic troubles of his city he had ascribed them to the fact that "formerly only here were artificers to be found, but now they have spread all over the world."[76]

CHAPTER VI

RESILIENCE IN THE COUNTRYSIDE

In sharp contrast to the decline and atrophy that afflicted the urban economy of Lombardy in the seventeenth century, the rural economy displayed a record of continuity, despite temporary setbacks and losses,[1] of adaptation to changing conditions, and finally of vigorous resilience and progress. While in the cities the sources of capital and enterprise were drying up, the opposite was true in the countryside; while the cities turned their backs on their glorious and highly promising past and settled down as dormant centers of administration and consumption, the rural communities managed to preserve their heritage basically intact and proved capable of scoring some significant, if limited, gains as well.

The continuity in the life of the Lombard countryside is discernible, first of all, in the preservation of those sophisticated farming practices that had long been the pride of the irrigated plain; it can also be seen in the persisting commercial orientation of agriculture, even in the darkest decades of the century, when rents and land values had collapsed and the countryside had been subjected to the depredations of the soldiery and the rapacity of the tax collector. In the 1640s and 1650s in the low plain, the system of convertible husbandry continued to be practiced much as it had been before, even in the darkest decades of the century (see Appendix C). This system was characterized by the close integration of arable farming and stock raising and by a continuous rotation pattern, in which fallowing was totally eliminated—cereals and industrial crops being alternated with artificial grasses to ensure the fertility of the soil. These features of agriculture in the plain are vividly described in documents dating from the mid-seventeenth century;[2] and elicted astonishment and admiration from the English traveler Arthur Young.[3]

The strong commercial orientation of Lombard agriculture, too, survived the ordeals of the seventeenth century. From the irrigated plain near Binasco it was reported in 1640 that "on gentlemen's estates crops greatly exceed local needs" and that the grain surplus "for the most part is sold in Milan." Similarly, grain produced in another locality halfway between Pavia and Milan was shipped to the latter city "for sale in the Broletto" (the city's granary and cereal market). Of the residents of a village near Melegnano it was noted in 1652 that "two-thirds of them ply diverse trades such as carrying butter, cheese, poultry, eggs, and fish to Milan or weaving linen." In other parts of the Lodi province the sale of grain, dairy products, and flax to nearby urban centers continued to provide the mainstay of the rural economy in the second half of the century. In some areas specialization had, by the last quarter of the century, if not earlier, reached the point where the peasantry no longer grew enough grain and other basic necessities to meet their own needs, an increasing proportion of available land having been turned into irrigated meadows, "the latter being more profitable than the fields under wheat."[4]

A marked commercial slant persisted in the adjacent Cremona province as well, despite all the trials and tribulations that province had endured in the 1640s and 1650s. Around 1640, for instance, the irrigated country near Soncino had lost neither its taste for wine nor its ability to pay for it: 60,000 lire were reportedly spent every year to import wine, mostly from Brescia; in return, flax and wheat were sold "to foreign merchants." Other communities similarly solved their balance-of-trade problems by selling cheese, cereals, flax, or coarse linen in the nearby towns. The district of Casalmaggiore, for its part, continued to depend on the wine trade: at the opening of the eighteenth century it had an annual production estimated at around 700,000 liters, and wine was exported in large quantities. In Casalmaggiore itself there were said to live "many merchants who own boats for carrying wine to Lodi, Pavia, Cremona, Pizzighettone, and Gera, and occasionally to Mantua and Ferrara as well." At mid-seventeenth century, the countryside around Vigevano was known to be a net exporter of grain, the proximity of the city of Vercelli in Savoyard territory representing a convenient and attractive outlet for the landowners' surplus. In Lomellina, it was claimed, "when the harvest is good, the tenant's share is enough to feed the local population, while the landlord's share is for sale."[5]

The high, dry plain had long had an agriculture based on the marriage of cereal and tree crops, with the former intended mainly for local consumption and the latter (whether vine or mulberry) for the market. The same pattern is discernible in the second half of the seventeenth century: in the Geradadda, a large stretch of coarse, porous lands just east of the Adda river, the local grain harvest was said to cover about three-fourths of local needs, the shortfall being made up with imports from the irrigated Crema district further south; on the export side, some wine and large amounts of silk provided the necessary purchasing power. In the plain north of Milan, rye, rather than wheat, seems to have been the main arable crop in the late seventeenth century, and some of it may have been available for sale; but the main marketable crop was no doubt silk, if we are to judge from common observations about "the large number of mulberry trees" in that area. Further west, along the main highway that linked Milan to Lake Maggiore, rye and silk were still important, but maize (*melegone*) is also mentioned, possibly for the first time, in 1652. Occasionally, as near Gallarate, wine replaced silk as the major cash crop.[6]

The vine continued to hold a prominent place and may have made further headway in the economy of the hill zone where, along with chestnuts, it formed the main resource in an otherwise barren agricultural picture. The districts of the upper Brianza, while unable to grow all the cereals they needed, shipped a surplus of wine and chestnuts to Milan; the small community of Merate prided itself on producing in good years some 5,000 *brente* (375,000 liters) of "excellent wine which is mostly hauled to Milan partly on packhorses and partly by waterway down the Adda river."[7] At higher elevations the shortfall of cereals was paralleled by that of wine and, much as in the past, mountain communities met both deficiencies by combining the profits of their pastoral economy with the earnings of their emigrants and, whenever possible, with the sale of metal goods and of wood. For Ossuccio, a village ensconced on the mountainside overlooking Lake Como, the sale of wood to the city of Como was the only link with the market economy: "Wood is what helps the poor to meet their needs," as one villager put it. Likewise, in the mountains of Valdossola, one way for villagers to earn a living was "to carry wood and charcoal down to Domodossola on their backs, the terrain being too rugged for packhorses to be used." In the Valsassina, where practically no wine was produced, where cereals "did not suffice for two months of the year," and where, so it was claimed, people lived on chestnuts for half the year, mining and metallurgy remained a major source of livelihood, and so did seasonal outmigration and stockraising on the high alpine pastures.[8]

The impression that throughout the vicissitudes and trials of the seventeenth century Lombardy's rural economy lost none of its traditional features, nor its dependence on the market, nor its pattern of intraregional trade is confirmed as soon as we turn to the rural trading centers and market towns, which had played such a vital role in binding together the diverse and partly complementary zones that make up the Lombard countryside.

To be sure, the dislocations caused by warfare, depopulation, and taxation left their ugly marks on a number of those nodal points of the rural economy. Scant and fragmentary though the evidence unquestionably is, it is sufficient to assure us that losses and setbacks were serious. When a document for 1642 tells us rather curtly that the once prosperous cattle and linen market in Luino, on the shores of Lake Maggiore, had in recent years been discontinued, we cannot help but connect this loss to the unsettled conditions of the time. Another document makes precisely that point when it mentions a similar development in Soncino, a once-thriving trading center of the upper Cremona province: its weekly market, we are told in 1640, had not been held for twenty years "owing to the evil quality of the times" (*attesa la mala qualità de tempi*). Not far from Soncino, Caravaggio fared somewhat better, but was not left unscathed: in the 1640s it still featured a weekly market and an annual fair, but these were "no longer what they used to be, for poverty keeps many people away."[9]

If more information were available, we would no doubt hear of many similar instances of commercial decline and paralysis. Even then, we can be sure that the picture would not be uniformly bleak, for archival research does, in fact, yield more examples of continuity and vitality than it does of dislocation and blight. Consider, for instance, the case of Gallarate, a large village which in the late sixteenth century had been described as "a place of traffic" and which had harbored a good many substantial wholesale merchants. In the 1650s Gallarate, with a population of 2,000, or 20 percent below what it had been eighty years earlier, still featured a weekly market "very rich in all sorts of merchandise." Much as before, it was still the residence of "many merchants who deal in livestock, cloth, wool, hemp, and other commodities brought hither from Piedmont," and six of its leading merchants, it was further pointed out, "have assets of over six thousand *scudi.*" In those same years, Busto Arsizio, only a few miles away, held its own market on a different day of the week, but its residents also shopped in Gallarate when looking for clothes and went as far as Milan when they wanted to buy silk items. At the opposite end of the State of Milan, Casalmaggiore, too, somehow managed to survive the devastations visited on it by the French and Modenese soldiery in the late forties: in the early eighteenth century, if not earlier, it was still the home of numerous wine merchants and of "all sorts of artisans." In the Lodi province the weekly cattle market of San Fiorano was still held in the 1640s much as it had been in earlier and happier years.[10]

In the second half of the century, more substantial trading centers existed in larger communities of the Lodi province. One was Casalpusterlengo, where on market day flax, silk, and hides were actively traded; as a trading center with a population of nearly 2,000 and some fifty retail shops, it was described as "very prosperous" at the close of the century, and we know from another source that villagers (*paesani*) from the surrounding countryside came there to buy "clothes and other things"—an indication that the local peasantry did have some money to spend. Halfway between Casalpusterlengo and San Fiorano, Codogno, too, had its weekly market and an assortment of retail merchants, barbers, shoemakers, grocers, and even two physicians, and we can presume that business there depended on the patronage of the local residents as much as on that of the nearby villages.[11]

Trade involving farm products and simple manufactured goods on the one hand and peasant customers on the other could reach even a small village such as Castelponzone: "In said village Thursday is market day and the peasants of the surrounding countryside come there in large numbers, . . . and a few heads of cattle are traded, and most business involves only chestnuts, poultry, flax, and other things of little value."[12] Market day in Castelponzone, a village of but eighty households with seventeen retail shops, was a far cry from similar events in Casalmaggiore and Gallarate, and its existence would be of no historical interest whatever except as a reminder that commercial transactions trickled down into the recesses of rural society and that the peasantry did not live in a closed world of self-sufficiency, as has too often been assumed.

The influence of trade continued to be felt in the hills and mountains as well. In the Valassina, the narrow, rugged valley ensconced in the mountainous wedge that separates the two branches of Lake Como, the large village of Asso was described by a local antiquarian in the 1660s as being "thronged with people and well off, thanks to the market which is held there at the end of each week."[13] West of Lake Como, Valle Intelvi depended on the community of Porlezza across Lake Lugano for such commercial contacts as its narrow resource base required. At the lower end of the valley a regular ferry was in operation every Saturday to carry people from Osteno to Porlezza to attend the weekly market. Traffic on the ferry must have been considerable: in 1676 the ferry was leased out to a local boatman for an annual rent of L.28 s.15; as the fare to Porlezza was set at half a *soldo* per person, the rent alone was the equivalent of 1,150 passengers per year, or an average of 20-25 each week; and since the valley's total population at the time was probably less than 3,000,[14] it is obvious that attending the weekly market at Porlezza was a common experience for a great many residents of the valley.

If the enduring vitality of numerous trading centers and small market towns throughout rural Lombardy reflected first and foremost the high productivity of the land—which was made possible by elaborate farming practices and specialization of crops—it also reflected the fact that in the countryside, unlike the cities, such industrial activities as had been typical of rural Lombardy in the preceding century remained in existence in the next, while a few new ones emerged that added to the diversity and complexity of the rural economy. The evidence at our disposal is more abundant for the seventeenth than for the sixteenth century. It can, however, be ambiguous at times, as when a document reveals the existence in the late seventeenth century of an industry for which no earlier mention is available to us: in such cases it would be clearly wrong to assume that what we have here is a totally new industry, for it is just as possible that the industry itself had long been in existence but had left no previous trace in the surviving documents. In other and more numerous cases the connection with the past is well documented, and in a few others still there is enough evidence for us to speak of entirely new forms of industrial activity. The three cases must, of course, be kept distinct.

Papermaking belongs to the first group. One of our earliest references to it comes from the 1660s, and we learn that at the time there were nineteen paper mills (*folle da carta*) in the province (*ducato*) of Milano alone.[15] Whether, in fact, papermaking in the countryside was a long established tradition or a new development is impossible to tell on the basis of the available, scant evidence. All we can do, besides taking due notice of its presence in the countryside, is to observe that papermaking in the Milan province was a rather modest affair: with only nineteen mills, the province could not compare with the two districts of northern Italy where papermaking was concentrated at the time—namely, the tiny Salò district on Lake Garda, with its thirty mills, and the Voltri district on the Genoese coast, with nearly a hundred mills feeding a flourishing export trade.[16] The making of "exquisite brass lamps," for which Soncino apparently had a considerable reputation in the late seventeenth century,[17] is another case in which we cannot decide whether it represented a recent development or an established tradition.

When it comes to iron mining and metallurgy, on the other hand, we can confidently speak of continuity with the past. This holds true, first of all, for the chief mining district in Spanish Lombardy, the Valsassina. Although iron production there suffered a severe setback in 1636, when a French army led by the Duke of Rohan invaded and laid waste the valley, destroying a number of furnaces and forges in its path,[18] recovery had been swift: that same year an enterprising ironmaster from Bergamo rebuilt or restored a number of furnaces and was able to deliver large consignments of cannonballs and other hardware to the Spanish army then stationed in the State of

Milan—much to the dismay of the Venetian government, which had hoped that the destruction inflicted on the Valsassina would make the fortune of its own mining districts near Bergamo and Brescia.[19] By 1647 the iron industry of the Valsassina, galvanized by the Spanish war effort, had apparently regained its full momentum and the representatives of the valley could claim that

> In this valley enough iron is extracted and wrought to meet the needs not only of the whole State of Milan but of His Majesty [the King of Spain] as well for his artillery. This industry gives employment to large numbers of people of divers skills, for it requires miners to dig out the ore, lumbermen to cut wood and turn it into charcoal, muleteers to haul all those things down from the mountains, ironmasters to smelt the ore, others to refine the metal and give it a first rough shape, and many others to make the finished goods . . . One can say that two thirds of the people of the valley work in this industry.[20]

These claims contain no doubt a good dose of hyperbole, for we know that in the 1640s and 1650s the Spanish authorities in Lombardy secured large quantities of military hardware from Brescia to supplement an obviously inadequate domestic production. The statement just quoted, however, clearly points to a vigorous and buoyant industry and fits in well with the fact that throughout the century new mining pits were opened in the Valsassina.[21] Whether in the long run this resulted in a larger output of iron is hard to tell, for it is quite possible that the opening of new pits simply offset the closing-down of old ones as they became exhausted. All we know is that in 1719 there were five blast furnaces active in the Valsassina, as against seven at the close of the sixteenth century.[22] Assuming, as indeed we must, that no dramatic improvement in the smelting process had taken place in the meantime, we are led to the conclusion that over the century iron production in that area decreased somewhat or, at best, remained the same.

A total loss, on the other hand, was registered in the 1630s in Busto Arsizio, whose long established iron-wire industry died out as a result, it would seem, of the depletion of nearby forests.[23] The making of wire, however, continued throughout the century in Lecco, and in the 1660s it was claimed that the fine wire produced there and used in musical instruments was exported throughout Europe.[24] Concorezzo, the old center of the needle industry, held its own as well: at the close of the century it was reported that "in this village the chief trade is that of needle making and most men and women who do not tend the fields are employed in it."[25]

The textile industries, too, remained very much alive in the countryside at a time when they were being rapidly dismantled in the cities; in a few cases to be discussed later, some dramatic progress did, in fact, take place. Admittedly, in the Brianza and the Valassina, where ordinary woolens had traditionally been manufactured, production was at a low ebb in the 1640s, when but a handful of small firms managed to survive.[26] But beginning in 1649 the old industry exhibited a renewed vitality and, by moving into better quality fabrics, posed a serious threat to the dying industry of Milan.[27] In the eyes of the Milanese guilds, Canzo in the Valassina was the worst offender,[28] but another threat lurked from an unexpected quarter, the village of Gorgonzola east of the capital.[29] How large the output of the new rival centers may have been, we do not know. It is likely, however, that it remained rather small—a conclusion suggested by the fact that much of the wool spun by peasant women in the Valassina in the late seventeenth century found its way not to local looms but to those of the Bergamo province in Venetian territory, where cloth making on a large scale remained prosperous throughout the seventeenth century.[30] And yet, the making of woolen fabrics in the Valassina must have been far from negligible, if we are to judge from the persistent outcry of the Milan weavers' guild.

In the Gallarate district, where the manufacture of cotton fabrics (*fustagni*) and of fabrics mixed of cotton and flax (*bombasine*) had developed quite vigorously in the sixteenth century, the dislocations created by the plague of 1630 threatened the industry with extinction: a local chronicler writing in those years foresaw disaster for the entire district, because, in his view, the welfare of the district itself totally depended on an industry which, he contended, had provided employment to "five or six thousand people, bringing income and profit to all, spinners, carders, weavers, finishers, dyers, and lastly merchants."[31] His worst fears, however, proved unfounded: the village of Busto Arsizio recovered and remained a major and

burgeoning center of the cotton industry:[32] twenty years after the
plague it was noted that "the greater part of its people are engaged in
making *bombasina* and *fustagno* with cotton fetched in Milan, Genoa,
and Leghorn;"[33] by the first half of the eighteenth century, if not
earlier, the industry had spread to nearby Gallarate and Somma
Lombardo; in 1760 Busto Arsizio and Gallarate had a combined
output of about 100,000 pieces of fustian, far more than what
Cremona had produced at the zenith of its prosperity two hundred
years earlier.[34]

In rural Lombardy, however, the most widely spread forms of
handicraft activity in the seventeenth century were those connected
with flax. This holds true, first of all, of the laborious and
time-consuming operations needed to extract usable fibers from the
stalks: since retting, drying, scutching, combing, and spinning had to
be performed *in loco* as soon as the stalks had been pulled from the
ground, we can safely assume that they constituted an important form
of secondary employment for the peasants (and especially for the
peasant women) living in the flax-producing districts of the low
plain.[35] The weaving of flax into linen fabrics, on the other hand, was
not tied to the localities where flax itself was grown, and we have
already seen that skeins of linen thread were actively traded in rural
markets as well as exported abroad. We also know that
sixteenth-century Lombardy had been a heavy importer of linen from
northern Europe and that a similar situation obtained in the eighteenth
century, when linen thread held a prominent place among Lombardy's
exports, and linen fabrics from the Low Countries and Germany
among its imports.[36] Nevertheless, the weaving of linen was
commonly practiced in the Lombard countryside (see Appendix D).
This had been noticed, as will be recalled, by an English visitor in the
Lodi province at the opening of the seventeenth century. In later years
it was true (as is abundantly confirmed for a wider area) by the
relative frequency with which linen weaving is mentioned in our
sources: out of eighty villages in which some trace of industrial
activity is recorded, as many as forty-eight harbored linen weavers, as
against a mere ten where woolen cloth was made; not surprisingly, the
heaviest concentration of linen weavers was found in the villages of
the low plain where flax was grown, although a few were found in
other districts too.[37]

How can one reconcile the diffusion of the linen industry in the Lombard countryside with Lombardy's heavy dependence on foreign sources for linen? The answer seems to be that what was produced in the Lombard countryside was low-grade, coarse linen, while finer grades had to be imported. This was no doubt the situation prevailing at mid-eighteenth century when an official survey of thirty-seven localities across the State of Milan revealed that linen was manufactured in twenty-six of them, on a total of nearly 1,500 looms: in virtually all instances the linen fabrics produced were "ordinary and coarse" (*tele ordinarie, tele grossissime.*)[38] For earlier periods we cannot be so sure. And yet there are a few, isolated facts that are consistent with the view that native production was mainly low quality, while better stuffs had to be imported. In the inventory *post mortem* of a great nobleman in the late sixteenth century, we find an astonishing profusion of bed sheets, pillowcases, tablecloths, and napkins, and many of those articles are listed as coming "from Flanders."[39] On the other hand, when we read the petition submitted by "some poor men from Saronno" to be allowed to peddle undisturbed in the streets of Milan "pieces of linen for making aprons and infants' swaddles,"[40] we are inclined to assume that what was being sold from door to door was low-grade linen produced in local cottages. An unusual report drawn up in 1704 on the losses suffered by some villages near Vigevano at the hands of the soldiery provides another glimpse of the production and use of linen among the Lombard peasantry: not only did every household report, among other things, the loss of linen articles (a pair of sheets here, a few shirts there), but some of them also reported the loss of skeins of linen thread, thus suggesting that weaving was done in the household itself, presumably to provide simple articles for ordinary use.[41]

The diffusion of the linen industry in the Lombard countryside need not, of course, be interpreted to mean that this was the most important rural industry, in terms of either the labor force employed or the value of aggregate output. Any attempt to rank rural industries in those terms is clearly beyond our reach. Concerning the linen industry, in order to keep a sense of proportions it is well to remember that its wide diffusion throughout the low plain was offset by its astonishing dispersion: in only a few villages does one meet more than a dozen weavers; in most, only two or three.[42] To put it another way, the linen industry in seventeenth-century Lombardy looks like a dust of minuscule units of production scattered in the interstices of the agrarian landscape. Even so, its total output must have been far from negligible. For if it be true that the role of the linen industry was basically that of supplying the peasantry and the urban poor with simple, inexpensive articles of apparel and household linen, while the more extravagant needs of the well-to-do were met by imported goods, then the size of the output of the native industry ought to be measured by the size of aggregate consumption of coarse linen fabrics. The latter is, of course, impossible to estimate, but it is well to recall once again that the peasantry dressed in coarse linen, that the urban poor made a relatively large use of inexpensive linen fabrics, and also that waxed linen continued to be the material commonly used to make windowpanes, glass being a luxury that only the rich could afford.[43] In short, we have every reason to believe that the rural linen industry did represent a significant element in the Lombard economy of the seventeenth century. Its survival at a time when so many urban manufactures were being dismantled certainly cushioned the impact of a prolonged depression in the economy as a whole.

The story of Lombardy's rural economy in the seventeenth century is not merely one of continuity with the past. Although the preservation, in the face of the severe hardships and dislocations endured between 1620 and 1660, of elaborate and highly productive farming methods, a high degree of regional specialization, and an assortment of industrial activities would in itself have been no mean achievement, possibly the most remarkable thing about the countryside was its ability to achieve progress and to innovate— something the Lombard cities conspicuously failed to do.[44]

In the low irrigated plain one of the most significant changes was the expansion of fodder crops and artificial grasses at the expense of either waste or cereal crops. It has been estimated that the surface given over to fodder crops increased threefold between the mid-sixteenth and early eighteenth century.[45] It is difficult to know precisely when the change occurred, but in view of the price movements that favored cereals until about 1630 and animal products thereafter,[46] it is not fanciful to assume that stock raising gained ground sometime after 1630, and most likely after 1660 when peace and security had been restored. Such a chronology is borne out by what is known about a large estate in the low plain of the province of Pavia: there the last three decades of the seventeenth century witnessed the expansion of irrigation, an increase in the proportion of land assigned to meadows, and a sharp increase in the ratio of cattle to land. Not surprisingly, these changes were accompanied by a reversal in the downward trend exhibited by agrarian rents in previous decades.[47]

The winds of change also blew, in that same period, on the estate that the bishop of Pavia held on the right bank of the Po. The first task vigorously pursued by the bishop's steward was that of mending the ravages caused by warfare, epidemics, and foul weather in the grim decades between 1620 and 1660: tenants were bailed out of insolvency by advances of seed grain, draft animals, and implements; new buildings were erected to replace those that lay in ruins or to accommodate additional peasant families; land that had been allowed to return to waste when the plague and military operations had combined to thin out population, was now reclaimed. More importantly, in the long run, the traditional practice of share tenancy was gradually replaced with direct management, the bishop's stewards and bailiffs supervising the work of hired laborers. The results of all these changes were impressive indeed: between 1649 and 1720 the production of wheat doubled, that of leguminous crops rose fourfold, that of maize sevenfold, and there was a very substantial increase in the number of cattle, while traditional but inferior crops such as spelt disappeared altogether.[48]

Churchmen in early modern times have not enjoyed an especially good reputation as imaginative, efficient entrepreneurs, and the performance of the bishops of Pavia need not be considered typical of the Lombard clergy in the late seventeenth century. It is all the more interesting, however, to detect the same new spirit of enterprise at work on a large estate that the Augustinian monks of Cremona owned near the junction of the Po and the Adda rivers. That something new was stirring there is borne out by a comparison of two contracts between the monks and their tenants, drawn up in 1658 and 1681 respectively.[49] The type of tenure contemplated in both deeds is the same: a rather complicated form of share tenancy. The wording and format of the two contracts is also very similar, and a number of provisions in the later deed are merely repetitions from the older contract. The 1681 contract, however, is considerably more detailed and comprises twice as many clauses as its predecessor. While in 1658, for example, it was simply stated that the tenants (a farmer and his sons) "shall work the land as honest men do according to the custom of this district," in 1681 it was also specified that the tenants "shall give five furrows to the land," a probable reference to the number of times arable fields must be either ploughed or harrowed. In the earlier deed twelve *pertiche* of land were allocated to the tenants for feeding "their oxen or other animals as they please;" the later version, more generously and at the same time more stringently, allocated sixteen *pertiche* "on condition, however, that the tenants keep four pairs of oxen." The 1681 contract, moreover, goes into minute details that its predecessor ignores, such as the exact procedure by which the grain harvest was to be divided between tenant and landlord, and the upkeep of irrigation canals. In short, by comparing the two versions one cannot escape the definite impression that at the later date a new, more businesslike approach had replaced earlier informality and reliance on custom.

But of greater interest in the present context are the differences between the two deeds on the subject of crops. The 1658 version mentions grains (*biave*) and hay repeatedly, but such things as vines, flax, and mulberry trees are referred to only briefly; of flax it is merely stated that "the tenants shall be allowed to sow two *pertiche* with flax and to retain the entire crop thereof"; as for mulberry trees, nothing is said except that the landlord "shall let the tenants enjoy the three mulberry trees near the house at no charge." In 1681, on the other hand, the two crops are of a sufficient size to justify the landlord's interest in them: in that year it is stipulated that "all cocoons [*galette*] of the silk worms [*cavallieri o bigatti*] shall be divided in half," and, further, that should the tenants choose not to raise silkworms the landlord "will lease out the mulberry trees to whomsoever it shall please him"; concerning flax it is now specified that both the seed and the harvest shall be divided in half. A new twist suggesting a more businesslike approach is discernible in the case of the vineyards as well: the 1681 contract, besides repeating the usual provisions about the proper care of the vines, stipulates that at harvest time an overseer (*camparo*) shall be hired at the landlord's expense. Lastly, in 1681 a new root crop is mentioned as being subject to division in half, namely, cole (*ravizzone*). In summary, it is clear that by 1681 a good deal had changed on the Augustinian monks' estate: flax and silk had ceased to be mere trifles left to the tenants' judgment for their own use, but had become sufficiently important for the landlord to expect and seek a return from them; the grape harvest was now subjected to the control of a professional overseer, which may indicate either an expanded scale of operation or a greater concern for efficiency on the landlord's part, or (and more likely) both of these things; lastly, an effort was made at diversifying and improving cultivation with the introduction of a root crop.

The expansion of rice fields in Lomellina and Vigevanasco provides another and more impressive example of agrarian change. The magnitude of the change itself is borne out by the only two reliable figures we possess concerning the overall acreage under rice in that area: a mere 3,500 *pertiche* in 1549, and as many as 180,000 in 1723.[50] The chronology of the change, however, is not so easily traceable. A recent study suggests that in the eastern parts of Piedmont adjacent to Lomellina the great upswing in risiculture got under way in the later part of the seventeenth century.[51] As for Lomellina, we have at least one bit of precise information that fully confirms this view and points to the 1670s as the turning point: an inquiry conducted in 1677 at Olevano near Mortara informs us that "rice fields have been introduced here in the last six or seven years." Significantly, the new development, much as in nearby Piedmont, was the work of a great landlord who owned "most of the land located in this jurisdiction."[52]

Signs of change and adaptation are discernible even in the hill zone, where holdings were generally small and where peasant property was widespread. In the Como province change took the form of a reduction in the acreage devoted to cereals and an increase in the cultivation of tree crops (vines, olive trees, and mulberry trees),[53] a clear and sensible response to falling grain prices. At the opposite end of the State of Milan, in the large village of Montaldeo, perched on the hills near the Genoese border,[54] the late seventeenth century witnessed considerable change and progress, too. This is the more interesting in that we are dealing here with an area of relative backwardness, both economically and socially, and one where not only had subsistence agriculture traditionally predominated, but where archaic forms of copyhold (*livelli perpetui*) and heavy seignorial obligations lingered on well into the eighteenth century. Nonetheless, after the fateful middle decades of the seventeenth century, signs of change and progress were numerous and unmistakable. There was a definite tendency toward the concentration of property into the hands not only of the feudal lord, but also of a new class of substantial landowners recruited from among newly enriched merchants and tax farmers. Older forms of tenure began to give way to more rigorously defined arrangements blending sharecropping and leaseholding. The vine, clearly one of the most suitable crops in the hill zone, made headway at the expense of woodland and health, and so did the mulberry tree; the latter's diffusion, in turn, created an important new source of peasant employment in the raising of silkworms and in silk reeling and spinning. Progress took other forms as well: in 1675 clover and sainfoin made their first appearance in that area and their introduction clearly points to a new emphasis on stock raising; the yield of cereals per acre was on the rise, either as a result of heavier manuring, or of improved rotation patterns, or both. In 1678, moreover, maize was also introduced into the hill zone.[55]

All the evidence of agricultural progress recited so far is not only fragmentary, but bears, for the most part, on individual localities—two estates in the low irrigated plain, one in the dry plain, another in the hill zone—rather than on large geographical areas. For all that, one is justified in drawing from these separate strands of information some broad, if tentative, conclusions as to the general upward trend of Lombard agriculture from the late seventeenth century onward. What is striking about the cases that have been discussed is that, representing virtually all the evidence currently available for the period, they all tell, albeit in different forms, one same story of progress and improvement. This is obviously more than sheer coincidence; the more so as each case is based on independent and widely different sources and has been studied by a different scholar. Moreover, all those cases seem to be consistent with prevailing market signals; they reflect, in other words, economic choices such as we would expect from landowners, large or small, who had an eye on costs and profits. It would be very strange indeed if those choices represented exceptions, and if they were coincidentally confined to those few localities for which evidence has, in fact, survived.

The shift from cereals to livestock in the plain, for instance, was a perfectly rational response to falling grain prices and more stable meat prices. The gradual phasing-out of the vine from the low plain[56] is what one would expect in a period when wine prices were plummeting: under the pressure of low prices, it made sense to do away with a crop that was clearly marginal in the plain, just as it made sense for the peasant owners of the hills to specialize in wine production since their land was especially suited for it. That the Augustinian monks of Cremona should have tightened up the management of their estate may have merely reflected the presence of a new, efficient abbot at the head of their community; and yet it is unlikely that he was alone in grasping the advantages of turning to industrial crops such as flax, silk, and cole oil in a period when cereal farming was at a low ebb of profitability. The expansion of rice cultivation in the Lomellina, too, reflects a keen sensitivity to changing market conditions, and more specifically to changing factor proportions. In his study of the expansion of rice cultivation in the Piedmont plain during the second half of the seventeenth century, Pieraldo Bullio has convincingly shown that the expansion itself was a response to an acute labor shortage resulting from the epidemics of 1630 and the war devastations of the following decade.[57] Confronted with a depopulated landscape, the landed class turned increasingly from wheat and rye to rice, because the latter—grown as it was on large estates with the help of migrant labor hired for short periods of time to handle the laborious operations of weeding, transplanting, and harvesting—did not require a large, stable labor force and could, in fact, draw on a pool of transient labor recruited from a wide area. Similar considerations must have obtained in the western districts of the State of Milan as well. It is interesting, however, that in the village of Lomellina, where rice was introduced in the 1670s by a local magnate, depopulaton seems to have followed rather than preceded the introduction of the new crop.

"The air is not too healthy around here," asserted a local peasant, "on account of some rice fields laid out by Signor Hieronimo Olevano, and in the last two years more than forty families have moved out."[58] Presumably, in this instance the landlord's decision to switch to a crop such as rice, which required only cheap migrant labor, was motivated not by an actual labor shortage, but by a desire to reduce costs in the face of sagging farm prices.

In the second half of the century, progress, as distinct from mere continuity with the past, is discernible in a few rural industries too. The making of fine felt hats is an example of moderate industrial progress in a rural setting. Until the close of the sixteenth century this manufacture had been the jealously guarded privilege of the hat makers' guild of Milan, and legislation had long ago been enacted that barred hat making from the countryside and even restrained the Milan hat makers from putting work out to hired artisans who lived outside the city walls (*submissae personae extra civitatem Mediolani*). Despite such restrictive legislation, however, hat making began to take root in Caravaggio and Monza in the beginning of the seventeenth century, much to the displeasure of the Milan hat makers, who ascribed most of their troubles to the competition of those new rustic rivals. In Monza, at any rate, the new manufacture prospered in the course of the century, while it became virtually extinct in Milan, and hats from Monza found a market both in Lombardy and abroad (*in partibus etiam longiquiis*). Its rural character remained unmistakable, however, and is brought out by a complaint filed by the few hat makers left in Milan in which they described the labor force in Monza as consisting of "men who all have another occupation (besides hat making) and who should, in the final analysis, tend the fields."[59]

Before the end of the seventeenth century a fresh development was reported from Vigevano, one of the smallest *città* of the State and one which was more a rural market town than a real city. Once a modest center of the wool industry, Vigevano suffered irreversible economic losses in the course of the century and was never to recover its traditional manufacture.[60] In 1699, however, it was reported that "even the silk merchants of Milan purchase silk fabrics in Vigevano, and from Vigevano silks are shipped to other parts of the State and even abroad."[61] How large the newly established manufacture may have been at the time is not known. By mid-eighteenth century, at any rate, Vigevano harbored 305 looms for the making of silk cloth and 571 ribbon looms.[62]

By far the most impressive industrial development in the country-side, however, involved not the weaving but the reeling and throwing of the silk thread. The appearance of hand-operated silk mills was a relatively late development in the Lombard countryside.[63] Until the early seventeenth century the traditional division of labor between town and country had been preserved, with the latter specializing in the raising of silkworms and the first preliminary processing, namely the unwinding of cocoons, and the former carrying on from there through the successive stages of throwing, dyeing, and weaving. In 1658, however, grave concern was voiced in Milan over the fact that in recent years silk mills had sprung up in the countryside (as many as two hundred, it was claimed, in the province of Milan alone) and that large quantities of silk thread were being exported clandestinely from rural locations, much to the detriment of the city's silk spinners.[64] Stringent measures were then enacted to curb the disturbing new trend, but four years later new mills were reported operating in Varese, in Brianza, and in Como province, as well as in areas just over the Milanese border, such as Lugano in Swiss territory and Bergamo in the Venetian Republic, in places, that is, where raw silk from the State of Milan could be easily smuggled.[65] By the mid-seventies the silk spinners' guild in Milan was said to be on the brink of extinction, and two main reasons were given for its rapidly declining fortunes: first, the exportation of cocoons to other countries and notably to the Venetian Republic—a fact which, it was lamented, "deprives our own people not only of the benefits they would otherwise derive from spinning, but also robs our poor women of the earnings they used to receive for unwinding the aforesaid cocoons"; and second, "the intro-duction and increase in recent years of silk mills in villages and ham-lets throughout the State and the relocation of silk mills from this city to rural districts."[66] "The transfer of silk mills from Milan," reads a 1678 memorandum, "has caused innumerable families in this city to fall into such poverty . . . as not to be ashamed to beg in order not to starve to death."[67] This was probably hyperbole, but not untypical of the period. Yet, the blunt fact that, "as everybody knows, a great many silk mills have of late been dismantled [in Milan] and moved to the villages" was fully borne out by a survey made in 1679.[68] The findings were ominous enough: in Milan 270 silk mills were counted in that year, as against 384 only a few years earlier; most of the 270 mills still in the city were found inactive. In the province of Milan, on the other hand, 359 mills were reported in operation, with the heaviest concentration in and around Varese, and it was known that a great many others were scattered throughout the other provinces of Spanish Lombardy. In 1698 a new survey indicated that only 100 mills were left in Milan, of which 25 were active, while the province harbored 348 mills. And the divergent trend continued unabated in the next century: in 1762 Milan was left with a paltry 34 silk mills, while the entire state could boast a total of 748 such establishments.[69]

In sharp contrast to its cities, then, the story of Lombardy's rural economy in the seventeenth century is one not only of basic continuity, but also of remarkable resilience and even fresh expansion after the serious, but not irreparable, losses experienced in the grim period between 1620 and 1660. It is not hard to find reasons for these contrasting records. The countryside was, and had always been, free from the guilds, those typically urban institutions that tended to hinder adaptation and stifle innovation. Moreover, and more importantly, the rural economy, devoted as it was to the production of foodstuffs, raw materials, and simple manufactured goods, was not likely to be adversely affected, as the cities were, by some "barbarous" nations acquiring skills and know-how and thus closing the gap that had long separated them from their Lombard purveyors and mentors. On the contrary, the progress of manufacturing north of the Alps, by increasing the demand for industrial raw materials such as silk and flax, opened up new opportunities for the Lombard farmer at the very time when it deprived the urban craftsman of his erstwhile supremacy.[70] Lastly, as will be seen, in the course of the seventeenth century a number of restrictions on trade in agricultural commodities and on rural industry were gradually relaxed, thus allowing the rural entrepreneur a wider range of choices.

All these favorable conditions and developments, however, could not have effectively helped the countryside if an adequate supply of capital and enterprise had not been available (as it conspicuously was not in the cities) to repair the damages wrought by decades of warfare, to reclaim deserted land, and, finally, to introduce new crops and start new industries.

The question of the supply of capital and enterprise to the rural economy can best be approached by raising first the question of how continuity was ensured in Lombard agriculture in the midst of devastations, trade dislocations, and the mounting pressure of taxation, billeting, and requisitions. That farming somehow went on is obvious enough; that it retained even in the darkest decades of the century its highly refined techniques has been argued earlier in this chapter; what needs clarification at this point is how these results were achieved, for there is no a priori assurance that they should have been. The evidence recited earlier about deserted farms and fugitive peasants is a stark reminder that in the countryside, no less than in the city, economic activity could grind to a halt or be seriously curtailed.

If the partial or total stoppage of production was averted, as in most instances it certainly was, even in the face of severe hardships, the reason must be found, first of all, in the ingrained, almost compulsive attachment peasants felt for their land: it is conceivable that many of them, and notably the owner-occupiers, somehow managed to weather the storm merely by expending additional effort in order to maximize production while, at the same time, reducing consumption. The tax system itself, paradoxically, tended to pressure them in that direction: based as it was on a fixed assessment of land values (*estimo del perticato*) and predicated on the principle that taxes must be paid annually regardless of whether or not the land was cultivated and regardless of the size of the harvest, the system had a built-in incentive for the owner to keep as much of his land under crop as possible, even when the expected return from it would not, in the absence of taxation, have justified the effort; and the incentive, of course, grew all the stronger in periods of depressed farm prices, such as the middle decades of the seventeenth century.[71]

But however strong the pressures, sentimental or fiscal, inducing owners to hold on to their farms and keep them in operation, there were no doubt instances when either a rising tax burden, a series of crop losses, or falling grain prices brought deprivation to intolerable levels and spelled ruin for the peasants. Under those circumstances, it is not surprising that some of them, presumably after exhausting the patience of a local moneylender, simply deserted their holdings and joined what seems to have been a growing fringe of vagrants and bandits.[72] In more numerous instances, however, no such desperate course of action was resorted to. In the hill zone, where peasant ownership had traditionally been widespread, many peasant holdings were sold rather than deserted, and their former owners were allowed to stay on as tenants. In this way continuity was ensured in the operation of the farm, and what made this result possible was the presence of individuals—mostly *petit-bourgeois* from a nearby town who had made money in trade or, more often, in tax farming and government loans—willing to invest in the ownership of one or more small farms.[73]

The position of the large landowner was no doubt less vulnerable than that of the peasant: the very size of his estate and the fact that more often than not his income from land was supplemented by seignorial rights or the perquisites of office presumably gave him greater flexibility and staying power in the face of economic hardships and made it easier for him, in an emergency, to borrow on the security of his lands. The landed class, to be sure, had to contend not only with taxation, the vagaries of the weather, and the ups and downs of the grain market, but also with their inveterate penchant for extravagant spending. From the late sixteenth century, however, this last threat to financial stability was to some extent held in check by the widespread practice of *fedecommesso,* a rigid form of entail whereby successive heirs were prevented from alienating parts, and even the whole, of the family estate.[74] Admittedly, entails, insofar as they interfered with the free operation of the land market, were bound to have, in Lombardy as well as in other countries where the practice became widespread in the seventeenth century, adverse effects on the optimal allocation of productive resources. But to the extent that they curbed the prodigality of a class notoriously prone to spending beyond its means, they must have bolstered the level of savings in the economy as a whole.[75]

For all this, there were members of the landed aristocracy who, as a result of either bad luck, mismanagement, or extravagance, did meet with financial disaster and, having secured the necessary authorization from the Senate, sold the family estate. One case in point is Count Niccolò Alberti, who in 1637 found himself unable "in the face of the current hard times, war, and other well-known misfortunes, to support himself and to raise his children in a manner befitting their rank"; accordingly he was authorized to sell his property and seignorial rights at Colico on the shores of Lake Como to a local magnate.[76] Another example, and one on which our sources shed greater light, is that involving the property owned by Marquess Agostino Omodei at Piovera near Alessandria.[77] Ironically, the marquess had made a reputation for himself as an improving landlord. A member of the Milanese patriciate, he had purchased his Piovera estate in 1614 from a Spanish nobleman who wanted to return to his native country and over a number of years had done much for his newly acquired possession: "He has turned 40 *biolche* of land that lay waste and brought very little income into meadows that now yield a good return . . . he has extended and enlarged irrigation canals which now bring water from twenty springs, spending a great deal every year for the upkeep of the same . . . and he has also planted over four thousand willow saplings and about a hundred mulberry trees." Despite such promising beginnings, things had turned sour for Omodei, and by 1650 he was on the brink of bankruptcy. In that year he found himself confronted with a host of angry creditors from whom he had borrowed money years before by issuing bills of exchange; that money he had used to make a huge loan to the Treasury, but reimbursement had been effected only in part and after long delays. Now, at the very moment when he had to realize his assets to repay a huge backlog of debts and accumulated interest charges, land values had sunk to half what they had been at the time of purchase and buyers were hard to find "on account of the heavy tax burden." Eventually, a buyer did come forth in the person of Francesco Maria Balbi, a Genoese patrician and a leading figure in government finance at the time,[78] and the Piovera estate passed into new and less impecunious hands.

The intervention of a great financier on the land market was, of course, no rare occurrence. In the late sixteenth century, we have the example of Gottardo Frisiani, a self-made man who had rapidly established himself in Milan as a financial tycoon and who had invested a good portion of his growing fortune in land: in one instance he had acquired a sizable farm from a Milanese patrician who had borrowed money from him but had defaulted on his debt; in another, it was the property of an insolvent merchant that fell into Frisiani's lap.[79]

Gottardo Frisiani no doubt had many imitators: it is only the paucity of our sources that allows us but occasional glimpses of social mobility and the turnover of landed property. It is the more interesting to observe at close range one case on which information happens to be unusually detailed.

In 1685 Marquess Francesco Guidoboni Cavalchini petitioned the Senate for permission to sell his estate and his fief located at Brignano and Frascata in the province of Tortona. Sadly reduced circumstances were given as reasons for the request: the marquess, a witness confirmed in the course of a hearing, "lives in poverty and at times would be in deep trouble without the help of friends." The castle of Brignano which, as feudal lord, it was his responsibility to keep in a state of repair, was reported as "nearly in ruins," while the land nearby had in recent years been flooded by the Curone river, and, the marquess "being unable to fund the necessary works of embankment," a number of houses had been washed out and whole meadows had been lost as a result of erosion. To bring things to a head, one of the marquess' creditors had now filed suit to recover a large unpaid loan. Marquess Cavalchini, however, was able to avoid the indignity of bankruptcy proceedings by selling all his possessions to a friend. This was a wealthy commoner, Signor Francesco Ferrario by name, who owned a house in Milan and a *bellissimo palazzo* near Brignano, lived in style with servants and a horse-drawn coach, had married off his daughter to a nobleman, and whose brother was known to be "one of the chief agents in the salt farm and a very wealthy man too." As for Signor Francesco himself, he had made his fortune "dealing in bills of exchange," but had recently had the discretion to withdraw from active participation in business, preferring instead "secretly to invest his money in large transactions through intermediaries." Needless to say, with such qualifications and family connections, Ferrario's offer to buy was accepted by the Senate, all the more readily as he promised to undertake all necessary repairs in the castle and on the estate.[80]

Whether small peasant holdings or large noble estates were involved, the importance of land transactions such as those we have just discussed is plain enough. To be sure, it would be wrong to see the investments effected by those who purchased land as acts of capital formation, for what took place were mere transfers of assets, one man's investment offsetting another's disinvestment.[81] Nonetheless, those transactions in land did help ensure continuity in agrarian life: it stands to reason that, unless money had been forthcoming whenever a landowner or peasant owner was going under, more farms would have been deserted, land values would have sunk even lower than they actually did, and more resources would have been wasted or would have remained idle.

Continuity was also fostered by changes in agrarian contracts, introduced in response to the strains and dislocations of the agrarian depression and aimed at shifting the burden of risk and the responsibility of supplying working capital for the farm from the financially weaker to the stronger party. Thus in 1637, on a noble estate near Lodi where conditions had reached "a parlous state, due to onerous billetings, the flight of several tenants, and other evil accidents," the owner, in an effort to reverse the situation and attract a new tenant, switched from the customary leasehold to a sharecropping arrangement under which all risks (and profits) were equally shared by landlord and tenant.[82] On the right bank of the Po River by mid-century the leasehold had given way to a form of tenancy under which the landlord not only shared risks with his tenant, but also took it upon himself to provide the latter with "oxen, wagons, implements, seed grain, and all the rest." The reason for the change was, according to a local farmer, that "if an individual tried nowadays to let his land [for a fixed rent], he would find no one willing to assume the risk on account of the many taxes and burdens of war."[83]

The supply of working capital—in the form of draft animals, implements, and seedgrain (the so-called *scorte*, or "movable stocks")—was possibly the most common and crucial contribution that landlords made toward ensuring the continuity in farm production in a period of agrarian depression and widespread tenant insolvency.

Besides the cases just quoted for the Lodi province, we find similar arrangements in the Como province: there the customary contract had called for a fixed rent payable in grain, plus a share of the grape harvest, and the tenant had normally been expected to supply his own movable stocks; in the course of the seventeenth century, however, as agrarian conditions deteriorated and tenant insolvency grew alarmingly, the responsibility to provide *scorte* was increasingly assumed by the landlord.[84] Similar adjustments were made in Lomellina as well: according to a tenant farmer speaking in 1631, "formerly share tenants received no *scorte* because they were well-off [*perché stavano commodi*] . . . but in the past six, seven, or eight years it is the landlord who has provided the said *scorte*," clearly on account of the tenants' inability or reluctance to do so themselves. When even this arrangement failed to solve the problem, landowners had no choice, short of allowing the land to go to waste, but to assume the direct management of their estate and to farm it with the help of hired laborers.[85]

Roles, however, could at times be reversed, as substantial tenants—the forerunners of the wealthy *fittavoli* who down to the present day have been typical of the Lombard low plain—drew on their own resources to rescue a large estate (and its noble owner) from financial disaster. A case in point is provided by the vicissitudes of the Stanga family, owners of eight farms covering a total of about 400 hectares in the rich Cremona province. In 1639, of those eight farms, seven were under lease and one was sharecropped; only one tenant had received movable stocks as part of his contract; the rest had to provide their own. It was stipulated that all taxes (including the onerous billeting of troops) for the eight farms were to be paid by the landlord. In actual practice, however, not only was the Stanga family unable to pay those taxes, but it was their own tenants who did so for them, thus, in fact, acting as their masters' creditors. Said one of them: "I have paid the land tax on behalf of Signor Joseffo [Stanga] and have incurred other expenses too, so that I reckon to have paid out more than I owe him to date." "I have acquitted my entire rent," declared another, "and have also disbursed some money as an advance on the next installment [of my rent] in order to help my lords who are overburdened with the billeting of troops and other charges."

"Not only have I received no *scorte*," chimed in a third tenant, "but I have also helped Donna Francesca by paying 200 *ducatoni* in Cremona on account of the tallage [*taglione*] that was due on her estate."[86]

Genuine capital formation, as opposed to mere transfers of property or shifts in the supply of working capital, did, of course, take place whenever idle resources were brought into use, or changes were made in land use, or new crops and new industries were introduced—and here, too, we have every reason to believe that the individuals involved spanned the social spectrum of seventeenth-century Lombardy.

The role of the great landowners is illustrated by what was said earlier about agrarian improvements and innovations in various localities of the plain, the introduction of risiculture in Lomellina, and the diffusion of the mulberry tree in the hills at the hands of patricians, churchmen, and bourgeois. All this, however, should not obscure the role played by countless peasant-owners and small tenants, who certainly contributed to the reconstruction and the growth of the rural economy through a myriad of infinitesimal repairs, adaptations, and improvements. By their very nature these contributions have gone unrecorded, but it would be rash, not to say absurd, to assume that recovery and progress in the Lombard countryside after 1660 was solely the work of improving landlords directing the efforts of a totally passive peasantry.

When it comes to investment in rural industries, the role of the peasantry can be safely assumed, for much of the fixed equipment used in rural cottages (handlooms and spinning wheels, tenters and dyeing vats, anvils and hammers) represented lumps of capital small enough to be within the reach of the peasant family. Only when exceptionally large investments were called for was the peasant craftsman replaced by his social superiors.

The point is well brought out by the example of the power-driven mill. Whether used to grind grain, crush metal ores, or turn rags into paper pulp, the water-driven mill represented in those days one of the largest and more costly items of fixed industrial equipment. Not

surprisingly, water mills were owned (and presumably had been built)
by individuals who were rich enough not to have to tend such facilities
themselves. Thus, we find a large flour mill and a fulling mill attached
to the castle of Brignano and operated by two men who paid the landlord a fixed rent; in Valdintelvi, millers in general did not own their
facilities, but held them as share tenants, the profits of milling being
divided in equal parts betwen them and the landlord, and major
repairs being the responsibility of the latter.[87] Paper mills represented
an even larger investment, for, in addition to the power-driven
stamping mill, they also included several large rooms where paper was
manufactured and hung to dry, an assortment of large copper vats, a
press, and other lesser equipment. Few papermakers, it would seem,
could afford such an investment, and in fact of sixteen paper mills
reported in the countryside around Milan in 1666 only two were
owner-operated; the rest were rented from "absentee landlords," and
among the latter were two marquesses, a count, a lawyer, and a
monastery.[88]

Members of the upper class, and especially noblemen, loomed even
larger in the mining industry, where investment had to come in sizable
lumps and where, by ancient custom, no social stigma accrued to the
individual involved. In the seventeenth century, as new mining pits
were sunk in the Valsassina, the capital was provided by some of the
most prestigious families of the Milan patriciate, such as the D'Adda,
the Borromeo, the Medici, and the Marliani, as well as by government
officials, lawyers, and country gentlemen such as the Manzoni, the
Arrigoni, and the Monti.[89] The exact nature and extent of noble
investment in mining is not known. What those capitalists did was to
secure a mining concession from the state in return for a cash
payment; they probably also provided the necessary funds to get a
new pit opened; as for the actual management and operation of the
mine itself, this was no doubt entrusted to a local master miner either
for a fixed payment or, as seems more likely, for a share of the output.
It is more difficult to decide whether members of the ruling class invested in ironworks as well. All we know is that the D'Adda family
owned at one time a blast furnace at Locarno and that Giulio Monti,
the iron magnate who at mid-century managed to acquire feudal
rights over the entire Valsassina, not only owned a number of mining

pits in the valley, but had a blast furnace built there in 1651, to which, some twenty years later, he added a forge.[90]

Participation by members of the propertied class and the aristocracy probably did not go beyond the smelting process. Further downstream the iron industry splintered into a multiplicity of tiny forges, smithies, and metal workshops owned and operated by independent craftsmen who provided the fairly simple equipment required for turning iron bars into nails, wire, and implements. Even so, it is likely that in Lombardy, as elsewhere in Europe,[91] most of those metal craftsmen actually worked, under the putting-out system, for an ironmonger who supplied them with the raw material, paid them on a piecework basis, and took care of marketing the finished products. When, on the other hand, production was intended for military purposes, as much of it was in the seventeenth century, a major source of capital was the royal treasury. Although the government itself rarely built and operated its own gun foundries and forges, it did provide arms manufacturers with the working capital they needed, and it did so in the form of advance payments for the goods that were to be delivered at a future date.[92]

The rural industry that experienced the fastest growth in the late seventeenth century—namely, the manufacture of silk thread—is also the one about which least is known, as far as ownership and the supply of capital are concerned. A reasonable guess would seem to be that while the silk mills themselves were owned and operated by independent artisans, working capital, in the form of raw silk and wages, was provided by wholesale merchants or by the landowners on whose estates silkworms were raised.

Although our knowledge about the sources of capital and enterprise that made recovery and expansion possible in the countryside remains tantalizingly limited and fragmented, what evidence is available does point to two important facets of the Lombard economy in the seventeenth century.

In the first place, one cannot help noticing the wide spectrum of people—peasants and landowners, patricians and financiers, craftsmen and churchmen—who, in varying degrees and in different ways, contributed to the rebuilding and the progress of the rural economy. This diffuse pattern would not deserve special notice were it not for the fact that it can serve as an antidote to hasty generalizations about the role of any one social group in the process of capital formation; it should also make one suspicious of the curt way in which historians have occasionally dismissed the landed class of this period as being "parasitic" and incapable of contributing to economic growth;[93] and, lastly, it should make one aware of the obscure, but no less crucial, role played by the anonymous crowd of peasants, tenants, and rural artisans.

In the second place, our evidence indicates, however dimly, that some of the capital invested in the countryside came from individuals, high-born and low-born, whose fortunes had been made, at least in part, in transactions directly or indirectly connected with public finance—tax farming, government loans, speculation on those fairs of exchange where much private money was channeled, at the expert hands of the Genoese, into Spain's insatiable war machine. We have seen instances of this in the case of wealthy financiers such as Frisiani, Omodei, Balbi, and Ferrario, but it will also be remembered that lesser bourgeois who had made money in tax farming and government loans invested in rural property, too. What is worth stressing in all this is that, in an age of escalating government indebtedness and massive concentration of income in the hands of the wealthier members of the community, some liquid funds were being recycled back into the economy: not the stagnant, unappealing economy of the cities, but the more vital and resilient economy of the countryside.

CHAPTER VII

THE LEGACY

In the literature devoted to the economic history of Spanish Lombardy the seventeenth century has been generally portrayed as an age of unrelieved gloom, as a tragic break along the path of development that Lombardy had so successfully trodden until the close of the preceding century. The accepted picture is one of a country that for centuries had seemed to hold the highest promise of continuous growth along precociously modern lines; a country which, in retrospect, would seem to have been predestined for a rapid and unimpeded transition to industrial capitalism—and yet one which conspicuously failed to fulfill that promise and to achieve that transition. As a result of either misgovernment, warfare, or "flagrant misinvestment" in conspicuous consumption—so runs the argument—by 1700 Lombardy found herself recast in a mold of agrarian backwardness. Not until the closing decades of the eighteenth century would conditions begin to improve, thanks to the sweeping reforms introduced by her enlightened rulers in the field of taxation, internal trade, the guild system, and the administration of justice.[1]

This picture is but a half truth, as the foregoing chapters have shown, for while it is beyond dispute that the urban economies experienced a severe and indeed irreversible decline during the seventeenth century, the same cannot be said of the lesser towns, the villages, and the countryside in general. Admittedly, the latter went through a very serious crisis, but there was no discontinuity, no irreparable fracture in their development. More importantly, as early as the 1660s, recovery got under way in the countryside, and some improvements and gains are already discernible in the following decades, nearly a century before the advent of enlightened absolutism. And if one keeps in mind that even in its halcyon days the Lombard economy had been predominantly rural and that agriculture had been by far its largest industry, one is bound to conclude that the debacle of the cities and the obliteration of their celebrated manufactures could hardly have had crippling effects on the economy as a whole.

It could be countered, of course, that what gave the decline of the cities such a far-reaching and negative influence on the future of Lombardy was not so much the drop in the gross national product that it obviously entailed, but rather the extinction of an urban economic elite (craftsmen, merchants, and financiers) whose skills, talents, and enterprise had made possible the astonishing rise of the Lombard cities to the forefront of European economic life, and whose continued existence could presumably have carried Lombardy further along the ascending path of modern economic development all the way to industrialization. This, however, is most unlikely. Not only is it worth remembering that, throughout Europe, none of the old centers of early capitalism (whether Antwerp or Venice, Amsterdam or Genoa, Bordeaux or Florence) played a leading role in the advent of modern industrialization,[2] but in Lombardy itself the cities, for all their undeniable achievements during the late Middle Ages and Renaissance, had few of the traits that we associate with modern industrialization and, in fact, had some that were diametrically opposed to it. Their growth and early success had been made possible by the superiority of their craftsmen and merchants over a still "barbarous" Europe and had been powerfully assisted by the cities' privileged position vis-à-vis their hinterland, on which they freely drew for revenue, supplies, and manpower. Their much-vaunted manufactures had consisted primarily of expensive luxury items that other countries could not yet produce, rather than of low-cost ordinary goods intended for a mass market. Lastly, the very precocity of their success had tended, in the long run, to breed complacency and an excessive reliance on traditional techniques and designs. The cities were thus clearly ill-suited to serve as the cradle of large-scale industrialization; far from being the vanguard of the modern economy, they must be viewed as anachronistic relics of a rapidly fading past.

To find the harbingers of the modern economy, it is to the countryside that we must turn, for it was there that economic progress, after a temporary setback around the mid-seventeenth century, continued, however slowly. In the low plain, works of reclamation and irrigation acquired new momentum in the course of the eighteenth century, and at the close of that century no less an authority than Arthur Young could still regard the area as "one of the richest plains in the world," for there, he proclaimed, "the arable lands never repose."[3] In the next century further progress was made in terms of higher yields, while the construction of the Villoresi canal (1886) completed the transformation of the rural landscape initiated by the Cistercians seven centuries before and added 55,000 hectares to the irrigated plain.[4] The output of silk, which had stood at about 200,000 kilograms per year in the mid-eighteenth century, topped the 300,000 mark before 1800 and grew fourfold in the next fifty years,[5] thus providing the base for a growing processing industry that served as leading sector in the early stages of Lombard industrialization.[6]

In the light of later developments, the growth of industry in the countryside deserves special attention, for when the modern factory made its appearance in Lombardy in the 1820s, it did so in the countryside rather than in the cities, and for much of the nineteenth century factories continued to be located in the countryside. More importantly, those early factories were built in the very areas which for at least two centuries had been studded with rural industries. The large, power-driven silk mills (*filande*), which represented the first intrusion of the machine age into many Lombard villages, were erected in the hill zone stretching from Varese to Lecco,[7] the same zone to which silk spinning had migrated in the second half of the seventeenth century after deserting the city. The modern cotton industry developed and thrived in the Gallarate district, where the manufacture of fustians had become established as a typical cottage industry in the late sixteenth century and had gained fresh momentum in the eighteenth. From 1820, when the first large spinning mill was built there, down to the present day, the Gallarate district has been the home of the largest and technologically most advanced concentration of textile mills in the Italian peninsula.[8] As for modern ironworks, they too made their first, if belated, appearance between 1830 and 1850 in or near the Valsassina, an area with a long established and not undistinguished tradition in iron metallurgy.[9]

Industrial progress in upper Lombardy was slow and did not gain strong momentum until the close of the nineteenth century. Nor is it

difficult to see why. On the one hand, agriculture in densely populated Lombardy had traditionally been very labor-intensive, with high
yields being secured at the cost of low output per man-hour; this undoubtedly placed a rather rigid ceiling on the proportion of the labor
force available for nonfarm production, while at the same time keeping peasant incomes down and thus limiting the demand for manufactured goods among the rural populace. On the other hand, the expansion of agriculture (which persisted in Lombardy until the agrarian
crisis of the 1870s) tended to discourage the shift of capital and manpower to alternative, nonagricultural uses.

For all this, some significant progress was made in industry well
before the close of the nineteenth century, and it is no mere historical
accident that Italian industrialization had its cradle in the high plain
and hills of Lombardy. The presence of waterfalls and fast-running
streams in that region was certainly of crucial importance, especially
in a country where coal deposits are virtually nonexistent; no less
important was the availability of cheap labor in an area where poor
soil conditions, combined with high population density and terrain
unsuitable for large irrigation projects, created conditions of rural
underemployment that were favorable to the recruitment of an industrial labor force, at least on a part-time basis.[10] But, as indicated by
the history of areas with similar conditions, water power and cheap
peasant labor are not by themselves sufficient to give rise to modern
industry. What was distinctive about upper Lombardy, in addition to
the availability of inanimate energy and cheap manpower, was the
proximity of a rich food-producing area, the quality of the available
labor force, and an uncommon concentration of entrepreneurial
talent.

The first point seems obvious enough: the viability of an economy
such as that of the landlocked hill zone of Lombardy, with its chronic
grain deficit, depended, until the coming of the railroad in the second
half of the nineteenth century, on easy access to a food-producing
area; the breadbasket of the low plain nearby fulfilled precisely that
function and also served as a vital outlet both for the seasonal employment of migrant workers from the upper reaches of Lombardy and for
simple manufactured goods produced in the peasant cottages of the
high plain and the hills. As elsewhere in Europe, moreover, this pattern

of regional specialization was reinforced in the seventeenth century by the low grain prices that prevailed at the time, for a consequence of these was to discourage cereal cropping on the clearly marginal soils of the hill zone, thus forcing the local peasantry to look for alternative sources of livelihood.[11]

As for the quality of the labor force, it is clear that the cottage industries that had existed in upper Lombardy since the late Middle Ages and had produced, at least in part, for the market were responsible for the formation of a large labor force trained in a broad range of skills (from spinning and weaving to metallurgy), accustomed to work for wages and thus amenable to the strenuous demands, the discipline, and the incentives of factory work. Under the circumstances, it is hardly surprising that, when the first factories were built, there was little trouble recruiting factory workers in that region, and that down to the present day the *alto Milanese*, as the area north of Milan is now known, has been a nursery of skilled, highly disciplined, and indeed docile industrial workers. The transition from the peasant cottage to the modern factory in the nineteenth century, moreover, was facilitated by the fact that for several decades the latter lived in a kind of symbiosis with the former—the typical example being the early machine-operated spinning mills, which fed cotton yarn to a multitude of peasant weavers working in their own homes.[12]

When we turn to the entrepreneurs, the picture is rather dim, because of a lack of detailed studies on the backgrounds and careers of the early Lombard industrialists. Nonetheless, we know that in the Gallarate district these were, as a rule, local people and that the process of industrialization there was essentially an indigenous and autonomous one initiated and carried forward by native entrepreneurs with little, if any, assistance from outside, and notably not from the larger cities.[13] This being the case, we must assume that the district itself was not wanting in entrepreneurial talents. Nor is it difficult to see why it was not: the traditional cotton industry of the high plain had depended on a network of merchants and middlemen for its supplies of raw material from overseas sources, as well as for the distribution of the finished product to markets other than the purely local; accordingly, its rise and expansion from the sixteenth century onward must have been accompanied by the formation of a sizable group of merchant-manufacturers with considerable financial means, commercial expertise, and a thorough familiarity with textile technology. In all probability, it is from this group that the cotton manufacturers of the early nineteenth century emerged to transform the industry from a galaxy of dispersed peasant cottages to a cluster of modern centralized factories.[14]

The economic recovery and subsequent progress that the Lombard countryside, unlike the cities, was able to achieve from the late seventeenth century looks like the very negation of all that the city-state system stood for; and, at first sight, it seems rather surprising that rural recovery and progress were allowed to occur at all under a system that was predicated on the cities claiming for themselves the lion's share of whatever riches the economy was able to produce—the more surprising in that the system itself was not formally dismantled until the second half of the eighteenth century, when the reformist legislation of the enlightened despots did away with the guilds, the tax privileges, and the restrictions on trade in agricultural commodities and on the location of industry, which for centuries had represented so many bastions of urban supremacy over the countryside.[15]

In actual practice, however, while the old, anachronistic institutional facade remained intact until the late eighteenth century, the edifice that stood behind it had been tampered with, modified, and weakened for nearly two centuries, and all the changes had been in the direction of a more modern, more "egalitarian" system favoring the countryside at the expense of urban privilege and foreshadowing the reforms of Maria Theresa and Joseph II. No one, of course, would want to deny the importance of those reforms and their contribution to the emergence of a genuinely modern institutional framework, as well as to the acceleration of economic growth in Lombardy. A close analysis of the record, however, leads us to conclude that what those enlightened rulers did was to bring to completion a process that had been under way, however erratically, since the late sixteenth century.

Consider, first of all, taxation—a field where the inequality between the city and *contado* had been especially glaring. In the second half of the sixteenth century, the introduction of a new direct tax, the *men-*

suale, had given rise to two issues that pitted rural against urban interests: Should farmland owned by townsmen be treated on a par with peasant land? and, secondly, Should movable, and notably commercial, assets be taxed as well? In both cases, despite the cities' dogged opposition, the Spanish government ruled against urban interests: it proceeded to levy the new tax on the townsmen's country estates, it denied any further extension of the distinction between land owned by townsmen and land owned by country residents, and lastly it forced the merchants and the guilds to contribute their share of the *mensuale*. In subsequent years, as we have seen, the cities were stripped of other fiscal privileges as well, notably in the matter of military billets.

Nor was the erosion of urban privileges and the trend toward a greater measure of equality confined to taxation only. The silk trade, too, was affected. Here the traditional policy had been two-pronged: on the one hand, the export of raw silk (whether in the form of cocoons or of skeins) had been prohibited, or had been authorized only in years of plenty after the needs of the Milan manufactures had been fully met; on the other hand, producers of raw silk had been required to sell only to members of the appropriate merchant guild in Milan. The intent of those policies, of course, had been to ensure as abundant a supply of raw material as possible to the city and its manufacturers. In 1593, however, the Congregazione del Ducato, speaking on behalf of rural interests, denounced those restrictive measures, and the unrestricted export of raw silk was temporarily authorized, possibly for the first time, despite the loud protests of the Milan guildsmen.[16] This new liberal policy apparently remained in force until 1640.[17] The following year, however, a resumption of the old ban on exports was advocated as a sure means of restoring prosperity to the declining silk industry of Milan.[18] The government must have heeded the advice: throughout the 1650s and 1660s, at any rate, repeated proclamations (*gride*) were issued by the Spanish governors that reaffirmed the old restrictive policies.[19] How effective those proclamations actually were is open to doubt, for in the same breath as they prohibited the export of silk the governors invariably denounced its smuggling across the borders of the state, thus indicating that violations of the law must have reached alarming proportions. Significantly, the chief offenders were said to be "noblemen, grandees, churchmen, officers, and other persons of rank [who] stockpile [silk] near the border and hide it in churches or in the houses of local parsons so as to prevent customs officials from making the necessary searches." In 1673 Governor Ossuna apparently bowed to the inevitable and granted total freedom to the silk trade;[20] five years later his successor adopted a new policy, and one that was more consonant with the diffusion of silkmaking abroad and its decline at home: an embargo was declared, but it was confined to the export of cocoons; the export of silk in skeins was permitted and no word was made of the obligation to sell exclusively to city merchants.[21]

Ironically enough, the new policy had been recommended by the highest municipal authority in Milan, the Vicario di Provvisione. Requested in 1676 to express his opinion on a petition submitted by the Milan silk spinners' guild that the free export of silk be prohibited, the Vicario found against his fellow townsmen and argued not only that "it would be impossible for all our silk to be processed here," but also that "it is unadvisable as a matter of good policy totally to restrict our trade with foreign nations as the latter draw from us much of the silk which they use in their manufactures and in return money is introduced here to the great benefit of those among His Majesty's subjects who raise silk on their land."[22] Rural interests, in other words, were given priority over those of the city.

A relaxation of old regulations and restrictions originally intended to favor the city artisans at the expense of rural interests is also discernible in the case of industries that had illegally sprung up in the countryside. During the seventeenth century the ruralization of industry continued to be frowned upon in official quarters, and, at times, stiff new measures were enacted to curb it, including instructions to local officials to destroy all looms and silk mills in the villages.[23] But the persistence and indeed the growth of rural industries suggest that enforcement was far from rigorous, if it was attempted at all. Neither cloth making in the Valassina nor hat making in Monza nor silk throwing in the Varese district seem to have been curbed or interfered with in any serious way by government officials. At one time, in fact, the Tribunale de Provvisione explicitly rejected the use of coercion against offending silk makers in the countryside and advocated milder, and probably ineffectual, fiscal measures as the only means for discouraging the proliferation of silk mills in the countryside.[24]

Whether in matters of taxation, trade, or the location of industry, it is clear that the cities' privileged position had begun to erode in the second half of the sixteenth century. We are still a long way from the sweeping, systematic legislation of the late eighteenth-century reformers, but the drift is very much the same: the city-state system was being slowly replaced by the equalizing structure typical of the modern bureaucratic state—and the beneficiary of this new trend could only be the countryside.

Needless to say, behind this trend there was no deliberate design aimed at galvanizing the countryside's latent energies, no laissez-faire ideology, but rather some very practical considerations dictated by necessity and expediency. Their source lay, first of all, in the mounting needs of the state treasury. The need for fresh revenue and the burden of taxation were on the rise since the days of Philip II, in response to the growing demands of war. Not surprisingly, contemporaries saw in the increasing pressure exerted by the government on the resources of their small country the main, if not the only, cause of the many ills besetting the economy. For our part, while we can subscribe only partially to their indictment of the tax collector, we can, from the vantage point of hindsight, detect other and, in the long run, more far-reaching effects of Spain's financial policies. For an inevitable, if unintended, result of those policies was precisely to undermine the privileges of the city and thus to narrow the gap that separated it from its rural hinterland.

The Congregazione del Ducato, for instance, was originally set up merely as an instrument for the apportionment of a new tax (the *mensuale*) among hundreds of rural communities; but, once in existence, it became a spokesman for the rural taxpayer and an advocate of greater fiscal equality between the latter and his privileged urban counterpart. It was at the Congregazione's request, in combination with the Crown's pressing need for revenue, that urban craftsmen and merchants were made to contribute their share of the *mensuale* and

were thus deprived of the traditional exemption from direct taxation.
Likewise, it was military and fiscal necessity (and possibly pressure
brought to bear by the Congregazione) that led Spanish authorities to
require the cities to provide money and accomodations for the
soldiery.

While major changes in fiscal policies emanated from an impecunious government in Madrid, decisions concerning the export of raw
materials or the toleration of handicraft industries outside the city
walls were probably made, or at least strongly influenced, by the
authorities in Milan—the Senate, the Finance Magistracy, the Tribunale di Provvisione—by agencies, that is, staffed and directed almost
entirely by Milanese patricians and presumably dedicated to the defense and promotion of urban, rather than rural, interests. That in the
seventeenth century those very agencies should, in fact, pursue policies detrimental to the city clearly suggests that by that time the patriciate had ceased to espouse urban interests.

This change in the attitude of the patriciate is illustrated by the
policies adopted in the course of the seventeenth century on the question of the silk trade and rural industries; but it is also dramatically
revealed in the events of Martinmas 1628, when famine struck the
State of Milan and a bread riot of alarming proportions exploded in
the capital, with the mob directing its outrage at the city bakeries and
indulging in plunder and violence. Anxious to calm things down, the
Spanish governor (or rather his deputy, the chancellor) proposed a
freeze on the price of bread. How effective such a measure—had it
been implemented—would have been in coping with the plight of the
populace is hard to tell. The point is that it was not implemented,
because of the determined opposition of the municipal authorities.
Speaking with the voice of the Milanese patriciate, they opposed the
Spanish governor and sided with the bakers, the grain dealers, and the
landowners who had everything to lose from a price freeze; rather,
they advocated, and eventually persuaded the governor to carry out,
repressive measures against the mob and a laissez-faire policy in regard to food prices.[25] A somewhat similar scenario, albeit without
violence, repeated itself in 1635 when grain prices soared once again
in the wake of a crop failure: the Spanish governor's attempts at securing fresh supplies of grain from abroad "were thwarted for a whole

month," according to a chronicler, due to "the great malice of the bakers and some gentlemen."[26]

In 1641, in a less dramatic but no less revealing context, we find the patriciate once again pitted against urban interests—this time the interests of the craft and merchant guilds rather than of the consumers. At issue were the policies to be adopted in order to save the chief urban manufactures, namely, wool and silk, both of which had suffered severe setbacks since about 1620 and were now on the brink of extinction. The guilds found an articulate spokesman in the person of a draper named Tridi, the author of a tract to which frequent reference has been made in these pages. Tridi's battle cry was protection and a return to the old system of controls in favor of urban industries. To save the ailing manufactures he called for a total ban on foreign industrial imports, for the strict enforcement of existing legislation against rural industries, for an embargo on native silk, and finally for a reduction of the excise and for suppression of the infamous *estimo mercimoniale*, with any loss of revenue resulting therefrom to be offset by higher land taxes.[27]

Although Tridi did find qualified support for his views among a few high-ranking officials in Milan, he also met with stiff opposition from the city government, and notably from the Tribunale di Provvisione, the patrician-dominated center of municipal administration and the chief regulatory agency in charge of economic matters both within the city of Milan and throughout the province.[28] It is revealing of the mood then prevailing among the city fathers that the Tribunale took issue with Tridi's every proposal: it rejected a shift in the tax burden from town to country as seriously detrimental to agriculture; it opposed protective measures in favor of native industries on the ground that keeping foreign goods out would raise prices at home and create "vicious monopolies"; it rejected the idea of a silk embargo as being "repugnant to every sound polity" and "destructive of that intercourse thanks to which commodities flow from one nation to another to their mutual benefit"; it candidly argued that a reduction or a stoppage of silk exports would "bring down the price of silk thus forcing noblemen to cut down their mulberry trees."[29] In 1679 the same body took up the defense of the rural silk spinners who had been threatened with the destruction of their workshops and mills: "no one should be deprived of his natural liberty to earn a living in whatever place he can best do so."[30]

The persistent, outspoken, and, at times, ruthless defense of agrarian interests by the patrician-dominated government of Milan should come as no surprise in view of the fact, recorded in an earlier chapter, that by the close of the sixteenth century the patriciate had assumed all the traits of an exclusive landed aristocracy and had deliberately excluded from its ranks any upstart whose wealth had been made in the countinghouse or the workshop. This shift away from the traditional sources of urban wealth has generally been interpreted as an ominous sign that Lombard society underwent a process of involution or retrogression that was to have disastrous consequences for the economies of the Lombard cities and of Milan in particular. For here, it would seem, was a class that had been the agent of a precocious, remarkable experiment in commercial and industrial growth, and which, on the very threshold of modern capitalism, had "betrayed" its progressive role and had adopted the mores and outlook of an agrarian aristocracy, thus contributing to the country's economic and social decadence.

The evidence, however, admits of a different interpretation and one that was proposed, although not pursued in detail, by Gino Luzzatto some forty years ago.[31] In discussing the economic decline of Italy in the seventeenth century, and its slow, partial recovery in the following century, Luzzatto remarked that what had really declined were the economies of its cities, with their corporate privileges and parochial outlook, and what had emerged from their debacle was a modern, "national" economy, one, that is, in which both town and country could participate as equals. Luzzatto, unlike most historians, considered the decline of the cities a necessary, if painful, step toward modernization; and he went on to contend that the crucial transformation from a narrow municipal perspective to a larger one was made possible by the shift of the urban patriciates' economic interests from the city to the countryside.

The case of Hapsburg Lombardy certainly supports Luzzatto's insight. Long before enlightened despotism swept away once and for all the anachronistic structure of the city-state, the structure itself had been seriously eroded as a result both of fiscal necessity and of the ruling elite's loss of interest in the traditional, but rapidly dwindling, sources of urban wealth. Although one should not minimize the merits and the achievements of Maria Theresa and Joseph II and their undeniable contributions to the modernization of Lombardy, one must recognize that what they cleared away so effectively and irreversibly were largely the debris of an edifice that lay already in ruins.

If this be true, then some generally accepted notions about the course of Lombard history in early modern times stand in need of revision. Rather than portraying the sixteenth, and even more so the seventeenth, century as a dismal age in which the cities' commercial and industrial elite traded their ideals and their ethos for the security and prestige of a country estate, thus allowing the country to drift into economic stagnation and social sclerosis, we must rather conclude that the urban-elite-turned-landowners did more to bring about the modernization of their homeland than their fellow townsmen who, true to a glorious past, still sat at the loom or in the countinghouse and upheld the cherished traditions of the guilds, old and prestigious standards of workmanship, and the city's exclusive role as commercial and industrial center. It is ironic, but all the more revealing, that as early as the 1640s the new landed class used in defense of its own interests terms that Adam Smith would not have repudiated, while the city merchants and guildsmen, in a last-ditch, futile attempt at shoring up the ailing urban economy, appealed to tradition, protection, and privilege.

CHAPTER VIII

A POSTSCRIPT ON FEUDALISM

In recent years the economic crisis that swept Lombardy as well as the rest of the Italian peninsula in the central decades of the seventeenth century has increasingly been viewed, especially by scholars of Marxist persuasion, as resulting from a process of social involution, variously labeled "refeudalization," "feudal restoration," or "neofeudalism"; from a process, that is to say, whereby the precociously modern, capitalistic character of Italian society was allegedly displaced by rigid, stifling ties of command and dependence, privilege and subjection, typical of feudalism. In the words of one historian:

> Widely accepted now is the notion that in the seventeenth century Italy experienced a far-reaching process of refeudalization which, if it did not entirely obliterate the achievements of earlier centuries, nonetheless caused a clear break on the path of expansion that Italy had trodden since the days of the *Comuni.* [Refeudalization] manifested itself, as is well known, in the stoppage of that commercial and industrial growth that had been at the root of the civilization of the city-states; but in the countryside too, property and production relationships underwent a process of involution, as ecclesiastical and noble privileges in economic, social, and political matters gained fresh ground . . . This was a time of consolidation and expansion for the large church and feudal estates . . . and of the reappearance of a whole set of privileges, prerogatives, abuses, and shackles that the feudal system imposed on productive activity.[1]

Referring to northern Italy in particular, S. F. Romano has spoken of the once-buoyant urban economies being "smothered by neofeudalism,"[2] and Giorgio Candeloro, after subscribing to the view that at the root of their crisis lay the shift of merchant capital from trade to landownership, has asserted that the new landlords adopted, vis-à-vis the peasantry, methods and attitudes of "a feudal or semifeudal character," with the result that as early as the fifteenth century "peasant conditions experienced a slow, but continuous deterioration."[3]

Spanish Lombardy itself, it has been argued, "did not escape the process of refeudalization," in the sense that not only were a large number of "free" villages sold in fief by an impecunious government, but also, and most importantly, that fresh burdens were fastened on the peasantry by the nobility as the latter tried to compensate for the loss of income resulting from the agrarian crisis of the seventeenth century. This the nobility did "by reviving long forgotten seignorial rights, by seizing communal pastures and forests, or by tightening and extending the jurisdiction of feudal courts"—in short, by introducing all sorts of "abuses, pressures, violence, and impositions which, in the final analysis, generated direct and, to an even greater extent, indirect economic advantages" for the feudatories.[4]

In the absence of detailed studies on the subject, what has led several scholars to speak so confidently of the "refeudalization" of seventeenth-century Lombardy are two broad facts: first, the massive sale of fiefs during the Spanish period, notably in the 1640s when the needs of the treasury were at their highest; and, second, the fact that, when given the opportunity to choose between enfeoffment and free status, a number of communities chose the latter even though their choice involved heavy financial sacrifices.[5]

At this point it is well to recall that any community that was part of the royal demesne (*regio demanio*)—that is to say, any village community that had never been subject to the rule of a feudatory—could be granted (and, in practice, sold) in fief by the Crown. In this event the community itself had the option to request, within a year, that the act of feudal investiture be rescinded—provided, however, the community itself could come up with a sum equal to two-thirds of the price paid by the new lord. By so doing, the village was said to have "redeemed" itself or to have "acquired the royal demesne" in perpetuity; henceforth it could not be sold in fief again unless it explicitly waived its right to remain free. A similar option was open to any community under feudal rule whenever its lord died without issue in the direct male line, in which case the fief reverted, or escheated, to the

Crown by devolution: here again, by paying a ransom or "price of redemption" (*prezzo della redenzione*), the community ceased to be liable to future enfeoffments. On the other hand, a free community could, by majority vote, renounce its freedom and ask to be infeudated—provided, of course, it had found someone willing to purchase it in fief from the Crown.[6] There were thus three cases in which the choice between freedom and enfeoffment presented itself to a village: first, when the Crown decided to sell a hitherto free community in fief; second, when a fief was up for resale following devolution; and third, when a community that had "acquired the royal demesne" in the past considered waiving the rights it had previously acquired.

The fact that several rural communities did purchase their redemption from feudal rule—at considerable cost to the residents—when the option to do so presented itself has, therefore, been interpreted as clear proof that feudal rule was sensed as a very real burden, and one that must be avoided at almost any price. According to Bruno Caizzi, enfeoffment represented a dreaded prospect for Lombardy's villages, because it meant "falling under an authority which was probably harsher and certainly more arbitrary than that of the central government"; therefore, "great efforts were expended by the communities so threatened in order to avoid enfeoffment even at the cost of supporting financial sacrifices in order to pay the required ransom."[7] And Ruggiero Romano has concluded that "If the Lombard fief had not been extremely burdensome for the people involved, how could we account for the incredible efforts those people undertook in order to secure redemption from, or in order to avoid being subjected to, feudal rule?"[8]

Although both the large-scale sale of fiefs and the requests for redemption are facts beyond dispute, the conclusions that have been drawn from them are open to question and deserve close examination. There is no question that the Spanish rulers resorted to the sale of fiefs whenever they could in order to raise revenue; it is probable, moreover, that well over a thousand villages were sold in fief, at one time or another, during the nearly two centuries of Spanish domination. It is, however, a mistake to infer from this that the Spanish period witnessed a dramatic revival of feudalism and represented a radical departure from the age of the Visconti and Sforza dukes. As Cesare Magni has convincingly shown, the State of Milan was already studded with fiefs when Charles V took power: of the 1,600 rural communities that were under feudal rule when Spanish domination came to an end in 1714, a good three-fourths had already been in fief two centuries earlier when Lombardy had fallen under Spanish rule. The Spaniards may have added as many as 500 new localities to the roster of fiefs, but a majority of their sales involved communities that had long been enfeoffed and had simply become available for resale following their devolution to the Crown.[9]

The view that Spanish policies concerning feudalism, far from representing a sharp break with earlier practice, were in fact its continuation has recently been confirmed by Giorgio Chittolini in an essay showing that, in the fourteenth and fifteenth centuries, the dukes of Milan not only did not destroy feudal institutions, but used them very effectively as tools for state-building: while asserting their own supremacy over the most recalcitrant and unruly feudatories, they carefully preserved the existing feudal structure and lavished feudal grants on their own supporters, thus in fact turning them into docile representatives of ducal authority in the countryside. They also tightened the chain of command from the center to the periphery by placing fresh emphasis on the loyalty owed by the vassals to their liege lord, by couching the extent and the limits of feudal authority in precise legal terms, by reserving to themselves the right to levy certain taxes (and notably the hearth and salt taxes), even within a fief, and, lastly, by upholding the right of appeal from feudal to ducal courts.[10]

Such was the streamlined, tightly supervised feudal system the Spaniards inherited, which was embalmed in an even more rigid form in the *Nuove Costituzioni* issued by Charles V as new ruler of Milan. The creation of new fiefs in the sixteenth and seventeenth centuries, then, followed a well-established pattern and was basically a continuation of a long-standing tradition. The main difference, it would seem, was that the Hapsburgs viewed feudalism less as an instrument for keeping the aristocracy loyal then as a convenient mechanism for extracting additional and urgently needed revenue from their wealth-

iest Lombard subjects: hence their policy of granting fiefs in return for
a cash payment proportional to the size of the fief, of making the concession of any new title of nobility contingent upon the purchase of a
fief, and of trying to maximize the chances of a fief reverting to the
Crown as a result of failure in the line of succession by insisting on the
rule of primogeniture.[11] Nor was this overriding financial concern
kept a secret: when in 1647 a new rash of sales was ordered, the pertinent royal proclamation explained in all candor that this was done "in
order to raise money for the upkeep of His Majesty's army and the
defense and preservation of this State."[12]

If the creation of new fiefs in the Spanish period was no departure from past policies, it is still possible that the nature and
extent of the power exercised by the feudal nobility over the peasantry
was modified in the course of the sixteenth and seventeenth centuries
and that, in fact, that power became more oppressive and arbitrarv,
ultimately resulting, as some authorities have contended, in the deterioration of peasant conditions. No clear evidence of an increase in
peasant obligations and dues has, to my knowledge, been provided,
nor have I found any such evidence myself. And yet, the mere fact
that a number of rural communities were prepared, when given the
opportunity, to disburse the heavy "price of redemption" has been
interpreted, not unreasonably, as evidence that the feudal yoke was
heavy indeed and may have grown heavier during the long agrarian
depression of the seventeenth century. There is, in other words, a
strong presumption that, if a community was willing to tax itself in
order to fend off the threat of enfeoffment, it must have been because
living under feudal rule represented a bleak and dreaded prospect.

From presumption to formal proof, however, there is a gap, and
one that is not easy to fill, because in most instances all our sources tell
us about a redemption from feudal rule is that it had been requested
by a community, that the request had been either accepted or rejected
by the government, and, in the former case, what ransom was eventually paid by the community itself. How the peasants really felt
about the whole issue and whether opinions were unanimous or not is
something the documents seldom discuss. Only in a limited number of

cases can we catch a glimpse of peasant attitudes and feelings, and those cases obviously deserve close attention.

When a rural community was earmarked for sale in fief, either because it was still part of the royal demesne or because it had reverted to it by devolution, an official was sent to the village to interview a number of knowledgeable residents (older peasants or peasants holding some minor local office) in order to determine the size of the village itself, the kind of crops grown there, its sources of tax revenue, the presence, if any, of large landowners, and so on.[13] Occasionally, the investigating official also raised the question of whether or not the villagers had any objection to passing under feudal rule. Thus, in a village near the Adda River, to the question "Is this community inclined to be enfeoffed or would it prefer to remain without a lord?" one local informant replied in a mood of despondent skepticism, "Sir, I know not what to say, for without a lord we fare badly and only God knows how we would fare if we had one." Another villager expressed feelings of frank indifference: "As far as enfeoffment is concerned, it makes no difference [non importa niente] to us." Elsewhere the response was slightly more encouraging. In Robbiate the news that a local landowner, Count Corio, had offered to purchase feudal rights over the village elicited the following comment: "Since the said gentleman is a man of integrity and nobility, he is respected and esteemed by all and no one finds fault with his becoming lord of this village." In a number of villages near Lodi, to the question of how people would accept their new lord, one peasant replied that "no ill feelings are likely to develop between the lord and the residents," while two others cautiously asserted that "these communities raise no objections to being infeudated . . . provided no additional burden be imposed on them."[14]

At times the prospect of enfeoffment seems to have been greeted with genuine anticipation. In the Cremona countryside in the 1640s (at a time, that is, when the province was turned into a battleground), to the question whether the local residents "would like to live under a feudal lord," one man replied, "Yes, sir, we would, for we have suffered so much destruction and a lord could help us in our needs"; and another echoed him by saying, "I reckon it would be to our benefit to have someone here who could help us in our needs and who could give us some relief in our troubles"; a third one was even more emphatic, "This community will always fare better if it has a gentleman who can protect it."[15] What kind of help and protection these men had in mind and what kind of relief they expected from a feudal lord is not spelled out in our sources, but a reasonable guess is that the presence of a feudatory was seen as a safeguard against the worst scourge peasants were exposed to in wartime, namely, the billeting of troops. This is suggested by a comment made in 1656 by a resident of Gallarate when the absentee feudatory of that community, the German Count Altemps (or Hohemens) requested permission to sell his fief to two brothers, the marquesses Visconti di Cislago, who owned a great deal of land, held an assortment of fiefs in that very district, and had their residence nearby. The prospect of passing under the rule of the Visconti was said to be "welcome by all" and one reason for this was that "from the said Visconti, as residents [of this area], we can expect constant favors, protection and assistance in the matter of the billeting of soldiers, something Count Altemps cannot provide since he does not live here."[16]

It would, of course, be rash to generalize from so few examples and assume that the Lombard villages were, as a rule, either indifferent or frankly favorable to being enfeoffed, the more so as we know that a number of villages did pay large ransoms in order to be "redeemed from the feudal yoke," or at least expressed a desire to be free, but failed to achieve their intent merely because they lacked the money to do so.[17] Yet, the seeming contradiction between the peasants' attitudes we have just recorded and the efforts made to avoid enfeoffment is resolved as soon as one turns to what evidence is available on who, inside or outside individual communities, actually advocated or resisted redemption.

On this point the evidence, limited though it is, is clear and consistent: the initiative to avert enfeoffment never originated with the peasantry; it was rather the work of the larger landowners (*maggiori estimi, primi estimi*) and other notables in the community or, more rarely, of the authorities in a nearby town. As for the peasants, if they voiced any preference at all, they did so in favor of, rather than in opposition to, feudal rule and, in at least one instance, as will be seen, were ready to resort to arms to avoid redemption from it.

The role played by municipal authorities in trying to secure the redemption of a village can be seen in Bellagio and Brunate, two small communities in the Como province. When they were offered for sale in fief (in 1624 and 1656 respectively) it was the Como municipal authorities that took steps against such change: in Brunate's case they were apparently successful, while in Bellagio's their efforts failed in the face of the villagers' determination to have a feudal lord.[18] A similar, but far more dramatic, and indeed bloody, conflict between town authorities and the villages in the *contado* broke out toward the end of the seventeenth century in the district of Casalmaggiore. The market town of Casalmaggiore, along with fifteen nearby villages, had been sold in fief in 1649. Thirty years later, the Casalmaggiore municipal council had tried to free the town from feudal rule (and had offered to raise a handsome sum to that effect), arguing, on the dubious basis of ancient privileges, that the entire district had been illegally excised from the royal demesne. The attempt failed, but it is interesting to note that, on that occasion, the villages squarely opposed the town and declared to be "fully satisfied with the feudatory." In 1692, however, the death of the incumbent without issue gave Casalmaggiore the undisputable right to request redemption. The town council quickly voted to impose a new tax over the entire district in order to raise 50,000 gold *scudi* as ransom; the government, on its part, accepted the offer without much ado, "in view of the pressing need for cash." Out in the villages, however, news of the whole transaction was received in an angry mood: not only were "loud recriminations" heard "among the poor villagers" (*i poveri paesani*), but meetings were soon held to organize resistance and, despite the town council's threat of "raising the gallows on the public square," it was agreed that no one should pay the new land tax and that two delegates should be dispatched to Milan "to seek redress and to have this intolerable imposition voided." Meanwhile, however, the appearance in the villages of tax collectors, duly escorted by constables (*sbirri*), and the arrest of a few recalcitrant peasants touched off a riot in which firearms were used on both sides and in which eight constables and two peasants were killed. Only the threatened intervention of a cavalry troop and

an infantry regiment that would have been billeted on delinquent
taxpayers restored the public peace and sealed the redemption of the
villages.[19]

More commonly, opposition to enfeoffment came from local landed
interests. When, in 1648, a Count Arese offered to buy in fief Parabiago, his offer was at first rejected by a seemingly unanimous community. The rejection, however, was later denounced by the peasants
as a fraud perpetrated behind their backs by local landowners, and an
official inquiry confirmed that, indeed, the decision to seek redemption and to raise the necessary ransom money had been secretly made
by "a few individuals" who had then sent out "armed servants" to
notify "the will of the masters" (*la volontà dei signori*) to the peasants.
On the basis of these disturbing findings the offer to redeem was
voided and Parabiago was duly sold in fief to Count Arese, much to
the relief of the peasants who, we are told, had threatened "to flee and
desert the village" had the landowners had their way.[20] In Tradate,
that same year, a similar offer by a member of the Milanese patriciate
was vigorously and, as it turned out, successfully resisted by two
prominent local families (the Castiglioni and the Pusterla) also of
patrician rank.[21] In 1651 Albairate avoided being sold in fief thanks to
the efforts of "noblemen who owned land in the village";[22] in both
Castelseprio and Besana the local notables took similar action. "Sheer
deceit" was the charge leveled at the largest landowners (a senator,
several titled aristocrats, and two monastic houses) by the peasantry
of Zelo Surigone when a request for redemption was submitted to the
central government in 1649.[23]

The reasons behind the opposition of municipal authorities and
local notables against enfeoffment are not far to seek. To the former
the enfeoffment of a village meant that the village itself would be
excised from the town's *contado*, and thus it represented a loss of
revenue and of jurisdiction. As for the local notables, it would appear
that their opposition was largely motivated by reasons of prestige. In
resisting the sale of Tradate in fief, the Castiglioni and Pusterla families argued that enfeoffment would be "of prejudice to more than a
hundred [sic] illustrious households of ancient lineage" and that their
reputation and dignity would be irreparably damaged should they be
forced to render homage and fealty to "a fellow patrician" (*un compa-*

tritio).[24] In Castelseprio the gentry argued that no discernible "reason of state" could be invoked to justify their "surrendering the graves and the bones of their forefathers in feudal servitude."[25]

But more tangible and prosaic interests could also be at stake, and the little act of sedition that occurred in Albese in 1656 shows this well enough.[26] The feudatory of Albese, Dal Verme, had been duly authorized to sell his rights over the village to Signora Clemenza Carpano in 1656. But when she came to the village to receive, as the law prescribed, the oath of fealty from her newly acquired subjects, the latter simply refused to comply. Thereupon an official investigation was ordered of this rather unusual case of insubordination, and it revealed that two influential men—a priest named Tommaso Odescalchi who owned a palazzo in Albese itself and a prominent Milanese banker named Alessandro Parravicini[27]—had intimidated the villagers with threats of physical violence into refusing the oath and requesting redemption from feudal rule. It was further disclosed that the necessary ransom money was to be loaned by the friendly banker and that it was to be refunded to him in course of time out of the sale of timber from the communal woodland. "Tommaso Odescalchi," asserted one informant, "wants a good part of the chestnut trees belonging to this community to be sold so that the poor can repay the fief." The poor themselves, however, felt differently and had no intention of giving up what was probably the community's only asset. As one of them candidly put it in his sworn deposition, they much preferred "their village to be infeudated rather than spend money, becuase it is poor and loaded with taxes . . . and what is involved here is the sale of the community's timber." Only after the whole shady deal had been exposed and the two enterprising fellows, Odescalchi and Parravicini, had been served an injunction to stop harassing the peasants, did Signora Carpano receive the oath of her new subjects.

This espisode throws light not only on one of the possible motives that drove well-do-to individuals to advocate redemption from feudal rule, but also on the motives that drove the peasants to resist it. To the latter, redemption meant, first and foremost, the payment of a substantial ransom; ultimately, the money would have to come out of the sale of communal property or (as in Casalmaggiore) would have to be raised out of new taxes—in either case new sacrifices must be imposed on the community, and it is understandable that strenuous efforts were sometimes made to preserve the status quo. When trying to justify their overt rebellion against the signori's attempt to force them to pay the new land tax needed for redemption, the peasants of the Casalmaggiore district blamed the new imposition for "driving them into a desperate course of action" and bluntly asserted that "if they had not been harassed they would have been as so many lambs, but if they were going to be treated without regard to justice they would turn into so many tigers."[28]

To the peasants the choice of enfeoffment could mean more than just being spared an additional fiscal burden. Feudal rule could bring some positive advantages as well. Protection against the soldiery, as we have seen, was one such advantage, but not the only one. The "poor men" of Bellagio, for instance, openly advocated their enfeoffment to Ercole Sfondrati, Duke of Montemarciano, whose sumptuous residence had recently been built in the village itself, both because enfeoffment would make it possible for routine legal matters to be conveniently and expeditiously transacted in loco before the feudal judge, rather than in Como, thirty kilometers away, and also because they believed that their poverty-striken community had everything to gain from closer ties with the wealthy duke. In the petition in which they pleaded to be enfeoffed to him they argued that "thanks to his kindness, to the many buildings he has erected and is still erecting, to the wages he liberally pays, and to the generous alms he dispenses, many and indeed most of us poor folks have stayed in this village which would otherwise have been deserted."[29]

The need for protection and the resentment against the additional financial burden represented by the ransom were also behind the "renunciations of the royal demesne" (*rinunce del regio demanio*) whereby villages that in the past had purchased the privilege of being exempt in perpetuity from a new enfeoffment, reversed themselves and petitioned the government to be allowed to return under the rule of a feudatory.[30] In the few cases for which the details of the transaction are available, it was the peasantry that took the initiative to have feudal rule restored, and they did so, in open defiance of the wishes of the local notables and landowners, in order to ensure financial relief or protection.

The village of Oggiono provides a telling illustration at this point. In 1658, only six years after their community had chosen to redeem itself following the death of its lord without male issue, a nobleman had apparently offered to buy the village in fief and had found considerable support among the peasants. Although, in the end, the proposed "renunciation of the royal demesne" failed to receive a majority of the votes, it is nonetheless interesting to learn that it was some of the largest landowners (*alcuni delli primi estimi*) of Oggiono who first denounced the proposed change to the central government, while, on the opposite side, it was argued that "unless a new feudal lord be granted . . . who will relieve them of the debt incurred on account of redemption, will protect them in their needs, and will see to it that justice be done, the poor will be forced to leave this land."[31] Likewise, it was the "poor men" (*poveri homeni*) of Castelrozzone who in 1648, only one year after their village had been redeemed, waived their privilege and asked the Senate to be re-enfeoffed on the ground that a new feudatory not only would relieve them of the heavy debt contracted earlier in order to pay ransom, but would also protect them against the "arrogance" of the larger landowners (*maggiori estimi*).[32] And the same pattern repeated itself in Besana in 1656, in Cuggiono Minore in 1672, and in San Martino in Strada in 1689.[33] In 1713 it was Caravaggio's turn to "renounce the royal demesne" that it had acquired at great cost fifteen years earlier: the renunciation was supported by nearly three hundred heads of family and was opposed by "certain landowners."[34] Melzo, after several years spent as a free community, decided in 1703 to accept the offer made by a nobleman to purchase it in fief: within the community itself, however, opinions were divided, with the largest landowners (*maggiori estimi*) resisting the change, while the advocates of a new enfeoffment used the familiar argument voiced elsewhere by the poor: "the good of our community consists in getting rid of its debts and also in having someone who can provide protection."[35]

While all the sixteen cases discussed so far show that on the question of enfeoffment rural communities tended to split, with the landed class opposing and the peasantry favoring feudal rule, there are on record a few instances where opposition to enfeoffment might seem, on the surface, to have been close to unanimous and to have reflected the genuine aspirations of the peasantry.

The cluster of hamlets known as the ville di Bellagio is one such case. The hamlets had not been sold in fief in 1624 when Ercole Sfondrati had purchased feudal rights over Bellagio itself. In 1647, however, when a nobleman tried to acquire such rights over the ville, efforts to raise the "price of redemption" were quickly (albeit unsuccessfully) undertaken on grounds that "the people desire to live under His Majesty's direct rule" and that "enfeoffment is what causes the ruin of monarchies."[36] One is entitled, however, to doubt that these arguments accurately reflected the true feelings of the peasantry, not only because to the latter the ultimate fate of monarchies was probably a matter of little concern, but also because we know that in the ville of Bellagio most land belonged to absentee landlords, both lay and ecclesiastic, who lived in Como.[37] One can hardly avoid the suspicion that it was from them rather than from the peasants that opposition to feudal rule originated.

A similar and stronger suspicion is justified in the case of Cernusco in the Brianza, a village that the government had put up for sale in 1647 and which an absentee landowner, Marquess Corio, had offered to buy in fief. The community, apparently with no one dissenting, quickly gathered enough money to counter the Marquess' offer and to preserve its freedom. It did so, however, by borrowing the money at 7 percent from the largest resident landowner, Signorino Cernuschio by name. It is not rash to conclude that it was Cernuschio himself who masterminded the whole transaction: he obviously had cash to lend and the interest charged was not unattractive; he could probably influence the largest number of peasant votes since a third of the local labor force was in his pay;[38] lastly, by securing the redemption of the village, he could keep a high-ranking aristocrat out of the community's affairs.

The large market town of Codogno, too, was apparently unanimous in its request to be reintegrated into the royal demesne when its feudal lord died without issue in 1678:[39] "the people with one voice ask to be subjected to [the direct rule of] His Majesty the King Our Lord," explained a local official. But another official was not so sure:

"some people want a new feudal lord, others do not," he commented; and he went on to point out that the whole effort aimed at securing redemption had been organized by four individuals who had managed to persuade the other members of the town that redemption "would be a good thing for them" and had advanced the required ransom money at 5 percent. As for the townspeople themselves, it is doubtful that they fully understood what was in fact happening: far from rejoicing in their newly acquired freedom, some of them believed that the four men who had loaned the ransom money had, in fact, jointly purchased Codogno in fief and were now its "new lords."[40]

The Valsassina, the valley rich in iron ores that lies to the east of Lake Como, provides another intriguing example of seemingly general distaste for feudal rule. When in 1647 a local magnate, Giulio Monti, offered to buy the entire valley in fief, he met with vigorous opposition. The official representative (*sindico*) of the valley voiced it in these terms: "So much does this valley abhor being removed from the direct jurisdiction of the Crown and being subjected to a feudal lord that without any doubt a majority of our people would leave and cross the border into Venetian territory." In a more pragmatic vein, the sindico went on to remind the government that Valsassina was the chief source of military hardware and munitions for the Spanish forces stationed in Lombardy; he further stressed that the iron trade in the valley had always been free and open to all and any of the residents of the valley. He then concluded with a warning: "Once the valley be turned into a fief, there is no doubt that many will secure for themselves the favor and support of the new lord and that, as a consequence, the rest will be forced to quit; in which event military supplies will no longer be available so easily and at such moderate prices, for the iron trade will be restricted in a few hands rather than being in the hands of many."[41] The sindico's warning was clearly directed against the danger of monopolistic practices on the part of the would-be feudatory and his cronies; nor does it seem to have been entirely devoid of substance, for we know that Monti was himself very active in the iron industry of the valley.[42] Accordingly, it was only natural to suspect that his feudal ambitions concealed a design that had more to do with business than with knightly prowess.

Whatever Monti's ultimate goals may have been, one cannot help but ask: Whom did the sindico speak for when he opposed the proposed enfeoffment of the Valsassina? It is unlikely that he spoke for the many day-laborers, charcoal burners, carters, muleteers, and miners who formed the bulk of the valley's labor force and who must have cared little whether they would be hired by Monti or by someone else. Rather, the sindico must have spoken for those individuals referred to in his petition as being "free to deal in metal goods at their pleasure,"[43] that is, the owners of mining pits, the forge masters, and the ironmongers. These, rather than the common people, must have felt threatened by the prospect of one of their peers acquiring the lordship of the valley.

Only in two known instances have we every reason for believing that an entire rural community chose freedom rather than enfeoffment with near unanimity—and both are very unique instances indeed. When the whole of the Valsassina was sold in fief to Giulio Monti, the village of Vedeseta (a small pastoral enclave abutting on Venetian territory just beyond the watershed) loudly protested that it should not be included in the new fief and, to buttress its case, appealed to ancient ducal privileges, and notably to "the inalienable right of selecting its own judges, handling all cases both civil and criminal, retaining all judicial fines and confiscated property . . . and being exempt from all taxes." In short, the community argued, Vedeseta cannot be enfeoffed becuase "there is nothing to be granted in fief" (*non c'è materia di feudo*).

The government took a dim view of the petition, not so much on legal grounds, but rather because it had reasons to believe that Vedeseta's immunities posed a real threat to the public peace. In the words of the Milan Senate, from the village "there often come very pernicious men, bandits, assassins, and others who kill and rob on commission and are ready to commit any sort of felony, confident as they are that justice is so badly dispensed by the magistrate whom they themselves elect with the title of Vicar that criminals do not pay any attention to it, nor is he [the Vicar] subject to review every two years, nor are his verdicts referred to the Senate, and they live without acknowledging any superior." In view of this state of complete lawlessness, concluded the Senate, "it is better, for reasons of good governance and polity, that Vedeseta be incorporated into the fief of

Valsassina," for enfeoffment would automatically have stripped the community of its unique immunities and would have brought it under the jurisdiction of a feudal judge. But it is precisely for these reasons that Vedeseta asked "to be left alone": the grim picture drawn by the Senate may well have been somewhat overdrawn, but in an age when banditry was rampant, it is conceivable that a small isolated settlement ("fifty families living on barren land where nothing grows but hay and which is nearly inaccessible") could use its ancient privileges as well as its location near the border to serve as a haven for outlaws.[44]

In those same years Abbiategrasso, a large and prosperous village of the plain, resisted enfeoffment with arguments that bear some resemblance to those invoked by Vedeseta. From time immemorial, it would appear, the community had enjoyed the privilege of selecting its own magistrate (*podestà*) with full jurisdiction (*cum mero ac misto imperio et potestate gladii*), nor could the residents of Abbiategrasso "for any case whatsoever either criminal or civil be brought before any judge other than the said podestà." This ample judicial immunity, it was argued, "would be jeopardized as a result of enfeoffment, for if this community were subjected to the lower [feudal] magistrate, it would also be subjected to the higher magistrate in Milan" in appeals cases.[45] Understandably, then, a community endowed with such exceptional privileges would fight tooth and nail to preserve them. But precisely to the extent that those privileges were exceptional, Abbiategrasso, like Vedeseta, must be treated as an exceptional, atypical case.

The evidence recited so far, limited though it is to two dozen localities, reveals a consistent pattern: all efforts to avoid enfeoffment came not from the peasantry, but either from a nearby town or, more frequently, from the landed class whose estates lay in the community about to be sold or resold in fief; the peasants, when they voiced any opinion at all, expressed either indifference, mild satisfaction, or outright anticipation at the prospect of being enfeoffed and, in fact, never opposed it.

If one starts from the conventional assumption that enfeoffment

brought fresh burdens to the peasantry and opened the door to all
sorts of "abuses, pressures, violence, and impositions," the pattern
that has emerged in the preceding pages looks truly paradoxical. If, on
the other hand, that assumption is unfounded, then the diverse attitudes toward the fief may well make sense and may prove to be, in
fact, sensible, pragmatic responses to the reality of feudalism as it
existed in seventeenth-century Lombardy.

The truth of the matter seems to be that enfeoffment, far from
bringing an assortment of evils in its wake, basically left things unchanged in the life of rural communities and, in some instances, could
even bring some tangible advantages. Redemption from feudal rule,
on the other hand, invariably involved an increase in financial burdens.

This can best be understood if one considers the precise nature and
extent of feudal rule in Hapsburg Lombardy. It is well to recall that
investiture of a fief involved no grant of land or immovable property
(except, in some cases, a castle), no control over the property rights of
the people who lived within the fief, no right to exact labor services
from them.[46] What the feudatory received was the right to administer
justice, to levy a few, clearly specified taxes, and to charge a fee for
the operation of such public facilities as the village mill, the baker's
oven, or the local inn.[47] In other words, in granting (or selling) a fief
the crown alienated to the new lord (for a carefully computed price
representing the capitalized value of the estimated annual revenue
from legal fines, taxes, and fees) certain lucrative rights and functions
normally enjoyed and performed by the Crown itself through its own
officials.[48] As far as the people living within the boundaries of the fief
were concerned, enfeoffment brought no change either in the level of
taxation or in the type of laws they had known before. What did
change, of course, was the fact that both the profits of justice and the
revenue from specified taxes now accrued to the feudatory rather than
to the royal treasury, but while this shift was of obvious importance,
if for different reasons, both to the government and to the feudatory,
it did not per se affect the feudal subjects. This being the case, one can
understand why the peasantry was so reluctant to "redeem" itself from
feudal rule when the opportunity for doing so presented itself.[49] Redemption had to be paid for and the necessary money had to be raised

from new taxes or by selling communal land; once freedom had thus been acquired, it brought no relief whatever from the usual burdens that had to be paid anyway, fief or no fief. One can also understand why a community, after redeeming itself by dint of additional sacrifices and indebtedness, might wish to waive its dearly paid-for privilege: the prospective feudatory was bound to refund to the village whatever monies had been previously spent to secure "redemption."[50]

The judicial rights of the feudal lord were generally expressed, in the formal act of investiture, with the awesome formula of *merum ac mixtum imperium et potestas gladii*, which indicated the fullness of jurisdiction in both criminal and civil cases, not excluding those carrying the death penalty.[51] In practice, however, since the days of the Visconti and the Sforza, and increasingly under Spanish rule, those sweeping judicial rights had been curtailed or at least strictly construed and placed under the watchful eyes of the central government.[52] By the seventeenth century, and possibly earlier, not only had certain major crimes (such as sedition, treason, and counterfeiting) been reserved to the Senate, but the principle had become firmly established that all verdicts handed down by a feudal court could be appealed to the Senate, and in vain did the feudal nobility try to have this restriction lifted. Moreover, sentences involving capital punishment, mutilation, or confiscation of property could not be carried out unless duly reviewed and upheld by the Senate; any case to which the feudatory was a party automatically fell outside the purview of his court, while the royal magistrate was empowered to take any case out of a feudal judge's hands if he had reason to suspect that the defendant would not receive a fair trial. The judicial authority of the feudal nobility was further restricted in two other important ways. On the one hand, feudal lords were forbidden to dispense justice themselves, but were required to appoint professional judges selected from a list of university-trained lawyers approved by the Senate, and, after the first two years of service, no feudal judge could be confirmed in office without the consent of the community in which he served. The other restriction was the so-called *privilegium civilitatis*, whereby those individuals who could claim to be freemen (*cittadini*) of one of the nine cities of the State of Milan (and many large landowners could make such a claim) were immune from the jurisdiction of the feudal judge (*minor magistrato*) and fell under that of the city or royal judge (*maggior magistrato*), a privilege that extended to a *cittadino*'s dependents, servants, and tenants.

All these limitations and controls were clearly spelled out in the statute book or firmly based on legal precedent, but it is, of course, difficult to know to what extent they were enforced and how, in fact, feudal justice was administered. What evidence is available points to marked differences from place to place. At one extreme we have the case of Montaldeo, a small fief held by a Genoese patrician family in the Apennine Mountains near the Genoese border. A recent, detailed study has shown how its feudatories ruthlessly used their judicial and police power to lord it over the peasantry and to extract from them substantial economic benefits in the form of fines, confiscations and, above all, docility.[53] It must be noted, however, that Montaldeo, although part of the State of Milan, was one of a handful of so-called "imperial fiefs," that is, fiefs that recognized the Hapsburg emperor rather than his Spanish cousin as their liege lord and, on that basis, regarded themselves as exempt from the jurisdiction of the Milan Senate, forming as many legal (and generally troublesome) enclaves in Spanish Lombardy.[54] But even fiefs that had no legal claim to immunity could de facto evade the Senate's control, the more easily so the further removed they happened to be from the reach of the Milan authorities. Such was the case of Rocca Grimalda, also in the Apennine Mountains. In 1621 its lord, Count Andrea Grimaldi, was formally charged with and convicted of "harassing" one of his tenants: the Senate imposed a fine of 2,000 gold *scudi* on him and, as he refused to pay, declared his fief forfeited. This drastic intervention on the part of the Senate, however, does not seem to have had much effect either on the overbearing Grimaldi or on his defenseless subjects, for, years later, he appears still to have been very much master in Rocca Grimalda: in the words of a resident, "no one around here dares quarrel with our lord the Count, for he is so powerful that he can ruin anyone in no time."[55] Clearly, the location of the fief and the fact that the feudatory was a Genoese rather than a Lombard subject combined to make the Senate's control largely ineffective. It was these kinds of fiefs, "sold to foreign subjects" and located "along the Genoese border," that a 1661 memorandum on feudal abuses singled out

for special criticism and bluntly called "nests and refuges of male-
factors."[56]

Most other fiefs, however, and notably those of the plain, do not
seem to have caused undue concern to the Milan authorities, not only
because they did not enjoy the natural advantage of a remote, not
easily accessible location, but also because the judicial powers of their
feudatories were often reduced to little more than hollow formulas in
the face of the *privilegium civilitatis* enjoyed by large numbers of the
residents. A Milanese patrician named Cusani learned how worthless
his *merum ac mixtum imperium* actually was when, in the 1580s, he
purchased at great cost the handsome fief of Magenta in the rich plain
west of Milan. According to a report written shortly after his investiture, "He came to his newly acquired fief assuming that, as lord, he
would be respected and honored, but in fact nobody paid the slightest
attention to him and therefore he renounced the fief . . . the reason
being that in the area lived several gentlemen who [thanks to the *privilegium civilitatis*] were subjects to the higher magistrate and the said
marquess could give orders neither to them nor to their tenants and
day laborers."[57] In view of the fact that throughout the Lombard plain
so much land was owned by townsmen, we can safely assume that
conditions in Magenta were in no way unique. Similar cases are actually on record: in Oleggio Castello near Lake Maggiore it was reported that the administration of justice brought no revenue to the
feudatory because "most people are subject to the higher magistrate";
likewise in Paullo, where most land belonged to "eight gentlemen,"
feudal jurisdiction had little scope for action, because, as was pointed
out at the time, "all the tenants are employed by gentlemen and, as
such, are under the jurisdiction of the higher magistrate so that, in
effect, only the day laborers who are poor are subject to the feudal
magistrate"; and "although fines are occasionally inflicted, they can
hardly be collected due to the poverty of the individuals involved." In
Binasco, where virtually all land (but not the feudal title) belonged to
the Carthusian monastery of Pavia, the entire population was exempted from the jurisdiction of the feudatory. In one locality, ironically enough, the feudatory's judicial powers were effectively voided
simply because the villagers refused to pay the salary to the feudal
judge as it was their obligation to do; rather than assert his indisput-

able rights or pay the salary out of his own pocket, the lord chose to appoint no judge at all.[58]

Whatever the scope of feudal (as opposed to royal) jurisdiction, it does not seem to have caused any great anxiety among the peasants when they were confronted with the choice between enfeoffment and freedom for their community. Ironically, in the few cases when the peasants did express an opinion on the subject they came out, as we have seen, in favor of feudal justice, either as a matter of greater convenience (as in Bellagio) or as a shield against the arrogance of the local landowners (as in Castelrozzone and Melzo), or in order to have someone *in loco* who could "see to it that justice be done" (as in Oggiono) or, as in Inzago, as a shield against the rigors of the royal courts.[59] By and large, however, it is probably safe to say that to the peasantry it mattered little whether justice was dispensed by a royal magistrate or a feudal appointee: to them the whole judicial system must have appeared to be a fearsome and rather alien power totally in the hands of their social superiors, and their main concern was probably to stay clear of it as much as possible.

To the landowners whose estates happened to be located within the boundaries of a newly created fief, on the other hand, the change from royal to feudal jurisdiction might well cause genuine concern, especially when they did not enjoy the immunity attached to the *privilegium civilitatis*. Enfeoffment meant the presence in their midst of a magistrate (the feudal judge) likely to intrude upon their quarrels with tenants and day laborers, even when the landowners themselves would have preferred to settle such quarrels out of court, in a more expeditious if not more equitable way. Moreover, if a case had to be brought to court, it was probably to a rich man's advantage to have it tried away from the village, in a town where he was likely to have, as a mere peasant did not, friends and connections.[60]

To local landowners and gentry, moreover, enfeoffment brought other and more subtle causes of displeasure. It could represent, as we saw in the case of Tradate and Castelseprio, a serious blow to the pride of local notables, for there would now be a recognized superior in the community and one to whom all honor and deference were due, even though he might not be the largest landowner nor a member of one of the oldest families in the district. More importantly, the new lord's interests and outlook need not always be identical to those of the local landowners, for by virtue of his office as lord of the fief he was responsible for keeping the peace and, as such, likely to try to exert a moderating influence between conflicting interests rather than to side squarely with the local landowners against the peasantry. And he would be all the more inclined to do so if, as was sometimes the case, his revenue from the sundry taxes attached to the fief outweighed his income from landownership, for in that case his own interest as tax collector might well conflict with that of the landowners: to the latter an impoverished peasantry might mean a docile, low-paid labor force; to the former, an unattractively meager source of revenue.

There is one aspect in the story of Lombard feudalism of which we have caught only occasional glimpses, and yet one that is crucial to a full understanding of peasant attitudes toward feudal rule—namely, the role of at least some of the largest and more influential feudatories as "protectors" or "patrons" of the village community.[61] We have noticed more than once that in advocating the return to feudal rule the peasants and the poor referred to a feudatory as the man who could shield them against the demands of the quartermaster and the tax collector or the oppression of the landlords. How often and to what extent feudal lords played a role as protectors is impossible to tell. All one can say, in the present state of knowledge, is that in a number of instances that role looked important enough for the peasantry to request the preservation or the restoration of feudal rule in their community. In those instances the personality of a feudatory—his moral decency and his liberality—must have weighed heavily with the peasantry; but of even greater importance in the latter's eyes must have been the amount of influence, the political clout he could exercise in high places.

This point is well illustrated by events and feelings in Melzo, a market town that had been under the rule of Prince Antonio Teodoro Trivulzio until 1678, when he died without male issue. Prince Trivulzio had been one of the largest feudatories in the State of Milan, and, moreover, he and members of his family had held, at one time or

another, some of the highest offices in the state, including the gov-
ernorship; "he has acquired," commented a worried official in 1661,
"so many fiefs that one can virtually journey from the Piacenza border . . . all the way to the City of Milan without ever leaving his
fiefs."[62] Being the subjects of a man of such power and prestige could
pay off handsomely. We have it from a Melzo tenant that the late
prince "had assisted the town in every possible way, and notably by
securing for it exemption from the excise . . . to the great benefit of
merchants and traders." Trivulzio, we are further told, "in order to
attract people to come and settle here, used to publish edicts . . . in
which he promised exemption from half the taxes for three years to all
newcomers." His death had apparently changed all that: Melzo had
opted for redemption and its prosperity had waned, witness "the
many buildings and shops that are vacant as a result of declining
trade." Little wonder, then, that after a decade as a "free" town Melzo
asked to be reinfeudated to a relative of the late prince.[63] His death
had brought changes, albeit of a different kind, in nearby Inzago as
well: many peasants and craftsmen had been forced to leave, we are
told, because some Milanese landlords had caused "many shops and
cottages to be razed to the ground" in order to make room for their
new mansions.[64] The implication here is clear enough: although he
had no legal authority to meddle in the private affairs of his subjects,
let alone interfere with property rights, a feudal lord of Trivulzio's
stature and authority could have a restraining influence on the landed
class if he chose to exercise it.

On the basis of the available evidence, then, the idea that refeudalization represented a revival of institutions and practices
that placed additional and often arbitrary burdens on the Lombard
peasantry appears totally unfounded and indefensible. We have seen
that the enfeoffment of free village communities, although vigorously
pursued by the Spanish authorities, represented no new trend, but was
a continuation of traditional policies. We have also seen that opposition to enfeoffment—and the requests made by numerous communities to be "redeemed from the feudal yoke"—cannot be taken as proof
that feudal rule was viewed by the peasantry as a form of oppression

or as the embodiment of an arbitrary power that must be avoided at all costs. On the contrary, what evidence we have consistently suggests that it was the peasantry that opposed "redemption" and even advocated a return to feudal rule, while the local landowners took the opposite position.

All this, of course, should not be interpreted as a sign that feudal rule promoted the welfare of the lower strata of rural society, although an element of paternalism was probably present in Lombard feudalism and should not be discounted altogether.[65] To the Lombard peasantry it made precious little difference whether their village was free or infeudated, for in either case the legal system and the burden of taxation remained essentially the same. Only insofar as the presence of an influential feudatory seemed to ensure a measure of protection against the soldiery, the tax collector, or the local landowners was the peasantry inclined to advocate enfeoffment; otherwise, as one peasant put it, "it made no difference." The prospect of redemption, on the other hand, was generally feared and opposed by the peasantry because, requiring as it did the payment of a large ransom, it meant an additional burden on the community's strained resources.

But even though it is misleading to regard feudalism in Spanish Lombardy as an instrument of peasant oppression and as an index of social involution, its significance cannot be underestimated. Such significance, however, must be sought not in the way it affected peasant lives, but in the way it affected public finances and, indirectly, the distribution of income.

When a community was sold or resold in fief, the price of the transaction was set on the basis of two separate figures: one was proportional to the number of hearths (*fuochi*) in the community (usually L.40 per hearth), regardless of the relative wealth or poverty of the community itself and regardless of its ability to produce revenue; the other figure represented the capitalized value of the estimated annual revenue, if any, that the new feudatory could expect from the fief itself—judicial fines and fees as well as the yield of those select taxes and monopoly rights, known as *regalie*, that the treasury was prepared to alienate to the prospective buyer.[66] When those *regalie* had already been alienated or farmed out, as was often the case, and when the profits of justice were trifling, (as was also often the case) the first figure—based on the number of hearths—was all the new feudatory had to pay for the fief.

From the standpoint of public finances, the first payment (a flat rate times the number of hearths) must be viewed as equivalent to a tax levied on the rich in return for the privilege of securing a noble title and whatever marks of honor and deference went with it; in short, it must be viewed as a "tax on vanity."[67] Payment of the second figure, based as it was on such revenue as the new lord could reasonably expect in future years, amounted essentially to an advance the buyer made to the treasury on future revenue that would normally have accrued to the treasury; it thus represented a thinly veiled form of investment in the state's funded debt.

It is important to stress the different nature of those elements which, together, combined to form the price of a fief, because they had different, and indeed opposite, economic effects. As a tax levied on the rich, the first payment enabled the government to tap additional revenue from a class that, given the basically regressive nature of the system of taxation, contributed relatively little to the state budget; as such, this levy helped mitigate, however slightly, income disparities. On the other hand, the second payment, being essentially a funded loan, ensured the feudatory a steady flow of income from future taxes and, as such, had the effect of heightening income inequalities in favor of the feudal class. Which of the two effects was stronger in the aggregate is impossible to determine with any degree of precision on the basis of the available evidence. One can venture, however, that the first effect (toward equalization) was stronger than the second (toward disparity), for we know that, while all sales of fiefs invariably involved the "price of hearths," a great many (and possibly a majority of) sales involved no payment at all on account of future revenue, all sources of revenue having already been alienated by the time the village or district was sold in fief.[68] In other words, while all sales embodied a tax on vanity, not all of them embodied an investment in the public debt.[69]

Whether as a form of disguised taxation or as a form of borrowing, the sale of fiefs points to the basically fiscal nature of feudalism in Spanish Lombardy. It is in these terms, after all, that contemporaries saw it: the sale of fiefs, as will be recalled, was frankly acknowledged as a fiscal measure intended to generate additional revenue for an impecunious government. And it is in much the same terms that eighteenth-century reformers viewed the feudal system when they set about dismantling it as they did in the days of Maria Theresa and Joseph II.[70] To them the key problem was that of recovering for the government a myriad of small sources of revenue that had been alienated in the past and of providing adequate compensation to fief holders; their task, therefore, was one that required a great deal of careful bookkeeping, but which involved no far-reaching social changes. Not surprisingly, the virtual suppression of feudalism in the State of Milan in the late eighteenth century was carried out not by an outraged peasantry in the blaze of revolution, but by conscientious bureaucrats in the quiet decor of their chambers.

APPENDIX A

UNITS OF MEASUREMENT

These metric equivalents of the units of measurement in use in the State of Milan until the Napoleonic conquest are taken from *Istruzione su le misure e su i pesi che si usano nel Regno d'Italia*, 2nd ed. (Milan, 1806). I have rounded them to the second decimal point.

braccio = 0.59 meter (23.22 inches)

pertica milanese = 0.06 hectare (0.15 acre)

libbra grossa = 0.76 kilogram (1.6 pounds)

brenta (for liquids) = 0.75 hectoliter (19.84 gallons)

moggio (for dry goods) = 1.46 hectoliters (4.17 bushels)

In the Cremona province the pertica measured 0.08 hectare; in the provinces of Como, Lodi, and Pavia the local pertica amounted to approximately 0.07 hectare.

APPENDIX B

MONEY AND PRICES

In the State of Milan all prices, rents, and wages were expressed in the official monetary unit known as *lira imperiale* (L.) and its fractions, the *soldo* (s.) and the denaro (d.); one lira was equal to twenty soldi and one soldo to twelve denari. The lira of Milan was a money of account; actual transactions were effected with a variety of actual coins among which the gold *doppia* (with a content of about 6 grams of gold) and the silver *ducatone* (about thirty-one grams of pure silver) were the most commonly used for large payments. Smaller denominations made largely of copper and worth but a few soldi or denari included *parpagliole, sesini,* and *terlini;* these were used in small everyday transactions. (For a full discussion of the monetary system see Cipolla, *Mouvements monétaires,* from which the information that follows is also taken.)

In the course of the seventeenth century the gold and silver equivalents of the Milanese lira changed. This is indicated by the fact that the exchange rates, in terms of the money of account, of such stable coins as the *doppia* and the *ducatone* registered frequent and significant variations: the doppia was valued L.14 at the beginning of the century and L.23 10s. at the end; the ducatone was rated at L.5 17s. in 1605 and L.8 in 1700. From these rates one can easily determine that the gold equivalent of the lira fell, in the course of the century, from 0.43 grams to 0.25 grams, while its silver equivalent fell from 5.29 grams to 3.87 grams. In other words, the Milanese lira underwent a depreciation of about 40 percent in terms of gold and 25 percent in terms of silver. The year-to-year fluctuations of the lira's silver equivalent are shown in Table 4.

Commodity prices expressed in *soldi* (except for those of bricks, which are in *lire*) are shown in the accompanying figure. All prices are those quoted in Milan, except for veal, the price of which is that quoted in the nearby city of Pavia.

Table 4. Silver equivalent of the Milanese lira, 1605-1700

Year(s)	Silver equivalent (grams)	Year(s)	Silver equivalent (grams)
1605	5.29	1634	5.34
1606-1607	5.16	1635	5.25
1608-1609	5.39	1636	5.08
1610	5.16	1637	5.34
1611	5.39	1638	5.25
1612	5.16	1639-1641	5.16
1613	4.77	1642-1656	5.06
1614	5.16	1657	4.96
1615	4.70	1658-1671	4.42
1616	4.37	1672-1673	4.27
1617	4.03	1674-1675	4.13
1618	3.87	1676-1700	3.87
1619-1633	5.39		

Source: Silver equivalents have been determined on the basis of the annual rates of the ducatone in money of account, as given in Cipolla, *Mouvements monétaires*, pp. 65-67. As the silver content of the ducatone remained unchanged at 31 grams throughout the century, the silver equivalent of the lira in any given year can be known by dividing 31 by the rate of the ducatone in that year. Example: in 1606 the rate being L.6 per ducatone, the silver equivalent of the lira was 31/6 = 5.16 grams.

The units of measurement to which these prices refer are: for wheat bread and veal, the *libbra grossa* (0.76 kilogram); for wine, the *brenta* (0.75 hectoliter); for charcoal, the *moggio milanese* (1.46 hectoliter); for bricks, the *miaro* (one thousand bricks). For cloth it has seemed desirable to juxtapose the two price series as closely as possible in order to facilitate a comparison of their respective trends. Accordingly, while the price of low-grade cloth refers to one *braccio* (0.59 meter), that of high-grade cloth refers to one-third of a *braccio*.

The data on which my figure is based are taken from the following sources: De Maddalena, *Prezzi*, pp. 157-177, for wheat bread, wine, high-grade and low-grade cloth; Sella, *Salari e lavoro*, pp. 131-137, for charcoal and bricks; Zanetti, *Problemi alimentari*, pp. 170-179, for veal.

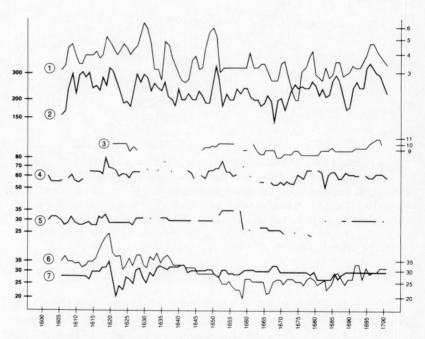

Prices of select commodities in seventeenth-century Lombardy:/
    1, bread; 2, wine; 3, veal; 4, charcoal; 5, bricks; 6, high-
    grade cloth; 7, low-grade cloth.

APPENDIX C

THE ROTATION OF CROPS
IN THE IRRIGATED PLAIN

Farming practices in the irrigated plain are outlined in chapter 1. This sketch can be filled in with more detailed information supplied by the peasants themselves, who answered questions posed to them by government officials in the course of inquests aimed at determining the nature and value of a fief (see the Note on Sources). Our evidence comes from ASM, *Feudi camerali p. a.* (abbreviated as *Fd.*). Although these inquests took place, for the most part, in the mid-seventeenth century, they reflect long-established patterns of cultivation as suggested by the expression, often used by respondents when describing their farming practices, "according to the custom of this land" (*conforme al stilo di questo paese*).

In the Lodi province, for instance, local peasants gave the following information as to the distribution of land between different uses: in one locality, meadows, cereal crops, and flax each covered one-third of the cultivated land; in another, the land was equally divided between meadows on the one hand, and cereals and flax on the other; in the three other villages meadows took up as much as two-thirds of the land, with the remainder under grain and flax (*Fd.* 264/1, "Sommario della qualità delle terre," Codogno district, 28 Sept. 1640; *Fd.* 568, Sigola, 28 Sept. 1640). It should be noted at this point that the terms used in the documents to indicate meadows, namely *prado, pradaria,* or *parte prativa,* do not include natural grassland or pasture; this was known as *pascolo.* And the latter was defined at the time as "uncultivated land [*loco zerbato*] which is never mowed [*nè si sega mai*]" (see Cipolla, "Ripartizione," p. 254 n.). Significantly, in one instance it is specified that while two-thirds of the land are covered by meadows, "there are no pascoli" (*Fd.* 264/3, Gattera, 17 May 1640), a clear indication of the sharp distinction being made between meadows and spontaneous grassland.

The *pradi* or meadows referred to in our sources, then, were manmade or artificial meadows in the sense that they were temporarily planted with grass or clover. More importantly, they formed a link in a rotation sequence in which grass or clover alternated with cereals or other crops. This is unmistakably brought out in one inquest that reads: "meadows are used at times for growing grass and at other times for growing wheat according to the custom of this land" (*Fd.* 544/5, S. Fiorano, 17 May 1617). Another source is even more explicit: "Two-thirds of the land are planted with flax and wheat and about one-third is meadows, and periodically the said arable land is turned into meadows and the meadows are ploughed up and sown with flax and wheat, and this is generally done every three or four years" (*Fd.* 87/7, Bertonico, 24 May 1656). As for the actual planting of the meadows, a description of the method used in northern Italy is provided by Camillo Tarello, the sixteenth-century agronomist, in his celebrated *Ricordo di Agricoltura* (Mantua, 1585), p. 89. "Meadows tend to wear thin and therefore they must be ploughed up in September and put under grain for three to four years, after which meadows must be restored by working the soil and sowing it with vetches mixed with hay seed (*seme del feno*) found in barn sweepings and in the dust that collects in mangers." Elsewhere in his book (pp. 124, 147) Tarello recommends clover (*trifoglio*) for meadows. It is interesting in this context to find large amounts of clover seed (*semenza de trefolio*) being bought on a farm south of Milan in the early seventeenth century (Archivio della Veneranda Fabbrica del Duomo, Milan, *Mandati*, 11 Apr. 1616).

What the exact rotation pattern may have been in the Lodi province, where artificial grasses alternated with grain or flax, is not at once obvious from the documents that have just been quoted, and the question is made more difficult to answer by considerable variations in land use and rotation patterns in each locality. In all of them, however, four main crops are mentioned as part of the rotation sequence: grass, wheat, flax, and millet. Where meadows occupied two-thirds of the land, the full rotation cycle probably spanned seven to nine years, with a particular piece of land remaining under grass for as many as five or six years and being planted with wheat, flax, and millet in three or four successive years—a pattern still practiced in the

Lodi province in the early nineteenth century (see Zaninelli, *Una grande azienda agricola*, pp. 91-93). On the other hand, where meadows claimed but one-third of the land, the full cycle may have spread over six years, of which two were for grass, two for wheat, and one each for flax and millet. An even shorter cycle of merely four years may have been practiced in the Cremona province, if we are to take literally a farmer's words: "For the sake of greater clarity I will say that a man who owns 100 *pertiche* will assign each year 25 of them to meadows, another 25 to flax, and the remaining 50 will be put under wheat or rye, and after harvesting his flax he will sow millet" (*Fd.* 430/3, Grontorto, 28 Aug. 1651).

But whatever rotation pattern was adopted (and local differences in the nature of the soil and the availability of irrigation water no doubt made for a good deal of variation from place to place), the crucial point is that on the best farmland of Lombardy a "green revolution" had taken place and had resulted in the suppression of the fallow and the marriage of arable farming and fodder crops. The beginning date of that revolution is, admittedly, not easy to determine, but it is certain, from what has just been seen, that by the seventeenth century it had become firmly established. It was, in fact, of much older vintage. According to Jones ("Medieval Agrarian Society," p. 375), artificial meadows and their concomitant, the suppression of the fallow, had been around in the Lombard plain since at least the fourteenth century, and this explains why our seventeenth-century sources refer to them as normal, customary elements in the agriculture of the time.

LINEN MAKING IN THE COUNTRYSIDE

The data on linen weaving shown in Table 5 come from the inquests on fiefs (*Fd.*), described in the Note on Sources. The expression "one or more" is used whenever one of the respondents in the inquest identified himself as "linen weaver" (*tessitore di tela*), but provided no further information on whether other weavers lived in his village. When a respondent asserted that there were "some" or "several" weavers, the word "several" has been entered in the table. "Several" has also been used in the few instances in which a respondent simply stated that in his community "linen is manufactured" (*si fanno tele*).

Table 5. Linen weavers in the countryside

Locality	Number of weavers	Date of document	Box number in *Fd.*
Mountain and hill zone (11 localities)			
Albizzate	3	3/30/1633	59
Appiano	several	7/27/1666	55
Arcisate	2 (women)	3/30/1633	59
Bosco Valtravaglia	2 (women)	3/31/1633	619/6
Caronno Ghiringhello	3	3/30/1633	59
Carpesino	1	3/18/1620	281
Castiglione Olona	8	3/30/1633	59
Inarzo	2	3/30/1633	59
Lurago Marinone	several	7/27/1666	55
Ossuccio	1	12/1/1637	217/6
Sumirago	1	3/30/1633	59

(cont.)

Table 5. (cont.)

Locality	Number of weavers	Date of document	Box number in *Fd.*
High plain (5 localities)			
Besnate	2	3/26/1630	90
Brenna	1 or more	6/28/1682	54
Brignano Geradadda	several	3/18/1603	116
Fagnano	5	3/24/1632	244
Porchera (Incino)	1 or more	6/28/1682	54
Low plain (31 localities)			
Bereguardo	1	7/28/1635	84/4
Bertonico	several	5/28/1656	87/7
Biraga	3	9/28/1640	264/1
Caravaggio	several	9/4/1607	140/15
Casalmaiocco	6	11/13/1623	550/13
Castelleone	several	1/20/1651	181/13
Caviaga	1	3/25/1657	75bis
Codogno	1 or more	8/2/1678	213/6
Consordi	5	11/13/1623	550/13
Cornaleto	5	8/19/1649	430/1
Dorno (Lomellina)	5	10/21/1635	240/9
Gattera	1 or more	9/11/1686	264/7
Gombito	8	2/23/1649	430/1
Gualdrasco	1 or more	9/17/1698	276
Landriano	20	1652	288/2
Maleo	1 or more	8/5/1678	320/2
Meleto	1 or more	12/12/1652	345/7
Olevano (Lomellina)	2	5/25/1631	415/3
Paderno (Cremona)	8	8/19/1649	430/1
Porchera (Binasco)	2	3/8/1632	94/7
Quattro Case	2	10/3/1649	154
Roncadello	"most women weave"	10/3/1649	154
Sant' Angelo (Lodi)	several	8/21/1680	530/1
San Bassano (Cremona)	30	8/19/1649	430/1
Santa Cristina (Pavia)	20	11/3/1630	542/6
San Fiorano (Lodi)	several	12/4/1644	545/1
Staffora	several	10/3/1649	154
Trecate (Novara)	12	10/31/1643	594/18
Vicomoscano	6	10/3/1649	154
Villareggio	1 or more	10/30/1670	640
Zorlesco	10	10/30/1632	657/4

NOTES

A NOTE ON SOURCES

With few exceptions, all the primary material used in the preparation of this book was drawn from the Archivio Storico Civico, Milan (ACM) and, to an even greater extent, from the Archivio di Stato, Milan (ASM). The series *Materie*, in the Archivio Storico Civico, proved especially valuable. In the Archivio di Stato I drew on the following series: *Apprensioni, Cancelleria spagnola, Censo p.a., Commercio p.a., Comuni p.a., Deroghe giudiziarie del Senato, Feudi Camerali p.a., Feudi imperiali p.a., Finanza p.a., Fondi camerali p.a., Militare p.a., Miscellanea lombarda, Potenza estere,* and *Uffici regii p.a.* Some of these archival series, notably *Censo, Commercio* and *Finanza*, are well known and have often been tapped by students of the Lombard economy. The series *Feudi Camerali p.a.* (abbreviated as *Fd.*), on the other hand, has generally been ignored by economic historians and yet I found it to be by far the most valuable source of information on economic and social conditions in the countryside.

Feudi Camerali p.a. is composed of close to seven hundred large bundles or boxes (*cartelle*) containing all sorts of documents relative to feudal lordships from the late Middle Ages to the end of the eighteenth century. Since the Spanish government consistently excluded the nine major cities from enfeoffment, only rural communities (*terre*) and market towns (*borghi*) show up in these documents. In this huge mass of material one type of document has proved to be especially useful for a knowledge of economic conditions in the countryside, namely the inquests (*informationi*). These were compiled by officers of the finance ministry (*Magistrato delle Entrate straordinarie*) whenever a rural community or market town was granted or, more commonly, sold in fief, or when a community already enfeoffed reverted to the Crown as a result of the feudal lord having died without issue. In either case the purpose of the inquest was to determine the value of the community to the royal fisc. To that end, explained a legal authority at the beginning of the eighteenth century,

> The *Magistrato* delegates one of its officers . . . and the latter, along with
> a notary, an usher, and a scrivener . . . betakes himself to the locality in

order to collect firsthand information about the quality and revenue of the vacant fief . . . about the existence, if any, of a castle, mansion, or other appurtenances to the fief; about the number of people subject to the feudal lord, their occupation, and their wealth; about the length and breadth of the land and its acreage . . . and about the fertility or barrenness of the land; . . . thereafter he interrogates the collectors or farmers of local taxes and feudal revenues . . . in order to determine how much money they yield . . . Upon returning to Milan, the officer submits a report to his superiors. (Benaglio, *Relazione istorica*, p. 220)

For the seventeenth century I was able to identify inquests relating to 381 communities. Although they all basically follow the format described above, individual inquests vary considerably in length and richness of detail. All of them start with the date and the actual location where the inquest was being conducted, as well as the names of the officials involved and of the individuals (generally petty local officials and older residents) called upon to testify under oath. Questions and answers are introduced with the Latin words *interrogatus* and *respondit* respectively, but the questions and answers themselves are always given in Italian; the answers, coming as they generally do from peasant folks, are often larded with expressions in the Lombard vernacular.

The 381 communities discussed in the seventeenth-century inquests that I have been able to see provide a good cross-section of the State of Milan: not only do they represent a sizable portion of the total, but they are scattered across the length and breadth of the whole state, with 112 communities from the mountain and hill zones, 137 from the high plain, and 132 from the low plain. Moreover, the fact that each became the object of an inquest can be considered purely coincidental, since it merely reflects the accident of a feudal family dying out or the government's decision to raise additional money by selling in fief one or more communities that still happened to be free.

To the student of the rural economy two points raised by the inquiring official are especially instructive: "What crops are grown here?" and "Are there any artisans [artefici]?" From the answers to these two questions a great deal can be learned about farming practices, the allocation of land between different crops, and the presence of handicraft or extractive industries. Unfortunately, not all officials seem to have been equally conscientious, and, while none of them failed to gather information on the number of hearths (*fuochi*), the acreage surrounding a village (*perticato*), and the revenues (*redditi*) raised in it—on the things, that is, which were indispensable for the determination of the price of a fief—a good many did not bother to inquire about crops and the presence of artisans. These omissions, of course, somewhat reduce the value of our sample and make broad conclusions about an entire zone the more tentative. At any rate, it should be obvious that when any mention of artisans is simply omitted, this does not mean that the village in question harbored no artisans at all.

ABBREVIATIONS

ACM	Archivio Storico Civico, Milan
Annales. E. S. C.	*Annales. Economies, Sociétés, Civilizations*
ASI	*Archivio Storico Italiano*
ASL	*Archivio Storico Lombardo*
ASM	Archivio di Stato, Milan
d.	denaro
EcHR	*Economic History Review*
Fd.	*Feudi Camerali p. a.* in ASM
FEHE	*Fontana Economic History of Europe*, ed. C. M. Cipolla, 4 vols. (London-Glasgow: Collins, 1972-1974).
JEH	*Journal of Economic History*
L.	lira imperiale of Milan
NRS	*Nuova Rivista Storica*
p. a.	parte antica
RSI	*Rivista Storica Italiana*
SdM	*Storia di Milano.* 16 vols. (Milan: Fondazione Treccani degli Alfieri, 1953-1966)

I. THE PARADISE OF CHRISTENDOME

1. Giovanni Botero, *Le Relationi universali* (Brescia, 1595), pp. 52, 148.
2. William Thomas, *The History of Italy*, ed. G. B. Parks (Ithaca, N.Y.: Cornell University Press, 1963), pp. 112-113. Originally published in 1549.
3. M. Tabarrini, "Relazione inedita dello Stato di Milano di G. B. Guarini," *ASI*, 3rd ser., 5 (1867): 14. Guarini served as diplomatic agent of the Duke of Ferrara in Milan from 1583 to 1592.
4. Michel de Montaigne, *Journal de voyage en Italie en 1580 et 1581*, ed. M. Rat (Paris: Garnier, 1942), pp. 230-231.
5. "Relazione di Milano, 1583," in *Relazioni degli ambasciatori veneti al Senato*, ed. Eugenio Alberi, 2nd ser., 5 (Florence, 1841): 480.
6. Quoted in Dante Zanetti, *Problemi alimentari in una economia preindustriale: Cereali a Pavia dal 1398 al 1700* (Turin: Boringhieri, 1964), p. 25.
7. Francesco Scoto (Schott), *Itinerario overo nova descrittione de viaggi principali d'Italia* (Venice, 1672), p. 155. First edition in Latin in 1600.
8. Sir Thomas Sherley, "Discours of the Turkes" (1607), ed. E. Denison Ross, *Camden Miscellany*, 16 (1936): 36.
9. Thomas Coryate, *Crudities* (Glasgow: MacLehose, 1905), 1: 238. First edition, 1611.
10. See K. J. Beloch, *Bevölkerungsgeschichte Italiens*, (Berlin: De Gruyter, 1961) 3: 169; Carlo M. Cipolla, "Four Centuries of Italian Demographic Development," in *Population in History*, ed. D. V. Glass and

D. E. C. Eversley (London: Arnold, 1965), pp. 570-573; Roger Mols, "Population in Europe, 1500-1700," in *FEHE*, 2: 38-39; and Fernand Braudel, *Capitalism and Material Life, 1400-1800* (London: Weidenfeld & Nicholson, 1973), p. 29.

11. On the difficulty of drawing a line between city, town, and village in past time see Philip J. Jones, "Medieval Agrarian Society in Its Prime: Italy," in *Cambridge Economic History of Europe*, vol. 1, ed. M. M. Postan (Cambridge: Cambridge University Press, 1966), pp. 349-350; Braudel, *Capitalism*, 374-377. According to a seventeenth-century source, Milan was a community "of artificers who support themselves exclusively with their manufactures" (ASM, *Commercio p. a.*, 153/2d, doc. of 1 Sept. 1631): despite the hyperbole, we have little trouble in classifying Milan as urban. But what can be done with Alessandria, a "city" in the legal sense of the term and yet one of which the same source claimed that in it "nearly everyone owns some land from which they draw their sustenance"? The market town of Gallarate, on the other hand, with a population of about 2,300 souls was "urban" in terms of its economic functions: among its 470 heads of household, only 92 were listed as farmers or peasants; 146 were listed as craftsmen, 84 as shop-keepers, 64 as merchants, and 30 as professionals (data drawn from Archivio della Curia Arcivescovile, Milan, *Archivio spirituale*, Sez.X, Stato delle anime di Gallarate, 1574).

12. On the administrative structure of the State of Milan the chief authority still remains Alessandro Visconti, *La pubblica amministrazione nello Stato di Milano durante il predominio straniero, 1541-1746* (Rome: Atheneum, 1913). A vivid account of the relationship and tensions between a *città* and its *contado* is provided in D. Olivero Colombo, "Mercanti e popolari nella Vigevano del primo Cinquecento (1536-1550)," *RSI*, 85 (1973): 116-127.

13. Data on the size of the Lombard cities have been derived from: Beatrice Besta, "La popolazione di Milano nel periodo della dominazione spagnola," in *Proceedings of the International Congress for the Studies on Population (Rome 1931)* (Rome: Istituto Poligrafico dello Stato, 1933), 1: 593; Domenico Sella, "Premesse demografiche ai censimenti austriaci" in *SdM*, 12: 459-478; Ugo Meroni, *Cremona fedelissima*, vol. 10 of *Annali della Biblioteca Governativa e Libreria Civica di Cremona* (Cremona: Atheneum, 1957), p. 6; Giuseppe Aleati, *La popolazione di Pavia durante il dominio spagnolo* (Milan: Guiffrè, 1957), p.22; Giuseppe Mira, *Aspetti dell'economia comasca all'inizio dell'età moderna* (Como: Cavalleri, 1939), p. 22; Giuseppe Agnelli, "Lodi e territorio nel Seicento," *ASL*, 3rd ser., 6 (1896): 81; Bruno Caizzi, "Economia e finanza a Vigevano nel Cinque e nel Seicento," *NRS*, 39 (1955): 359; and Salvatore Pugliese, *Le condizioni economiche e finanziarie della Lombardia nella prima metà del secolo XVIII* (Turin: Bocca, 1924), p. 60.

14. Unless otherwise indicated, this description of the Lombard country-side is based on the following authorities: Pugliese, *Le condizioni economiche*,

ch. 1; Gino Luzzatto, *Storia economica dell'età moderna e contemporanea,* 4th ed. (Padua: Cedam, 1955), 1: 88-96; Emilio Sereni, *Storia del paesaggio agrario italiano,* 3rd ed. (Bari: Laterza, 1972), especially chs. 39, 40, 55, 64; Carlo M. Cipolla, "Per la storia delle terre della 'bassa' lombarda," in *Studi in onore di Armando Sapori* (Milan: Cisalpino, 1957), pp. 665-672; D. F. Dowd, "The Economic Expansion of Lombardy, 1300-1500: A Study in Political Stimuli to Economic Change," *JEH,* 21 (1961): 143-160; Aldo De Maddalena, "Il mondo rurale italiano nel Cinque e Seicento," *RSI,* 76 (1964): 349-426; C. T. Smith, *An Historical Geography of Europe before 1800* (New York: Praeger, 1967), pp. 243-245, 524-528; Jones, "Medieval Agrarian Society," pp. 359, 363, 375, 382-383. Although primarily devoted to the period after 1800, the following have also proved very useful: J. M. Houston, *The Western Mediterranean World: An Introduction to Its Regional Landscapes* (New York: Praeger, 1967), pp. 380-384, 422-433, 485-490; and K. R. Greenfield, *Economics and Liberalism in the Risorgimento: A Study of Nationalism in Lombardy, 1814-1848,* rev. ed. (Baltimore: Johns Hopkins University Press, 1965), pt. 1, ch. 1.

15. Quoted in Gauro Coppola, "L'agricoltura di alcune pievi della pianura irrigua milanese nei dati catastali della metà del secolo XVI," in *Contributi dell'Istituto di Storia economica e sociale dell'Università Cattolica del S. Cuore,* 1 (1973): 284.

16. Ibid.

17. This expression, used by E. Le Roy Ladurie, *Le territoire de l'historien* (Paris: Gallimard, 1973), p. 164, in his discussion of the progress of farming and the disappearance of the fallow in the Netherlands as early as the fifteenth century, seems appropriate to Lombardy too.

18. See Coppola, "L'agricoltura di alcune pievi," p. 264, for the plain south of Milan; Carlo M. Cipolla, "Ripartizione delle colture nel Pavese secondo le 'misure territoriali' della metà del '500," *Studi di Economia e Statistica dell'Università di Catania,* 1 (1950-51): 254-257, for the area north and east of Pavia. For the Lodi and Cremona provinces see Appendix C. By 1600 rice, too, was grown in the irrigated plain, although still on a modest scale. See Aldo De Maddalena, *Prezzi e aspetti di mercato in Milano durante il secolo XVII* (Milan: Malfasi, 1949), pp. 43-45.

19. *Fd.* 449/5 (Piovera), 13 Oct. 1650; 480/2 (Redabue), 25 Apr. 1643. Similar conditions obtained in Lomellina: see *Fd.* 113/22 (Breme), 23 July 1653, and 240/9 (Dorno), 21 Oct. 1635. The abbreviation *Fd.* stands for ASM, *Feudi camerali p. a.;* the number following it refers to the file (*cartella*) in that series; the number after the bar (/) refers to the folder, if any, inside the file. Unless otherwise indicated, all documents in *Fd.* are inquests (*informationi*) and only the locality involved will be mentioned, followed by the date of the inquest itself. The nature of the inquests is discussed in the Note on Sources.

20. In the hill zone of Lombardy fallowing was generally practiced for

one or more years during the late Middle Ages; see Pierre Toubert, "Les statuts communaux et l'histoire des campagnes lombardes au XIVe siècle," *Mélanges d'archéologie et d'histoire de l'Ecole française de Rome*, 72 (1960): 486.

21. Pugliese, *Le condizioni economiche*, p. 64.

22. Sharp differences in the size of holdings and in the form of tenure were, of course, of long standing. For the medieval period see Jones, "Medieval Agrarian Society," pp. 412-413; George Duby, *Rural Economy and Country Life in the Medieval West*, trans. C. Postan (Columbia, S.C.: University of South Carolina Press, 1968), pp. 274, 324; and Toubert, "Les statuts communaux," pp. 450-451. For the sixteenth century see Fernand Braudel, *The Mediterranean and the Mediterranean World in the Age of Philip II*, trans. Sian Reynolds (New York: Harper, 1972), 1: 75; and Coppola, "L'agricoltura di alcune pievi," pp. 224-225. For a general discussion, see Giorgio Giorgetti, *Contadini e proprietari nell'Italia moderna. Rapporti di produzione e contratti agrari dal secolo XVI a oggi* (Turin: Einaudi, 1974), ch. 2. For details on the "mixed contracts" (fixed rents payable in grain and a share of all tree crops) in the hill zone and the high plain, see Bruno Caizzi, *Il Comasco sotto il dominio spagnolo. Saggio di storia economica e sociale* (Como: Centro Lariano per gli Studi economici, 1955), pp. 114-116. In the low plain, nine-year leases payable in money and in which the tenant provided his own movable stocks (seed grain, implements, livestock) seem to have been prevalent; examples of large estates so leased in the Lodi province are found in *Fd*. 633/15 (Vidardo), 13 Oct. 1613; 657/4 (Zorlesco), 30 Oct. 1632; 360/1 (Mirabello), 20 May 1655; 216/1 (Codogno), 27 Jan. 1679; in the Cremona province, *Fd*. 47 (Annicco), 1640. Even in the low plain, however, some form of share-tenancy was occasionally practiced: the farm "Musella" near Sant'Angelo Lodigiano was sharecropped in 1677 and let for money in 1680 (*Fd*. 527/1, 26 Jan. 1677 and 21 Aug. 1680). Other examples and the reasons behind the switch from one type of contract to another will be discussed in Chapter VI.

23. On the economy of the mountain region in general and on migration in particular see Braudel, *The Mediterranean*, 1:25-52, 334-338; also Toubert, "Les statuts communaux," pp. 488-501. On migration from the Lombard Alps see Domenico Sella, "Au dossier des migrations montagnardes: L'example de la Lombardie au XVIIe siècle," in *Mélanges en l'honneur de Fernand Braudel* (Toulouse: Privat, 1973), 1:547-554.

24. ASM, *Comuni p.a.*, 83 (Val Formazza), 2 Sept. 1581. Of Valsassina an eighteenth-century writer remarked that it was "rich in cattle which in winter are driven to the plain around Milan to be fed hay and to produce cheese and meat" (C. G. Reina, *Descrizione corografica e storica di Lombardia* [Milan, 1714], p. 83).

25. ASM, *Miscellanea lombarda*, IX, doc. 84 of 15 Apr. 1637.

26. *Fd*. 25 (Bognanco), 3 May 1655.

27. ASM, *Comuni p. a.*, 83 (Valtorta), 13 July 1572.

28. *Fd.* 627/4 (Vedeseta), 11 Sept. 1652.

29. Archivio della Curia Arcivescovile, Milan, *Archivio spirituale*, Sez. X, vol. 18, Stato delle anime di Valle dell'Olmo, 1606.

30. Sella, "Au dossier des migrations," pp. 549-550.

31. Braudel, *The Mediterranean*, 1:51.

32. *Fd.* 303/6 (Luino), 20 Feb. 1588; 619/6 (Bosco Valtravaglia), 31 Mar. 1633.

33. Sella, "Au dossier des migrations," p. 548.

34. *Fd.* 281 (Incino), 18 Mar. 1620. According to Giuseppe Ripamonti, *Historia patriae* (Milan, 1641), book 7, p. 209, the Brianza was then known as "the wine cellar of the City of Milan." The lower reaches of the Alpine valleys, too, were net exporters of wine. From Valdossola wine was shipped to the Vallais (*Fd.* 613/11, "1620. Notizie intorno alla Valle d'Ossola"). Vineyards also loomed large along the shore of Lake Como (Caizzi, *Il Comasco*, p. 144). In Bellagio, for example, it was reported in 1601 that cereal production fell far short of local needs, but that "the mainstay" of the village economy "consisted of wine and chestnuts . . . and some olive oil" (*Fd.* 81/7, "Copia relationis," June 1601).

35. Three examples from the high plain just north of Gallarate: in the 1630s Albizzate reportedly produced a surplus of rye that was marketed either in Varese or in Milan (*Fd.* 59, 30 Mar. 1633); in Fagnano, a few miles to the south and east, cereal production was estimated at twice local consumption (*Fd.* 244, 24 Mar. 1632); in nearby Besnate, as one local farmer put it, "the grain which is turned over to the landlords as rent payment is for the most part sold to merchants by the landlords themselves, and this proves that the grain we grow is over and above our own needs" (*Fd.* 90/5, 26 Mar. 1630).

36. Such was the case of Busto Arsizio where, according to a six-teenth-century informant, "the soil, for lack of water, is totally barren and bears no crop unless great efforts be expended in working it and unless it be manured at great cost . . . The people of this community, although they all own some land, make a living by plying diverse trades, some drawing wire, others weaving fustians and other cotton fabrics" (*Fd.* 129/4, 10 Mar. 1596).

37. ASM, *Commercio p. a.*, 228, "Consulta" of 1 July 1606: "On the basis of information supplied by the officials of the Excise (*Dazio della Mercanzia*), the average annual output of silk is of one million *libre*, to wit 300,000 from the Duchy of Milan, 150,000 from the Lodi province, 350,000 from the provinces of Pavia (Lomellina included), Tortona, and Alessandria, 100,000 from the province of Vigevano, and 100,000 from those of Novara, Como, and Cremona; this output is turned into cash [*si suol ridurre in contanti*] two or three months after it is produced." These figures are obviously very rough estimates and we have no way of testing their accuracy. All we can say is that one million *libre* (or about 330,000 kilograms) is not an unrealistic figure: at mid-eighteenth century, after the loss of the provinces

west of the Ticino river, the State of Milan produced a little over 200,000 kilograms of raw silk a year (see Chapter 7). Silk was weighed in *libre piccole* of 0.33 kilograms.

38. As indicated in the preceding note, the province or duchy of Milan was the largest producer of silk around 1600; within that province the northwestern district around Varese first witnessed the diffusion of the mulberry tree in the sixteenth century (Leopoldo Giampaolo, ed., *La cronaca varesina di Giulio Tatto (1540-1620)* [Varese: Società Storica Varesina, 1954], pp. xvii, xxix). In the high plain and hill zone north of Milan the mulberry tree spread in the next century (Sergio Zaninelli, *Vita economica e sociale,* vol. 3 of *Storia di Monza e della Brianza,* ed. A. Bosisio and G. Vismara [Milan: Polifilo, 1969]: 36,66).

39. Caizzi, "Economia e finanza," p. 360, for Vigevano. For Olevano, *Fd.* 415/3 (Olevano), 25 May 1631: "most villagers own small holdings . . . and hold larger ones as tenants."

40. *Fd.* 317/1 (Maleo), 19 Sept. 1644; similar conditions still obtained some thirty years later: *Fd.* 320/2 (Maleo), 5 Aug. 1678.

41. Cipolla, "Ripartizione delle colture," pp. 258-259.

42. Fynes Moryson, *An Itinerary* (Glasgow: MacLehose, 1907-08), 4:84. Moryson traveled between 1605 and 1617.

43. On grain exports to the Swiss Confederates see Federico Chabod, "L'età di Carlo V," in *SdM,* 9:198, 270; and De Maddalena, "Il mondo rurale italiano," p. 370. The political significance of those exports was recognized by a Venetian ambassador to Spain when he wrote (in 1602) that the Swiss kept on good terms with the State of Milan "because they are dependent on it for their grain, salt, and all other necessities" (*Relazioni degli Stati europei lette al Senato dagli ambasciatori veneti nel secolo decimosettimo,* ed. Nicolò Barozzi and Guglielmo Berchet, 1st ser., 1 [Venice, 1856]:103). In normal years grain from Spanish Lombardy also found a market in Venetian territory (Archivio di Stato, Venice, *Collegio, relazioni,* busta 35, 8 Feb. 1600).

44. These figures are very rough estimates based on a per capita consumption of grain of about 650 grams a day, as calculated by Zanetti, *Problemi alimentari,* pp. 60-62, for seventeenth-century Pavia. A population of about 120,000 was thus likely to require something like 28,000 metric tons of grain per year. On the assumption (to be discussed later) that good land under crop could yield at least one ton of grain per hectare, it would take 28,000 hectares to produce that amount.

45. The figures are found in ACM, *Materie,* 262, printed doc. of 19 July 1593, "Comparizione dei Sindici della Città di Milano a diffesa delli Mercanti." It is, of course, very hard to translate the number of beef cattle into actual weight of meat as so little is known about the average weight of cattle at the time. According to Giorgio Doria, *Uomini e terre di un borgo collinare dal XVI al XVIII secolo* (Milan: Giuffrè, 1968), p. 57, the largest cattle in the Apennine region barely reached 200 kilograms on the hoof, as

opposed to 700 kilograms in our day; one-year-old calves, which today would normally weigh 245 kilograms on the hoof, weighed 60 kilograms at best in the seventeenth century. Since the total number of cattle slaughtered, as given in our 1593 source, includes 7,050 cows and 20,436 calves, it is not unreasonable to estimate their total weight at about 2,600,000 kilograms and their meat equivalent at about half that amount. For a city of 120,000 this would give an annual per capita consumption of 11 kilograms of beef and veal.

46. *Fd.* 260/8 (Lachiarella), 1607; 344/16 (Melegnano), 12 Aug. 1600; 482/5b (Riozzo), 13 Jan. 1616; 542/4 (Santa Cristina), 24 Nov. 1621; 544/5 (San Fiorano), 3 Feb. 1617.

47. *Fd.* 555/4 (San Vito), 21 Dec. 1627. Of Corte Madama too it was said that flax "brings large profits to the villagers" (*Fd.* 226, 21 May 1607).

48. *Fd.* 153/11, "Relatione di Casalmaggiore," 18 Apr. 1618; see also *Fd.* 154, 4 Oct. 1649 for a reference to an early and unsuccessful attempt at raising livestock in that area.

49. For the late medieval period when a number of small market towns enjoyed a period of exceptional prosperity see Giuseppe Mira, *Le fiere lombarde nei secoli XIV-XVI: Prime indagini* (Como: Centro Lariano per gli studi economici, 1955).

50. *Fd.* 613/11, "Notizie intorno alla Valle d'Ossola," 1620.

51. *Fd.* 258/5, "Relatione sopra il feudo di Gallarate," 10 Apr. 1578. The commercial and manufacturing orientation of Gallarate is borne out by the 1574 listing of inhabitants (*stato delle anime*) referred to in note 11.

52. *Fd.* 140/15 (Caravaggio), 4 Sept. 1607.

53. *Fd.* 544/5 (San Fiorano), 3 Feb. 1617.

54. ASM, *Militare p. a.*, 165, "Bando generale di tutti i Francesi e suoi aderenti," 11 Oct. 1667, and "Lista de Forastieri che si ritrovano . . . a Castelnuovo Bocca d'Adda," 22 Oct. 1667; ibid., 165 bis, doc. of 13 Jan. 1674, and report of the *podestà* in Lodi of 20 Dec. 1673, concerning a number of French *resegotti* (sawyers). On the seasonal migration of farm laborers, sawyers, and hemp combers from Dauphiny and the Lyonnais into northern Italy at the time, see Henry de Boulainvilliers, *Etat de la France* (London, 1737), 5: 497 and 6: 19; also Raoul Blanchard, *Les Alpes occidentales* (Grenoble: Arthaud, 1952), 5, pt. 2: 743-744. Several migrant sawyers and hemp combers from the Lyons province were reported in or near Pavia in 1667 (ASM, *Militare p. a.*, "Bando generale . . . ," 1667).

55. On iron mining in Valsassina see Giuseppe Arrigoni, *Notizie storiche della Valsassina* (Milan, 1840), pp. 306-307; Amintore Fanfani, "L'industria mineraria lombarda durante il dominio spagnolo," in his *Saggi di storia economica italiana* (Milan: Vita e Pensiero, 1936), p. 175; Armando Frumento, *Imprese lombarde nella storia della siderurgia italiana*, vol. 2 (Milan: Società Acciaierie Falck, 1958), especially ch. 4; Domenico Sella, "The Iron Industry in Italy, 1500-1650," in *Schwerpunkte der Eisengewinnung und Eisenverarbeitung in Europa 1500-1650*, ed. H. Kellenbenz (Cologne-Vienna: Boehlau,

1974), p. 95. On gold, copper, and silver mines see Fanfani, "L'industria mineraria," 169-174.

56. Frumento, *Imprese lombarde*, 2: 61, 63, 65.

57. Carlo M. Cipolla, "Per la storia della popolazione lombarda nel secolo XVI" in *Studi in onore di Gino Luzzatto* (Milan: Giuffrè, 1950), 2: 153. In 1541 out of a total of seventy-four heads of family, twenty-five were listed as needle makers (*agugiari*). In the early eighteenth century Concorezzo was still renowned for its needles (Reina, *Descrizione corografica*, p. 96).

58. Luigi Ferrario, *Busto Arsizio: Notizie storico-statistiche* (Busto Arsizio, 1864), p. 54. According to a sixteenth-century source (*Fd.* 129/4, 10 Mar. 1569), "the inhabitants of the said *borgo* are all people who, although they may own some land, earn their living either drawing iron wire or weaving."

59. *Fd.* 303/6 (Luino), 20 Mar. 1588: the making of lime (*cozer la calcina*) is referred to as a major activity in Valtravaglia. See also ASM, *Autografi, Piazzeforti*, 230/3 for an undated (but clearly late sixteenth-century) petition by a contractor who was expected to supply lime for the castle of Milan: "to that end he has hired several workmen in Angera, Arona, Ispra, and Valtravaglia on Lake Maggiore who quarry the stone and make lime in the aforesaid localities."

60. Vermezzo, Gorgonzola, Crescenzago, and Cassano are mentioned as sources of supply for bricks intended for the construction of the Milan cathedral, in Archivio della Veneranda Fabbrica del Duomo, Milan, *Mandati*, under the following dates: 28 June 1603, 8 Aug. 1617, 10 Jan. 1650, and 12 Oct. 1684. According to a 1581 survey there were three brickmakers in Abbiategrasso; see Ambrogio Palestra, *Storia di Abbiategrasso* (Milan: Banca Popolare, 1956), p. 166. Bricks were also produced in Soncino; see Francesco Galantino, *Storia di Soncino con documenti* (Milan, 1869), 3: 389.

61. Archivio della Curia Arcivescovile, Milan, *Archivio Spirituale*, Sez. X, Stato delle anime di Boffalora, 1586.

62. Palestra, *Storia di Abbiategrasso*, p. 166.

63. Caizzi, *Il Comasco*, p. 101.

64. For the 1540s see Cipolla, "Per la storia della popolazione," 152-153; for the early seventeenth century, G. M. Tridi, *Informatione del danno proceduto a Sua Maestà* (probably printed in 1641), 10.

65. ASM, *Commercio p. a.*, 199, memorandum of 16 May 1647.

66. ACM, *Materie*, 571, doc. of 1 Mar. 1613: Lissone had 110 looms, Muggiò 13, Vedano 11, Desio 6.

67. *Fd.* 281, "relazione" on Incino, 18 Mar. 1620; for Lissone see preceding note.

68. Fustians were, as a rule, made entirely of cotton; see Franco Borlandi, "Futainiers et futaines dans l'Italie du Moyen Age" in *Eventail de l'histoire vivante: Hommage à Lucien Febvre* (Paris: Colin, 1953), 2: 135. *Bombasine*, on the other hand, had a linen warp and a cotton weft (ACM, *Ma-*

terie, 428/11, doc. of 30 July 1653).

69. According to Pio Bondioli, *Origini dell'industria cotoniera a Busto Arsizio* (Varese: Tipografica Varese, 1936), p. 11, the cotton industry there had its beginnings in the early fourteenth century, but did not experience a rapid growth until the sixteenth century. Writing in 1612, a local chronicler claimed that in Busto Arsizio "every able bodied man earns his living by plying some crafts . . . and even women and girls are busy spinning either flax or cotton; a great many of them prepare the warp, while others sort out and beat with sticks the cotton . . . which others weave and others dye in diverse colors." He went on to say that at the time the largest industry was wiredrawing "as it employs a larger number of people." Antonio Crespi Castoldi, *La Storia di Busto Arsizio e le Relazioni* (Busto Arsizio: Tipografia Orfanotrofio Civico, 1927), pp. 118-119.

70. Carlo M. Cipolla, "I precedenti economici," in *SdM,* 8: 339, points out that, although some fine linen was manufactured in Milan, the industry remained predominantly rural. Some Lombard linen was no doubt exported in late medieval times: Professor Maureen F. Mazzaoui has kindly brought to my attention a mention of Lombard linen passing through the Genoese customs in the early fifteenth century, in D. Giuffrè ed., *Liber Institutionum Cabellarum Veterum* (Milan, 1967), pp. 23-24.

71. Coryate, *Crudities,* 1: 254. In the early seventeenth century linen or flax in skeins were exported in large quantities from the Lodi province, according to Agnelli, "Lodi e territorio," p. 85.

72. *Fd.* 140/15 (Caravaggio), 4 Sept. 1607. At the time Salò was well known for its sewing yarn. See Ottavio Rossi, *Le Memorie bresciane* (Brescia, 1616), p. 214.

73. ASM, *Commercio p. a.,* 257, "Memoriale delli Abbati de Mercanti d'oro argento e seta" of 24 Feb. 1596.

74. In an age in which merchants often controlled industrial production through the putting-out system, *mercimonio* covered both commercial and industrial activities. As the cloth merchants of Milan explained in a 1554 statement, "it is well known that our *mercimonio* and trade (*trafego*) . . . consists for the most part of the manual work and industry of people, inasmuch as most raw materials in our business are brought in by foreigners from diverse parts and what is purchased from us goes to pay for the manufacture of cloth" (quoted in Caterina Santoro, *La Matricola dei mercanti di lana sottile di Milano* [Milan: Giuffrè, 1940], p. 190). On the putting-out system as practiced in the Milan textile industries, see Ettore Verga, "Le corporazioni delle industrie tessili in Milano: loro rapporti e conflitti nei secoli XVI e XVII," *ASL,* 3rd ser., 19 (1903): 66.

75. Giuseppe Aleati and Carlo M. Cipolla, "Aspetti e problemi dell'economia milanese e lombarda nei secoli XVI e XVII" in *SdM,* 11: 378-388: the total assessed value of the *mercimonio* (trade and manufacturing) for the whole State of Milan stood at L.45,404,000; of this total, L.29,512,000 represented Milan's share in the production of commercial services and manu-

factured goods. In the city itself the guild of "silk and gold merchants" was assessed for L.6,661,000 or about 15 percent of the statewide total and 22 percent of the city's assessment. Both the silk industry and the manufacture of gold thread had been firmly established in Milan at least since the fifteenth century; see Gino Barbieri, *Economia e politica nel Ducato di Milano, 1386-1535* (Milan: Vita e Pensiero, 1938), pp. 169, 190.

76. Aleati and Cipolla, "Aspetti e problemi," p. 389; Luzzatto, *Storia economica*, 1: 121 (in 1593 the total value of silk fabrics and gold thread produced in Milan was reported at 1,700,000 scudi; with the scudo at L.6, this meant L.10,200,000); ASM, *Commercio p. a.*, 228, "Consulta" of 1 July 1606.

77. Coryate, *Crudities*, 1: 247.

78. José-Gentil Da Silva, *Banque et crédit en Italie au XVIIIe siècle* (Paris: Klincksieck, 1969), 1: 264 (for exports to Poland and Hungary); Cesare Cantù, *La Lombardia nel secolo XVII. Ragionamenti* (Milan, 1854), p. 64 (for a quotation from Ludovico Guicciardini's famous description of the Low Countries); and Moryson, *Itinerary*, 4: 21: "The Germans . . . receive all kinds of silkes from Italy, whereof they use little quantity for their owne apparell, but send great store over land to those cities of the sea-coast where the English Merchants reside, to be sold unto them."

79. Ettore Verga, "Le leggi suntuarie e la decadenza dell'industria tessile in Milano, 1565-1750," *ASL*, 3rd ser., 13 (1900): 61.

80. Richard Gascon, *Grand commerce et vie urbaine au XVIe siècle: Lyon et ses marchands* (Paris-The Hague: Mouton, 1971), 1: 108-112.

81. The figure of 4,549 "pieces" or cloths in G. Frattini, *Storia e statistica dell'industria manifatturiera in Lombardia* (Milan, 1856), p. 32, is derived from the celebrated assessment of 1580 (*estimo Pigliasco*). The accuracy of the figure has been confirmed to me by Professor Giovanni Vigo who is currently working on a study of the *estimo*; he has also informed me that 3,195 of those cloths were shipped out of the city, while the rest were retailed in the city itself.

82. See Aleati and Cipolla, "Aspetti e problemi," p. 388: in 1580 the wool merchants were assessed for L.3,509,000, or about half as much as the silk merchants. It should be noted that in the first half of the fifteenth century, at a time when the silk industry was still in its infancy, the wool industry had held first place in Milan (Barbieri, *Economia e politica*, pp. 230-231).

83. In 1580, 3,575 broadcloths and 839 pieces of lower-grade fabrics were exported from Como (Mira, *Aspetti dell'economia comasca*, p. 157). Around 1550, Vigevano, with a population of about 5,000, could boast forty-one cloth manufacturers and a total output of perhaps 1,300 cloths a year (Olivero Colombo, "Mercanti e popolari," pp. 134, 162).

84. Fustians were all-cotton fabrics, *bombasine* were mixed cotton and flax (see note 68); *mezzelane* were a low-priced fabric mixing wool and flax (Maureen F. Mazzaoui, "L'organizzazione delle industrie tessili nei secoli XIII e XIV: i cotonieri veronesi," *Studi storici veronesi Luigi Simeoni*, 18-19 [1968-69]: 15).

85. Maureen F. Mazzaoui, "The Cotton Industry in Northern Italy in the

late Middle Ages: 1150-1450," *JEH*, 30 (1972): 285. At the time Milan, too, was a major center of the fustian industry, but had long passed its prime.

86. Meroni, *Cremona*, p. 15. By then the making of fustians had virtually died out in Milan.

87. See Agnelli, "Lodi e territorio," p. 86; Costantino Baroni, "La maiolica antica a Lodi," *ASL*, 6th ser., 8 (1931): 443-446; Meroni, *Cremona*, pp. 14-15; Giuseppe Aleati and Carlo M. Cipolla, "Il trend economico nello Stato di Milano durante i secoli XVI e XVII: il caso di Pavia," *Bollettino della Società Pavese di Storia Patria*, 49-50 (1950): 6-8; Caizzi, *Il Comasco*, p. 84.

88. ACM, *Materie*, 737, doc. of 23 Oct. 1606.

89. In the sixteenth century the French army relied heavily on Milan for its supplies of harness, arms, and armor (Gascon, *Grand commerce*, 1: 111); around 1600 the Duke of Rohan asserted that "qui veut avoir de belles armes, de belles étoffes, de beaux harnais de chevaux . . . il n'en faut point chercher ailleurs si Milan n'en fournit" (quoted in Cantù, *La Lombardia*, p. 22). In the early sixteenth century Milan already enjoyed a reputation for its sumptuously ornate carriages (Luzzatto, *Storia economica*, 1: 96).

90. On the Brescian arms industry, see Domenico Sella, "Industrial Production in Seventeenth-Century Italy: A Reappraisal," *Explorations in Entrepreneurial History*, n.s., 6 (1969): 243 and the bibliography cited therein.

91. On the export of firearms see Braudel, *The Mediterranean*, 2: 839. On the gunsmiths' guild see Jacopo Gelli, *Gli archibugiari milanesi: Industria, commercio, uso delle armi da fuoco in Lombardia* (Milan: Hoepli, 1905). On the armor industry, Bruno Thomas and Ortwin Gamber, "L'arte milanese dell'armatura," in *SdM*, 11: 700, 702.

92. Quoted in Verga, "Le leggi suntuarie," p. 62.

93. Alberi, ed., *Relazioni*, 5: 480.

94. Coryate, *Crudities*, 1: 247.

II. OLD CONSTRAINTS AND NEW PRESSURES

1. On the Milan guilds see Verga, "Le corporazioni"; also Chapter V.

2. On "subsistence crises" see Jean Meuvret's classic article "Les crises de subsistance et la démographie de la France d'Ancien Régime" in his *Etudes d'histoire économique* (Paris: Colin, 1971), pp. 271-278. The chronically precarious balance between food and mouths to feed in early modern Lombardy is discussed in Zanetti, *Problemi alimentari*, 13-23.

3. Zanetti, *Problemi alimentari*, table A; De Maddalena, *Prezzi*, p. 96.

4. See Cipolla, "Four Centuries," p. 573.

5. See Paul Bairoch, "Agriculture and the Industrial Revolution, 1700-1914," in *FEHE*, 3: 461.

6. Ester Boserup, *The Conditions of Agricultural Growth: The Economics of Agrarian Change under Population Pressure* (Chicago: Aldine, 1965), p. 30.

7. Data for the 1720s in Mario Romani, "I rendimenti dei terreni in Lombardia dal periodo delle riforme al 1859," in *Studi in onore di Amintore Fanfani* (Milan: Giuffrè, 1962), 5: 570. For the early nineteenth century, Pugliese, *Condizioni economiche*, p. 46. Pugliese's data for the 1720s are now superseded by Romani's.

8. Aldo De Maddalena, "Rural Europe 1500-1750," in *FEHE*, 2: 343, shows yields ranging from 0.2 metric tons per hectare in the hill zone of Lombardy to 0.6 in the plain in the second half of the sixteenth century. According to a 1667 document (published in Galantino, *Storia di Soncino*, 3: 419), from one *pertica* (0.08 hectares) of irrigated land one could expect 5 *staia cremonesi* (about 122 kilograms) of wheat; in other words, approximately 1.5 metric tons per hectare.

9. Yields of up to 1.5 tons per hectare were occasionally reported in the most fertile areas of northern France in the seventeenth century, according to Jean Jacquart, "French Agriculture in the Seventeenth Century," in *Essays in European Economic History, 1500-1800*, ed. Peter Earle (Oxford: Clarendon Press, 1974), p. 171. On the other hand, at mid-sixteenth century the clay soils of the plain near Modena produced a mere 0.2-0.3 tons of wheat per hectare; see Gian Luigi Basini, *L'uomo e il pane: Risorse, consumi e carenze alimentari della popolazione modenese nel Cinque e Seicento* (Milan: Giuffrè, 1970), p. 47.

10. Charles Hughes, ed., *Shakespeare's Europe: Unpublished Chapters of Fynes Moryson's Itinerary* (London: Sheratt and Hughes, 1903), p. 150.

11. Charles Bourdin, *Voyage d'Italie et de quelques endroits d'Allemagne fait ès années 1695 et 1696* (Paderborn, 1699), pp. 88-89.

12. See Domenico Sella, *Salari e lavoro nell'edilizia lombarda durante il secolo XVII* (Pavia: Fusi, 1968), pp. 21-24, 98, 120-127: farm laborers in Lombardy were paid about 20-22 *soldi* at the beginning of the century and 16-18 at the end; since the cost of living tended to fall in the second half of the century, real wages were not appreciably modified.

13. *Fd.* 87/7 (Bertonico), 24 May 1656. Chestnuts were an important source of food in the hill zone.

14. On the administrative structure of the State of Milan see Visconti, *La pubblica amministrazione*; Pugliese, *Le Condizioni economiche*, ch. 4; Mario Bendiscioli, "Politica, amministrazione e religione nell'età dei Borromei," in *SdM*, 10: 69-118; Giulio Vismara, "Le istituzioni del patriziato," in *SdM*, 11: 226-286.

15. On the subjugation of the countryside by the Italian medieval communes see Jones, "Medieval Agrarian Society," pp. 403-404; for the persistence of urban domination in the early modern period, Luzzatto, *Storia economica*, 2: 151-152.

16. The Senate is exhaustively discussed in Ugo Petronio, *Il Senato di Milano: Istituzioni giuridiche ed esercizio del potere nel Ducato di Milano da Carlo V a Giuseppe II* (Milan: Giuffrè, 1972).

17. Federico Chabod, *Lo Stato e la vita religiosa a Milano nell'epoca di Carlo V* (Turin: Einaudi, 1971), pp. 143-146.

18. Cesare Magni, *Il tramonto del feudo lombardo* (Milan: Giuffrè, 1937), pp. 160-161.

19. See Bruno Caizzi, "La ville et la campagne dans le système fiscal de la Lombardie sous la domination espagnole," in *Eventail de l'histoire vivante: Hommage à Lucien Febvre* (Paris: Colin, 1953), 2: 366; also Pugliese, *Condizioni economiche*, pp. 189, 265.

20. See Natale Cotta Morandini, *Il Censimento milanese* (Milan, 1832), 1: 100-106; Ettore Verga, "La Congregazione del Ducato e l'amministrazione dell'antica provincia di Milano (1561-1759)," *ASL*, 3rd ser., 8 (1895): 384; Pugliese, *Condizioni economiche*, p. 298; Meroni, *Cremona*, pp. 30-32. I am indebted to Professor Giorgio Chittolini for this last reference.

21. C. A. Vianello ed., *Considerazioni sull'Annona dello Stato di Milano nel XVIII secolo* (Milan: Giuffrè, 1940), pp. vii-xi; De Maddalena, *Prezzi*, pp. 27-35; Zanetti, *Problemi alimentari*, pp. 39-55.

22. Gian Piero Bognetti, "La seta in Lombardia," *Problemi Italiani*, 1 (1922): 27-28; Ettore Verga, "Il Comune di Milano e l'arte della seta dal secolo XV al XVII," *Annuario storico-statistico del Comune di Milano* (1915), p. xxiii (in 1474 a request from the Pavia municipal council for the manufacture of silks to be allowed in that city was denied by the Milan authorities). ASM, *Commercio p. a.*, 228, 7 Feb. 1587: silk looms in operation in some villages are ordered dismantled and brought to Milan. Similar examples are recorded for other years in ASM, *Censo p. a.*, 426, "Indice degli esempi."

23. Verga, "La Congregazione del Ducato," pp. 382-407.

24. Verga, "Le corporazioni," pp. 69-70, refers to a royal ordinance of 8 Apr. 1565 as instituting the tax on *mercimonio* and to 1591 as the year when, after much debate and legal chicanery, the new tax was actually levied. Professor Giovanni Vigo, who is currently conducting a study of the subject, advises me that, in fact, the new tax did not become effective until 1599.

25. Opposition to having movable wealth contribute to the *mensuale* was especially strong in Milan (Chabod, *Lo Stato*, p. 202 n.), but was not lacking in lesser cities. For the case of Vigevano, see Olivero Colombo, "Mercanti e popolari," p. 152.

26. Aleati and Cipolla, "Il trend economico," pp. 6-8.

27. Giuseppe Riva, *L'arte del cappello e della berretta a Monza e a Milano nei secoli XVI-XVII: Contributo alla storia delle corporazioni artigiane* (Monza: Tipografia Sociale Monzese, 1909), pp. 92-93, 109.

28. On the subject, see Braudel, *The Mediterranean*, 1: 330, 584-606.

29. De Maddalena, *Prezzi*, p. 32 n. A granary was also built in Como in 1573 (Mira, *Aspetti dell'economia comasca*, p. 242).

30. ASM, *Comuni p.a.*, 25, "Memoriale della comunità di Codogno," 16 Oct. 1591. In the 1590s crop failures seem to have affected the entire Po val-

ley: the futile attempts made by the Duchy of Modena to secure grain from adjacent areas, and notably from the State of Milan, are discussed in Basini, *L'uomo e il pane*, pp. 66-74.

31. ASM, *Miscellanea lombarda*, IV, doc. no. 51, 6 Feb. 1602.

32. ACM, *Materie*, 263, "Comparitione della Città di Milano," 20 Feb. 1598.

33. Public Record Office, London, *S. P.* 85/1, "A description of the fertilitie of the soile and countrie of Italie" (probably written in 1593). Internal evidence suggests that the author was familiar with conditions in Lombardy: when he wrote that "in some parts of Italie the soile ys so fertile that they make of the self same medowes fyve severall croppes of haie in the yeare," he must have had in mind the Lombard irrigated plain; similarly, his remark that in Italy land "never lightlie lyeth fallow" is a reference to the continuous cropping practiced in that same area.

34. Giovanni Botero, *The Reason of State and The Greatness of Cities* (London: Routledge and Kegan Paul, 1956), p. 275. On p. 155 we read: "Venice, Naples, and Milan do not exceed two hundred thousand inhabitants . . . because it is difficult to rear and feed more people in one place since the surrounding countryside cannot provide enough food and the neighboring territories, owing either to the unfruitful soil or to difficulties of transport, cannot supply the deficiency." On Botero's views, see Karl F. Helleiner, "The Population of Europe from the Black Death to the Eve of the Vital Revolution," in *Cambridge Economic History of Europe*, vol. 4, ed. E. E. Rich and C. H. Wilson (Cambridge: Cambridge University Press, 1967), p. 51. On the food crisis of the 1590s, see Jean Delumeau, *L'Italie de Botticelli à Bonaparte* (Paris: Colin, 1974), pp. 228-229.

35. In a 1669 petition the Milan hat-makers asked the government to put an end to the manufacture of hats in Monza; they pointed out that in Monza artisans "all have some other occupation" while their counterparts in Milan "have no other trade besides hat making" (quoted in Riva, *L'arte del cappello*, p. 275).

36. See Santoro, *La Matricola*, p. viii; Caizzi, *Il Comasco*, p. 84.

37. Sella, "Iron Industry in Italy," p. 105.

38. Frumento, *Imprese lombarde*, 2: 116-118, for a sixteenth-century description of blast furnaces in operation in Valsassina. By contrast, in Liguria, where the rich ores of Elba were smelted, open-hearth furnaces remained in use until the eighteenth century (Sella, "Iron Industry in Italy," p. 102). In England the transition from bloomery to blast furnace got under way after 1560 and in the northwest not until after 1695, according to D. W. Crossley, "The English Iron Industry, 1500-1650: The Problem of New Techniques," in *Schwerpunkte der Eisengewinnung und Eisenverarbeitung in Europa, 1500-1650*, ed. H. Kellenbenz (Cologne-Vienna: Boehlau, 1974), pp. 18-21.

39. Thomas and Gamber, "L'arte milanese dell'armatura," p. 702.

40. As late as the 1720s Jacques Savary des Bruslons could write of the Milan gold thread that "it consists of drawn silver which has been flattened into very thin and flexible bands . . . which are then gilded on one side only . . . This manner of gilding on one side only is a very ingenious and very singular secret known only to the craftsmen of Milan. Those of Paris and Lyons have repeatedly tried to imitate them, but have always failed" (*Dictionnaire Universel de Commerce* [Paris, 1723], 2: 908).

41. Bognetti, "La seta in Lombardia," p. 24, shows that by the late fifteenth century, when the mulberry tree was first introduced into Lombardy, the silk industry was already well established in Milan.

42. ASM, *Commercio p.a.*, 228, "Consulta" of 1 July 1606: "the raw silk which in our State is used to make both plain fabrics and gold cloth does not exceed 400,000 pounds, of which 300,000 are of native silk and 100,000 are imported; of the latter our merchants make use . . . because it is heavier than our own." The same document asserts that the State of Milan produced annually one million pounds of raw silk, most of which was exported.

43. The words are the Duke of Rohan's and are quoted in Cantù, *La Lombardia*, p. 22 n.

44. Borlandi, "Futainiers et futaines," p. 139; Mazzaoui, "The Cotton Industry," pp. 282, 284.

45. Thomas and Gamber, "L'arte milanese dell'armatura," p. 702.

46. The literature on the dislocations experienced by industries in northern Italy is reviewed in Carlo M. Cipolla, "The Economic Decline of Italy," and Domenico Sella, "The Rise and Fall of the Venetian Woollen Industry," both now reprinted in *Crisis and Change in the Venetian Economy in the Sixteenth and Seventeenth Centuries*, ed. Brian Pullan (London: Methuen, 1968), pp. 106-145.

47. In Como, cloth production had virtually stopped in the early sixteenth century as a result of the Italian wars (Giuseppe Mira, "Provvedimenti viscontei e sforzeschi sull'arte della lana a Como, 1335-1535," *ASL*, 95 [1937]: 397, 399), but had fully recovered by 1580 with an annual output of about 4,000 cloths (Mira, *Aspetti dell'economia comasca*, p. 157). In Milan the number of new admissions to the drapers' guild rose from an all-time low of about forty a year in the 1520s to about eighty in the 1550s (Santoro, *La Matricola*, p. xxviii).

48. Caizzi, *Il Comasco*, p. 89, speaks of "a noticeable decline of the Como cloth manufacture between 1580 and 1607." In Milan the number of new admissions to the drapers' guild fell sharply after about 1580 (Santoro, *La Matricola*, p. xxviii). On decline in Vigevano, see Caizzi, "Economia e finanza," p. 367; and in Alessandria, see Corrado Lodovici, "Alessandria sotto la dominazione spagnola (1537-1707)," *Rivista di Storia, Arte, Archeologia per le Province di Alessandria e Asti*, 66-67 (1957-1958): 50.

49. Bognetti, "La seta in Lombardia," p. 26: Henry IV also brought in a Milanese silk-maker, Enrico Turati, to train French workers. An echo of the

alarm created in Milan by the newly enacted French policy in ASM, *Commercio p.a.*, 1, document of 26 Apr. 1599.

50. British Museum, *Add. 12,496*, f. 311, "A true declaration of the state of the manufacture of gold and silver thread" dated 1624: the document asserts that "after many trials for the making of gold and silver thread" a way had been found to produce it "according to the manner of Milan in Italy."

51. Bendiscioli, "Politica, amministrazione e religione," pp. 14-15.

52. Chabod, *Lo Stato*, pp. 23, 37.

53. On the relative ease with which pontoon bridges could be built by army engineers, see Geoffrey Parker, *The Army of Flanders and the Spanish Road, 1567-1659: The Logistics of Spanish Victory and Defeat in the Low Countries' War* (Cambridge: Cambridge University Press, 1972), p. 82.

54. Ibid., pp. 56-68, for a full discussion of the stoppage of seaborne communications between Spain and the Netherlands and the establishment of overland routes from Genoa to Antwerp.

55. Barozzi and Berchet, *Relazioni*, 1st ser., 1: 103-104.

56. At the opening of the seventeenth century, Spanish garrisons were normally stationed in such heavily fortified towns as Milan, Alessandria, Novara, Mortara, and Valenza (Galantino, *Storia di Soncino*, 2: 108); in 1602 the garrisons' total strength was reported at 7,300 men (Barozzi and Berchet, *Relazioni*, 1st ser., 1: 104).

57. When Charles V took over as ruler of Milan in 1535, government expenditures stood at about 140,000 *scudi*; by 1543 they had risen to 770,656 *scudi* (Chabod, *Lo Stato*, pp. 107, 117). Alberto Cova, *Il Banco di S. Ambrogio nell'economia milanese dei secoli XVII e XVIII* (Milan: Giuffrè, 1972), pp. 19-20, provides the following figures on government expenditures (of which 80-90 percent were absorbed by the military) during the reign of Philip II: 604,000 *scudi* in 1562; 1,268,608 in 1576; 812,000 in 1581; and 1,552,000 in 1593. In a period of rising prices the doubling of expenditures may have reflected a fairly stable level of spending in real terms.

58. Chabod, *Lo Stato*, pp. 106, 109, 110, 124-133. In the last five years of Charles's rule unilateral transfers from Spain to Lombardy roughly matched all the revenue raised in Lombardy itself.

59. Cova, *Il Banco*, pp. 19-20: the shortfall was of 61,000 *scudi* in 1562; of 473,608 in 1576; and of 960,000 in 1593. In the 1590s large transfers of species from Spain helped alleviate in part the growing backlog of indebtedness (ibid., p. 21; also Carlo M. Cipolla, *Mouvements monétaires dans l'Etat de Milan, 1580-1700* [Paris: Colin, 1952], p. 45).

60. ACM, *Materie*, 263, "Comparitione" of 20 Feb. 1598.

61. Barozzi and Berchet, *Relazioni*, 1st ser., 1: 105.

62. The document is published in Carlo M. Cipolla, *Prezzi, salari e teoria dei salari in Lombardia alla fine del Cinquecento* (Rome: Edizioni di Storia e Letteratura, 1956), pp. 11-18.

63. Cova, *Il Banco*, pp. 23, 43, on the discussions leading up to the crea-

tion of the Banco on 14 Sept. 1593.

64. Tabarrini, "Relazione inedita," p. 33.

65. To the propertied classes Spanish rule may have been welcome insofar as it ensured internal peace and order. The point is convincingly made by Giorgio Politi, *Aristocrazia e potere politico nella Cremona di Filippo II* (Milan: SugarCo, 1976), pp. 451-456. This, of course, is true even though some of the most restless and overbearing magnates and some of the most dishonest officials in the State of Milan were at times dealt with severely by the Spanish government. On this, see Aldo De Maddalena, "Malcostume e disordine amministrativo nello Stato di Milano alla fine del Cinquecento," *ASL*, 9th ser., 3 (1963): 261-272.

III. WAR, DISEASE, AND DISLOCATIONS

1. For the following summary account of diplomatic and military events I have relied mainly on Romolo Quazza, *Preponderanza spagnola (1559-1700)*, 2nd ed. (Milan: Vallardi, 1950), pp. 408-520.

2. On the Alpine routes and their strategic importance at this time, see Parker, *The Army of Flanders*, pp. 70-78.

3. De Maddalena, *Prezzi*, pp. 99, 100, 102.

4. The best account is by Fausto Nicolini, "Il tumulto di San Martino e la carestia del 1629," in his *Aspetti della vita italo-spagnola nel Cinquecento e nel Seicento* (Naples: Guida, 1934), pp. 127-228.

5. Peaks of mortality are clearly discernible in Pavia (Aleati, *La popolazione di Pavia*, p. 58) and in Milan (Sella, "Premesse demografiche," p. 472).

6. See Carlo M. Cipolla, *Cristofano and the Plague: A Study in the History of Public Health in the Age of Galileo* (London: Collins, 1973), pp. 15-17.

7. Epidemics of the plague were at times preceded by famines, and contemporaries tended to assume a causal link between the two. An eyewitness account of the 1630 plague in Milan, for instance, refers to the famine that preceded it as "an omen of the coming pestilence" (Filippo Visconti, "Commentarius de peste quae anno Domini MDCXXX Mediolani saevit," *ASI*, Appendix 1 [1842-1843], p. 495), and an official report on the 1628 famine speaks of "the shortage of grain which has caused the wretched peasantry to make do with food of such poor quality that an outbreak of contagious disease is to be feared" (ASM, *Miscellanea lombarda*, IV, doc. 51, 19 Feb. 1628). Modern science discounts any direct, causal link between malnutrition and the plague. Although it is true that the plague mowed down far more victims among the poorer, and presumably more undernourished, segment of the population than among the well-to-do, this must have been primarily because the latter lived in more spacious quarters, enjoyed higher standards of cleanliness, and were thus less likely to be infected by disease-carrying lice. On this point, see Carlo M. Cipolla and Dante Zanetti, "Peste et mortalité

différentielle," *Annales de démographie historique* (1972), p. 201. Famine, however, could contribute indirectly to the spread of the disease: as masses of half-starved peasants flocked to the towns in search of relief, not only could they act as carriers of infection, but in the towns themselves the conditions of congestion they created facilitated contagion. See Jean Meuvret, "Demographic Crises in France from the 16th to the 18th Century," in *Population in History*, ed. D. V. Glass and D. E. C. Eversley (London: Arnold, 1965), pp. 510-511. The contemporary account just quoted did note "the refugees who poured into the city from all over the countryside to beg from townsmen the food which they no longer could secure from the fields."

8. On the progress of the plague, the policies adopted to combat it, and the manifestations of collective hysteria that accompanied it, see Fausto Nicolini, "La peste del 1629-32," in *SdM*, 10: 499-560.

9. Some contemporary and wildly exaggerated estimates are discussed in Catalano, "La fine del dominio spagnolo," in *SdM*, 11: 32, and Sella, "Premesse demografiche," p. 464.

10. Sella, "Premesse demografiche," p. 465; Aleati, *La popolazione di Pavia*, p. 22; Meroni, *Cremona*, p. 14; Caizzi, *Il Comasco*, p. 175.

11. ACM, *Dicasteri*, 329, "Relatione del presentaneo stato del Ducato" (1641). According to this document, in Monza "on account of the plague 3,800 souls are missing which is more than half"; in Busto Arsizio "as a result of the plague 1,400 persons are missing and 1,700 are left"; similar rough estimates are provided for other towns.

12. Inquests on fiefs (*informazioni sopra feudi* in *Fd.*) drawn up in the 1640s often provide some rough indication of whether or not individual villages had been visited by the plague in 1630. An examination of available inquests has netted the names of eighty-seven villages where the plague allegedly caused serious losses, twenty-two where losses were reported as minimal, and only fifteen which were totally spared. For the different incidence of the plague in the towns and the countryside, see Mols, "Population in Europe," p. 76.

13. K. J. Beloch in his *Bevölkerungsgeschichte Italiens*, 3: 169 and 242, estimated the population of the State of Milan at about 1,200,000 at the opening of the century and at 900,000 around 1650. One can safely assume that right after the plague of 1630 the population was well below the 900,000 mark. How far below can only be a matter of cautious guesswork. Yet, assuming that between 1630 and 1650 (when no serious epidemics struck the area) the natural rate of increase was "normal," that is to say around six per thousand annually (see Cipolla, "Four Centuries," p. 572), it is not unreasonable to estimate that in the wake of the plague population stood at about 800,000, or 30 percent below the level attained around 1600.

14. Demetrio Galli, "Informazione della Città di Lodi . . . negli anni 1609, 1635 e 1647," *Archivio Storico di Lodi* (1943), p. 44; *Fd.* 141 (Caravaggio), 5 Feb. 1643; Galantino, *Storia di Soncino*, 2: 203 and 3: 417-418.

15. *Fd.* 457/8 (Pontecurone near Tortona), 25 July 1639; 480/2 (Redabue near Alessandria), 25 Apr. 1643; 594/18 (Trecate Novarese), 31 Oct. 1643; 415/3 (Olevano Lomellina), 25 May 1631; Meroni, *Cremona*, p. 29.

16. *Fd.* 657/4 (Zorlesco), 30 Oct. 1632: the number of dairy herds in the village reportedly fell from five to three "due to the great mortality of cattle." Examples of plummeting feudal revenues (mainly tolls) in the late 1620s are found in Paola Zanoli, "Il patrimonio della famiglia Litta sino alla fine del Settecento," *ASL*, 9th ser., 10 (1971-73): 311-312; and Ludwig Welti, "Relazioni dei Conti di Hohemens con la città di Gallarate," *Rassegna gallaratese di storia e d'arte*, 27 (1968): 175 (for the years 1627-1631). Aldo De Maddalena, "I bilanci dal 1600 al 1647 di un'azienda fondiaria lombarda: testimonianza di una crisi economica," *Rivista Internazionale di Scienze economiche e commerciali*, 2 (1955), table I, provides data on the rents of some feudal rights along the Adda river: from an annual average of L.1,658 in the years 1616-1620 they dropped to L.1,400 in the period 1634-1643.

17. De Maddalena, "I bilanci," table VIII.

18. The land in question was the "Giardino del Castello," some 350 hectares outside the city walls of "meadows, arable fields, vineyards, and orchards." See Giuseppe Benaglio, *Relazione Istorica del Magistrato delle Ducali Entrate Straordinarie nello Stato di Milano* (Milan, 1711), p. 80. Data on rents are in ASM, *Fondi camerali p. a.*, 285, document of 28 Jan. 1647.

19. Aldo De Maddalena, "Contributo alla storia dell'agricoltura della bassa lombarda: appunti sulla possessione di Belgiojoso (secoli XVI-XVIII)," *ASL*, 8th ser., 8 (1958): 172 n.

20. G. L. Basini and P. L. Spaggiari, "Proprietà, redditi e spese del Collegio: Profilo Storico," in *I quattro secoli del Collegio Borromeo di Pavia* (Milan: Alfieri e Lacroix, 1961), pp. 172-173. On the Cathedral's estate (Rogorbella) see *Annali della Fabbrica del Duomo di Milano dall'origine fino al presente pubblicati dalla sua Amministrazione* (Milan, 1877-1885), 5: 95, 211.

21. Ferrario, *Busto Arsizio*, p. 95. A sharp drop in rents also occurred in the area around Novi (Doria, *Uomini e terre*, p. 102). On the agrarian malaise in the Brianza after 1630, see Zaninelli, *Vita economica e sociale*, p. 63.

22. Quoted in Catalano, "La fine del dominio spagnolo," p. 34.

23. ASM, *Fondi Camerali p.a.*, 285, report of 26 Apr. 1647 concerning the Giardino del Castello.

24. *Fd.* 415/3 (Olevano Lomellina), 25 May 1631.

25. *Fd.* 487/3e (Rivolta d'Adda), 30 June 1640.

26. Aleati and Cipolla, "Aspetti e problemi," pp. 392-395.

27. Although the collapse of the cloth industry in Como is beyond dispute, precise figures are hard to come by. According to a 1650 government report quoted in Cipolla ("The Economic Decline of Italy," p. 127), at the beginning of the century Como had produced an average of 8,000 cloths a year, while by 1650 output was down to a paltry 400 cloths. On the other hand, Caizzi, (*Il Comasco*, pp. 89, 93, 94), has proposed the following figures:

3,200 cloths in 1607, 1,820 in 1618, and 290 in 1628. Caizzi's figures are derived from the number of bales of raw wool imported into Como in those years. It is not clear, however, how the conversion from bales to cloths was effected.

28. The number of new admissions is given in Santoro, *La Matricola*, p. xxviii, as around twenty a year in the period 1580-1630; it fell to twelve in the 1630s and to only four in the 1640s. Little is known about cloth output in Milan: 4,500 cloths in 1580 (Frattini, *Storia e statistica*, p. 32) and possibly 3,000 around 1640. This last figure was provided by Tridi in his *Informatione*, p. 6. Tridi also claimed that in 1616 output in Milan had stood at 15,000 cloths, a figure which has often been quoted in the literature on the industrial decline of Milan, but one that is probably grossly inflated. It is unlikely that output rose threefold between 1580 and 1616: the number of new admissions to the drapers' guild over this period suggests stability rather than an increase of such magnitude. Then, too, internal evidence suggests that Tridi, in an effort to buttress his claim that a tax increase enacted in 1616 had crippled the wool industry, used his figures in a rather cavalier way. On p. 10 of his *Informatione* he claimed that the making of one cloth (approximately 30 meters in length) "provides employment to 25 people for a whole month so that a drop in output of 12,000 cloths deprives 25,000 individuals of their livelihood." From this statement one ought to infer that if production had really stood at 15,000 cloths in 1616, the work force employed in that year would have been of $15,000 \div 12 \times 25 = 31,250$ individuals. This is unrealistic: a city of about 120,000 people, such as Milan was around that time, could not possibly have one-fourth of its population employed in the making of woolen cloth, especially considering that, according to Tridi himself (p. 11), employment in the silk industry was comparable to, and possibly larger than, that in the wool industry.

29. Meroni, *Cremona*, p. 19; Ircas Jacopetti, *Le finanze del Comune di Cremona durante la dominazione spagnola*, vol. 14 of *Annali della Biblioteca Governativa e Libreria Civica di Cremona* (Cremona: Atheneum Cremonese, 1962), p. 114.

30. ASM, *Commercio p.a.*, 199, memorandum of Carlo Visconte, 16 May 1647. For Monza, see Zaninelli, *Vita economica e sociale*, p. 43.

31. The figure for 1606 is from ASM, *Commercio p.a.*, 228, "Discorso di persona incognita" of 1 July 1606. That for 1635 is from ASM, *Commercio p.a.*, 228, attachment A to the "consulta" of 26 Oct. 1640. For 1685, see M. Daverio, "Saggio storico sulle sete e serifici nello Stato di Milano," in C. A. Vianello, ed. *Economisti minori del Settecento lombardo* (Milan: Giuffrè, 1942), p. 446; and for the end of the century, see ACM, *Materie*, 572, doc. of 21 Dec. 1698.

32. See Paolo Mezzanotte, "L'architettura milanese dalla fine della Signoria sforzesca alla metà del Seicento," in *SdM*, 10: 630-645; and Cesare Jacini, *Il viaggio del Po*, 5, pt. 2 (Milan: Hoepli, 1950): 127-202, 449-455, 513-524.

33. See Paolo Mezzanotte, "L'architettura da F. M. Ricchino al Ruggieri," in *SdM*, 11: 441-478.

34. Ibid., p. 441.

35. Caizzi, *Il Comasco*, p. 112.

36. Aleati and Cipolla, "Il trend economico," p. 9.

37. J. W. S. Johnsson, ed., *Storia della peste avvenuta nel borgo di Busto Arsizio nel 1630* (Copenhagen: Koppel, 1924), p. 89.

38. Armando Novasconi et al., *La ceramica lodigiana* (Lodi: Banca Mutua Popolare Agricola, 1964), p. 23; Baroni, "La maiolica," p. 448.

39. John Evelyn, *The Diary*, ed. E. S. Beer (Oxford: Clarendon Press, 1955), 2: 501 (May 1646): Milan is "full of . . . rare Artists, especially for works in crystal." On the ribbon industry, ASM, *Commercio p. a.*, 145/1, petition of the ribbon merchants of 25 Nov. 1659. The merchants claimed to have placed orders for 130,000 *braccia* (about 70,000 meters) of ribbon with local ribbon-makers, but their orders were being delayed because the ribbon makers were said to be "busy making gold and silver articles, fringes, and trimmings for liveries and other ornaments." This suggests that the manufacture of haberdashery was doing well at the time. The figures in Table 1 confirm that there was an upturn in that line of business in the 1660s and 1670s.

40. The subject is discussed in Ferdinando Reggiori, "L'architettura militare durante il periodo dell'occupazione spagnola," in *SdM*, 10: 652-666. On Lodi, see Agnelli, "Lodi e territorio," pp. 82-105. For the iconography of seventeenth-century fortifications, see Vincenzo Coronelli, *Città e fortezze dello Stato di Milano e confinanti* (Venice, 1683), a collection of fine etchings. The quotation about Novara is from Galeazzo Gualdo Priorato, *Relatione della Città e Stato di Milano* (Milan, 1675), p. 132. For Tortona and Soncino, see Reina, *Descrizione corografica*, pp. 29, 73. A rough idea of the magnitude of fortification works can be formed from occasional information on the size of the work force employed in a given locality. In 1647, when new crown-works were being planned for the defence of Milan, it was estimated that "300 master masons will be working at the same time" (ASM, *Fondi Camerali p.a.*, 285/1, doc. of 26 Apr. 1647). In 1657 when a new fortress was being erected at Frascarolo, as many as 6,000 men were reportedly at work on the site (Archivio di Stato, Venice, *Senato, dispacci rettori Brescia*, filza 60, on 26 Apr. 1657).

41. And notably from Brescia, then a major center of the arms industry in Venetian territory. In 1641, for instance, Spanish authorities in Milan placed an order for "1,000 muskets and 1,000 gun barrels" with one Brescian gunmaker (Archivio di Stato, Venice, *Senato, dispacci rettori Brescia*, filza 43, on 6 Mar. 1641). Besides small firearms, its main specialty, Brescia also supplied helmets and breastplates (ASM, *Cancelleria spagnola*, ser. 22 (Mandati), reg. 64, 23 June 1646). Heavy ordnance, at least on one occasion,

was secured from Amsterdam (ibid., reg. 61, 14 Mar. 1640). At one time 2,000 muskets were purchased in Lucca (ibid., reg. 57, 9 May 1626).

42. Gelli, *Gli archibugiari milanesi*, especially pp. 89-99, for large government contracts with Milanese gunmakers; also Frumento, *Imprese lombarde*, 2: 87, 107, 124.

43. Examples of large consignments of common-service armor in ASM, *Cancelleria spagnola*, ser. xxii (Mandati), reg. 59, 23 May 1634 and reg. 64, 28 May 1646. See also Frumento, *Imprese lombarde*, 2:60, 77, 93.

44. The history of the excise is discussed in detail by Antonio Noto in his introduction to *Liber Datij Mercantie Communis Mediolani: Registro del secolo XV* (Milan: Università Bocconi, 1950). The register edited by Noto includes about a thousand commodities that were subject to the tax, from meat to spices, from scissors to millstones. Cereals are not mentioned, presumably because they were subject to a special milling tax (*dazio della macina*).

45. Significantly, feudal dues (mainly tolls) levied in the countryside fell sharply in this period. See note 16 in this chapter.

46. See Pugliese, *Condizioni economiche*, p. 182. Charitable institutions such as the Collegio Borromeo in Pavia, although not strictly ecclesiastical, were exempt as well (Basini and Spaggiari, "Proprietà, redditi e spese," p. 166).

47. On the crisis in its European dimensions see B. E. Supple, *Commercial Crisis and Change in England, 1600-1642* (Cambridge: Cambridge University Press, 1959), ch. 4; and Ruggiero Romano, "Tra XVI e XVII secolo. Una crisi economica: 1619-1622," *RSI*, 74 (1962): 480-531. Its impact on Lombardy is now fully discussed in Giovanni Vigo, "Manovre monetarie e crisi economica nello Stato di Milano (1619-1622)," *Studi Storici*, 17 (1976): 101-126.

48. Cavazzi della Somaglia, *Alleggiamento*, p. 684.

49. ASM, *Apprensioni*, 346, printed brief submitted on 17 Apr. 1630 by Gioacchino Marliani, farmer of the excise, in order to explain why he had defaulted on the last installment of his rent. He blamed the War of the Mantuan Succession for disrupting trade and especially foreign trade; he also mentioned military requisitions and the plague as causing serious dislocations.

50. ASM, *Finanze p.a.*, 530, memorandum of 12 June 1651 submitted by the person in charge of collecting a tax on all commodities in transit on the Naviglio Grande.

IV. CAUSES AND SCAPEGOATS

1. Quoted in Catalano, "La fine del dominio spagnolo," p. 52.
2. Agnelli, "Lodi e territorio," pp. 96-97; Antonio Barili, *Notizie storico-patrie di Casalmaggiore* (Parma, 1812), p. 61; for devastations in

Vigevano, see Catalano, "La fine del dominio spagnolo," p. 104; in Castelletto Ticino, *Fd.* 562/4, 25 Jan. 1640; in Soncino, Galantino, *Storia di Soncino,* 3:428.

3. Quoted in Meroni, *Cremona,* p. 126.

4. ASM, *Comuni p.a.*, 57, "Ordinazioni dei Sessanta, 1646-48," p. 90. Similar complaints addressed directly to Madrid by special envoys sent from Milan can be found in Angiolo Salomoni, *Memorie storico-diplomatiche degli Ambasciatori, Incaricati d'affari, Corrispondenti, Delegati che la Città di Milano inviò a diversi suoi Principi dal 1500 al 1796* (Milan, 1806), pp. 267-280 (for 1610), 313-332 (for 1640), 356-374 (for 1660).

5. Verri, *Considerazioni,* p. 36.

6. Cantù, *La Lombardia,* p. 16.

7. Caizzi, *Il Comasco,* p. 107. Even stronger words were used by Pugliese: "the monstrous Spanish fiscal system, far more than many disasters such as wars, epidemics, and famines, accounts for the rapid and severe decadence experienced by Lombardy" (*Condizioni economiche,* p. 309).

8. Between 1620 and 1658 the backlog of loans extended by the Banco to the city of Milan to enable the latter to meet its mounting fiscal obligations rose from L.6 million to nearly L.22 million (Cova, *Il Banco,* pp. 57, 69, 71, 72). For the situation in Cremona see Jacopetti, *Le finanze,* ch. 4 and p. 103. The Cremona municipal government borrowed mainly from monasteries and local magnates (ibid., p. 50). The role of the Genoese bankers in the finances of the State of Milan during the seventeenth century still awaits systematic investigation. That their role was very prominent indeed can, however, be inferred from scattered information in: Pugliese, *Condizioni economiche,* pp. 339, 341, 347; Cova, *Il Banco,* p. 80 n.; Da Silva, *Banque et crédit,* 1: 56, 246; and Giuseppe Felloni, *Gli investimenti finanziari genovesi in Europa tra il Seicento e la Restaurazione* (Milan: Giuffrè, 1971), pp. 213-215.

9. Wrote Cavazzi della Somaglia in his *Alleggiamento,* p. 13: "It can be concluded that from 1610 to 1650 the State of Milan has contributed (in revenue) 248,972,789 gold *scudi* at L.6 each . . . This does not include the more than sixty million in gold which His Majesty has sent here during this period." There is no way, given the present state of knowledge, of verifying the accuracy of these figures. We know, however, that vast sums of money were transferred from Naples and Sicily. According to Rosario Villari, *La rivolta antispagnola a Napoli: Le origini, 1585-1647* (Bari: Laterza, 1967), p. 121, in 1636 nearly 20 percent of all government expenditures in the Kingdom of Naples consisted of subsidies for Milan. Giuseppe Coniglio, *Il Vice-regno di Napoli nel secolo XVII* (Rome: Edizioni di Storia e Letteratura, 1955), p. 272, has data on such subsidies from 1631 to 1643. On the huge contributions extracted from Sicily a wealth of information is now available in two articles in *RSI,* 84 (1972): Maurice Aymard, "Bilancio d'una lunga crisi finanziaria," 84:988-1017, and Carmelo Trasselli, "Finanza genovese e pagamenti esteri, 1629-1643," 84:978-987.

10. In 1641 unilateral transfers (*rimesse*) from Naples alone were reported as averaging 1.2 million *scudi* a year (ASM, *Uffici regii p. a.,* 654, reg. 1, 6 Nov. 1641). This is not inconsistent with the figures in Table 3. According to the same source, transfers from Naples and Sicily were, as a rule, late in coming and in the meantime the Milan authorities had to borrow short-term (*di fiera in fiera*) from the Genoese at 8 percent.

11. See Appendix B for price trends; on wages, see Sella, *Salari e lavoro,* p. 14.

12. ACM, *Materie,* 268, doc. of 4 Feb. 1633.

13. Despite its name, by the seventeenth century the *censo del sale* had little to do with salt, but was really a poll tax. According to Pugliese, *Condizioni economiche,* p. 261, its yield rose from L.184,765 in 1536 to L.370,000 at mid-seventeenth century, and then to L.585,781 around 1700. The yield of the government salt monopoly (*gabella del sale*) increased from about L.1.1 millions around 1600 to twice that figure by 1700 (ibid., p. 192). In the Como province the land tax (*perticato*) rose threefold between 1616 and 1688 (Caizzi, *Il Comasco,* p. 131).

14. *Fd.* 640 (Villareggio), 22 Apr. 1630.

15. Johnsson, ed., *Storia della peste,* p. 89.

16. *Fd.* 85/3, "Comparizione" of 24 Feb. 1638.

17. *Fd.* 141 (Caravaggio), 5 Feb. 1643.

18. *Fd.* 449/5 (Piovera), 13 Oct. 1650. Similar statements in *Fd.* 293/19 (Rescalda), 15 Sept. 1647; Meroni, *Cremona,* p. 128; and Caizzi, *Il Comasco,* p. 164.

19. The land tax in the State of Milan had a built-in incentive for farmers to cultivate their land even beyond what would otherwise have been economical, for, as a seventeenth-century authority on taxation put it, "whoever puts only the good land under crop and allows inferior land to go barren is still required to pay taxes on the barren land as before" (Ambrogio Oppizzone, *Informatione per modo di discorso in materia delle Equalanze Terrere, Provinciali et Generali* [Milan, 1643,] s.v. "beni sterili" in "Tavola delle cose notevoli," no pagination). Not surprisingly, even emigrants, under the pressure of taxation, tried to keep under crop whatever land they left behind: "Although they do not live here," explained a peasant of Valsassina, "they pay their taxes just like those who do . . . Even those who have no relatives entrust their holdings to a tenant . . . for if they did not do so their land would lie uncropped, taxes would go unpaid, and the village community would sell the land at auction" (*Fd.* 616/3, Valsassina, 3 June 1647). For a discussion of the effect of direct taxation on the supply of effort in peasant societies, see P. T. Bauer and B. S. Yamey, *The Economics of Under-developed Countries,* 4th ed. (Chicago: University of Chicago Press, 1963), pp. 194-196.

20. On the agrarian crisis as a European phenomenon, see Wilhelm Abel, *Crises agraires en Europe, XIIIe-XXe siècles,* French trans. based on 2nd German ed. (Paris: Flammarion, 1973), chs. 5 and 6; B. H. Slicher van Bath,

The Agrarian History of Western Europe, A. D. 500-1850, English trans. (London: Arnold, 1963), pp. 206-220.

21. The crisis as it affected areas of northern Italy other than Spanish Lombardy is discussed in De Maddalena, "Il mondo rurale italiano," pp. 361-363; Gabriele Lombardini, *Pane e denaro a Bassano. Prezzi del grano e politica dell'approvvigionamento dei cereali tra il 1501 e il 1799* (Venice: Neri Pozza, 1963), pp. 48, 67-69; Gian Luigi Basini, *Sul mercato di Modena tra Cinque e Seicento: Prezzi e salari* (Milan: Giuffrè, 1974), pp. 96-115; and Mario Cattini, "Produzione, autoconsumo e mercato dei grani a San Felice sul Panaro, 1590-1637," *RSI* 85 (1973): 745-753.

22. When not indulging in recriminations against the tax collector, contemporaries sensed very clearly the connection between the agrarian depression and demographic and price changes. One small landowner, for instance, recalled that in 1631 "all things were altered as a result of so many people having died of the plague . . . Because of the shortage of labor, much land was left uncropped . . . and holdings which used to be let at two *staia* per *pertica* could hardly find a taker at one *staio*" (quoted in Ferrario, *Busto Arsizio,* p. 95). A few years later an official paper stated that "countless estates and spacious holdings are now uncultivated and deserted both because their owners are too poor to undertake the necessary work and because of the great scarcity of workers (quoted in Catalano, "La fine del dominio spagnolo," p. 34). In 1638 a landowner claimed that "since the plague . . . and the mortality of both tenants and cattle my income has dropped by two-thirds" (*Fd.* 85/3, Bereguardo, 24 Feb. 1638). The persistent depression of land values was, at times, recognized as a major cause of agrarian malaise (see docs. for 1640 and 1664 quoted in Meroni, *Cremona,* pp. 96 n., 130).

23. De Maddalena, "I bilanci," especially pp. 29 and 41.

24. The full title of this often-quoted tract is *Informatione del danno proceduto a Sua Maestà & alle Città dello Stato dall'impositione dell'estimo della Mercantia & dall'accrescimento del terzo del Datio & dall'introduttione delli panni di lana & altre merci forastiere; Et all'incontro dell'utile che ne risulterebbe a levarli, Rappresentata da Gio. Maria Tridi Cittadino Comasco.* This printed tract bears no date nor place of publication; the date of 4 June 1641 appears in handwriting on the front page of the copy preserved in ASM, *Commercio, p. a.,* 1.

25. Tridi, *Informatione,* p. 5. Actually the increase in rates occurred in 1613 (Pugliese, *Condizioni economiche,* p. 85).

26. Tridi, *Informatione,* pp. 10, 14, 18, 24.

27. See Chapter III, note 28.

28. Tridi, *Informatione,* p. 23.

29. ASM, *Commercio p. a.,* 1, printed copy of a letter to Senator Lambertengo of 14 Aug. 1641.

30. The expression "questo maledetto serpe dell'estimo mercantile" is

found in an undated brief written in support of Tridi's proposals (ASM, *Commercio p. a.*, 1, "Delle tre cause...").

31. Ibid., "Mezzi proposti dal Magistrato," 5 Oct. 1650.

32. Cavazzi, *Alleggiamento*, p. 695. On Cavazzi, see Verga, "La Congregazione del Ducato," p. 392 n.

33. ASM, *Censo p. a.*, 424, "Consulta dell'E. R. G." of 7 June 1732.

34. Verri, *Considerazioni*, p. 37.

35. Angelo Pavesi, *Memorie per servire alla storia del commercio dello Stato di Milano e di quello della città e provincia di Como in particolare* (Como, 1778), p. 2.

36. Pugliese, *Condizioni economiche*, p. 198.

37. According to Tridi, *Informatione*, pp. 6 and 18, around 1616 there were seventy firms (*lavorerij*) in Milan and sixty in Como producing cloth.

38. *Informatione*, p. 17.

39. On rural industries, see Chapter VI.

40. Ruggiero Romano, "A Florence au XVIIe siècle: industries textiles et conjoncture," *Annales E. S. C.*, 9 (1952): 508-511.

41. Sella, "The Rise and Fall of the Venetian Woollen Industry," pp. 108-110.

42. Domenico Sella, *Commerci e industrie a Venezia nel secolo XVII* (Venice-Rome: Istituto per la Collaborazione culturale, 1961), p. 130.

43. Gabriella Sivori, "Il tramonto dell'industria serica genovese," *RSI*, 84 (1972): 897.

44. Besides the titles quoted in the preceding three footnotes, see also Cipolla, "The Economic Decline of Italy," pp. 138-139, for additional evidence on this point.

45. ASM, *Commercio p. a.*, 1, "Consulta" (printed) of 4 July 1641.

46. See Verga, "Leggi suntuarie," p. 91. The 1646 decree (*grida*) is referred to and basically reproduced in the subsequent decree of 7 Mar. 1649 (*Gridario dell'Eccellentissimo Signor Luigi de Benavides, Marchese di Caracena* [Milan, n.d.], pp. 78-79).

47. ASM, *Uffici regii p. a.*, 655, "Intorno li panni forastieri," 5 Oct. 1650.

48. Ibid. The original reads: "essersi assottigliati gl'ingegnij e communicati questi lavorerij in somma isquisitezza."

49. Gascon, *Grand commerce*, 1:61.

50. ASM, *Commercio p. a.*, 228, doc. of 26 June 1635: "The thousands of looms that were formerly at work in the city of Milan are now to be found in France and notably in the City of Lyons."

51. See Chapter V.

52. Verga, "Le leggi suntuarie," p. 75; also Gascon, *Grand Commerce*, 1: 111.

53. Charles W. Cole, *Colbert and a Century of French Mercantilism*

(New York: Columbia University Press, 1939), 2: 195-196.

54. British Museum, *Add. 12,496*, p. 311, "A true declaration of the State of the Manufacture of gold and silver thread" (1624) already quoted.

55. Gascon, *Grand commerce*, 1: 111. The competition of German armorers has been discussed in Chapter II.

56. See Supple, *Commercial Crisis*, pp. 135-162; Charles Wilson, "Cloth Production and International Competition in the Seventeenth Century," *EcHR*, 2nd ser., 13 (1960-61): 209-221; D. C. Coleman, "An Innovation and Its Diffusion: The New Draperies," *EcHR*, 2nd ser., 22 (1969): 417-429.

57. R. W. K. Hinton, *The Eastland Trade and the Commonwealth in the Seventeenth Century* (Cambridge: Cambridge University Press, 1959), p. 8 (falling exports to the Baltic); Supple, *Commercial Crisis*, p. 140 (falling exports to Germany) and p. 160 (falling exports to the Mediterranean); also Margaret Priestley, "Anglo-French Trade and the 'Unfavorable Balance' Controversy, 1660-1685," *EcHR*, 2nd ser., 4 (1951-52): 44.

58. Pierre Goubert, *Beauvais et le Beauvaisis de 1600 à 1730* (Paris: SEVPEN, 1960), pp. 585-588; Pierre Deyon, "Variations de la production textile aux XVIe et XVIIe siècles: Sources et premiers résultats," *Annales. E. S. C.*, 18 (1963): 950.

59. Ibid., p. 952. See also Pierre Deyon and Alain Lottin, "Evolution de la production textile à Lille aux XVIe et XVIIe siècles," *Revue du Nord*, 49 (1967): 28.

60. See references in notes 40 and 41 of this chapter.

61. In the Bergamo district 26,000 woolen cloths were produced in 1596 and an average of 30,000 (two-thirds of which were low-grade fabrics) a year between 1685 and 1710: Sella, "Industrial Production," p. 238, and Richard T. Rapp, *Industry and Economic Decline in Seventeenth-Century Venice* (Cambridge, Mass.: Harvard University Press, 1976), p. 162. Apparently, much of the Bergamo production found its way into the State of Milan where it was "mostly used by people of lowly condition and purchased by hospitals and other charitable institutions to provide clothes to an infinite number of poor" (ACM, *Materie*, 571, doc. of 10 Feb. 1623). In the late eighteenth century the prosperity of the Bergamo wool industry was ascribed to "the wise policy of the Bergamasques who set up their manufactures not in the city, but in the valleys . . . where labor can be hired more cheaply than in the city" (Pavesi, *Memorie*, p. 78).

62. Data on the export of serges to Italy in Priestley, "Anglo-French Trade," p. 47. See also Richard T. Rapp, "The Unmaking of the Mediterranean Trade Hegemony: International Trade Rivalry and the Commercial Revolution," *JEH*, 35 (1975): 511-517.

63. Wilson, "Cloth Production," p. 214; see also Sella, *Commerci e industrie*, p. 121.

V. THE ATROPHY OF THE CITY

1. The upturn after 1659 has been noticed, although not analyzed in any detail, by Carlo Morandi, "La fine del dominio spagnolo e le premesse storiche delle riforme settecentesche," *ASI,* 94 (1936): 191; by Luigi Bulferetti, "L'oro, la terra e la società: Un'interpretazione del nostro Seicento," *ASL,* 80 (1953): 35 n.; and by Catalano, "La fine del dominio spagnolo," p. 149.

2. Gualdo Priorato, *Relatione,* pp. 10, 16. On the remodeling and expansion of the governor's palace see Carlo Torre, *Ritratto di Milano* (Milan, 1674), p. 362.

3. The two petitions are in ASM, *Commercio p. a.,* 264/2, 30 July 1670 and 9 Jan. 1672.

4. Verga, "Leggi suntuarie," pp. 95-96.

5. *Gridario dell'Eccellentissimo Signor Don Luigi de Guzman Ponze de Leon* (Milan, n.d.), p. 90, decree of 7 Aug. 1664.

6. *Gridario Caracena,* p. 78, decree of 7 Mar. 1649; *Gridario dell'Eccellentissimo Signor Conte di Fuensaldagna* (Milan, n.d.), p. 78, decree of 4 Aug. 1658.

7. See Vismara, "Le istituzioni del patriziato," pp. 254, 265.

8. Cova, *Il Banco,* pp. 80-83.

9. Caizzi, *Il Comasco,* p. 65 (on the easing of tax pressure) and p. 51 (on the reduction of interest rates). The animosity against government creditors is revealed by an undated (but unmistakably mid-seventeenth century) brief submitted by the rural communities and quoted in Verga, "La Congregazione del Ducato," pp. 403-404. After complaining about "the great burden of debts at 7 and 8 percent borne not only by the entire body of the Duchy, but by each individual community as well," and after asserting that the rural population "is so oppressed that their entire income does not suffice even to pay interest on their debts," the brief goes on to say that those interest charges "accrue for the most part to merchants, wealthy burgers of Milan, foreigners, etc. who, compared with the wretched peasantry, have hardly felt the devastations of war . . . and yet demand the prompt payment of interest so implacably that one hears nothing these days but stories of individuals driven to despair or thrown into jail."

10. Cova, *Il Banco,* pp. 83-89.

11. See Table 2.

12. Cipolla, *Mouvements monétaires,* p. 42: between 1581 and 1620 gold and silver issues had averaged about L.1,900,000 a year; during the next forty years annual averages had sunk to 1 million; from 1660 to 1700 they stood at about L.1,600,000.

13. See sources quoted in Chapter I, note 13.

14. ACM, *Materie,* 571, "Notificati delli numeri delle peze e saglie."

15. Meroni, *Cremona*, pp. 20, 21 n., 112.

16. Caizzi, *Il Comasco*, p. 107; Aleati̇e Cipolla, "Il trend economico," p. 13; Meroni, *Cremona*, p. 21.

17. See Chapter III, note 31, and Table 1.

18. ACM, *Materie*, 876, doc. of 7 Apr. 1698 for the 1674 and 1698 figures; the figure for 1678 is in Bognetti, "La seta in Lombardia," p. 29.

19. Gelli, *Gli archibugiari*, p. 103; Frumento, *Imprese lombarde*, 2: 124.

20. Frattini, *Storia e statistica*, pp. 39, 40.

21. Baroni, "La maiolica antica," pp. 448, 451.

22. Jacques Savary, *Le Parfait Négociant* (Paris, 1675), p. 62: "From Milan we import wrought silk for our manufactures in France, gold thread, satin velvets with large silk flowers and a gold and silver backdrop, and sundry silk articles which are very beautiful." According to a 1667 Milanese document, the export of wrought silk and gold thread to France was still brisk and, other manufactures having become virtually extinct, represented the last source "from which the people of this city draw their sustenance" (ACM, *Materie*, 269, petition of 20 Sept. 1667). See also Gualdo Priorato, *Relatione*, p. 131; and Richard Lassels, *The Voyage of Italy* (Paris, 1670), p. 130, for eulogies of the silk stockings, embroideries, and crystal made in Milan.

23. Verga, "Leggi suntuarie," p. 109 n.; and Rosita Levi-Pisetzky, "Le nuove fogge e l'influsso della moda francese a Milano," in *SdM*, 11: 565.

24. Verga, "Leggi suntuarie," p. 95. At the opening of the century it was stated that "the making of silk stockings is at present flourishing whereas in the past they had to be imported from Naples and Mantua" (ASM, *Commercio p. a.*, 228, "discorso di persona incognita" attached to *consulta* of 1 July 1606).

25. Caizzi, *Il Comasco*, p. 109.

26. Meroni, *Cremona*, p. 108.

27. Gualdo Priorato, *Relatione*, p. 131.

28. ASM, *Commercio p.a.*, 145, "1691. Notificazioni de Drappi e Bindelli forestieri." This dossier contains the itemized declarations of forty-one silk merchants in Milan; the foreign origin (Lyons, Florence, Venice, and so on) of the fabrics is indicated in most cases. The data for 1714 are in Pugliese, *Condizioni economiche*, p. 94.

29. Gualdo Priorato, *Relatione*, p. 131.

30. Anne Marie Piuz, *Recherches sur le commerce de Genève au XVIIe siècle* (Geneva: Jullien, 1964), pp. 164-165.

31. Such is the gist of Bruno Caizzi's exhaustive study, *Industria, commercio e banca in Lombardia nel secolo XVIII* (Milan: Banca Commerciale Italiana, 1968). Even the silk manufacture, possibly the most dynamic among urban industries, made but slow headway in the late eighteenth century; it had registered serious losses in the first half of the century (ibid., pp. 20, 108).

32. In 1766 a French visitor, after enumerating the many luxury productions of Milan (silks, jewelry, church ornaments, crystal, expensive car-

riages), commented that they all catered mainly to local consumers: "it is the numerous nobility living in Milan that causes the luxury trades to prosper." Abbé Richard, *Description historique et critique de l'Italie* (Dijon-Paris, 1766), 1: 271-272.

33. The same view was expressed in 1713 by the government of his Austrian successor, Emperor Charles VI, as it reaffirmed the desirability of noblemen engaging in business and blamed economic decline on the fact that "noblemen have been barred from trade." See Gianluigi Barni, "Mutamenti di ideali sociali dal secolo XVI al secolo XVIII: Giuristi, nobiltà e mercatura," *Rivista Internazionale di Filosofia del Diritto*, 34 (1957): 785.

34. Pavesi, *Memorie*, pp. 108-109. See also Carlo Antonio Vianello, *Il Settecento milanese* (Milan: Baldini Castoldi, 1934), p. 90 n., for a similar comment by a foreign observer twenty years later.

35. Cantù, *La Lombardia*, pp. 63, 66.

36. Carlo Cattaneo, *Notizie naturali e civili su la Lombardia* (Milan, 1844), p. xci.

37. A comprehensive discussion of the historiography on the subject is provided by Bulferetti, "L'oro, la terra e la società," pp. 5-29.

38. Chabod, *Lo Stato*, p. 199.

39. Ibid., p. 200.

40. Amintore Fanfani, *Storia del lavoro in Italia dalla fine del secolo XV agli inizi del XVIII*, 2nd ed. (Milan: Giuffrè, 1956), p. 21.

41. In addition to Chabod's and Fanfani's works just referred to, see Braudel, *The Mediterranean*, 2: 725-731: he uses the expression "defection of the bourgeoisie" to describe a Mediterranean, and not merely Italian, phenomenon typical of the sixteenth century. Giorgio Candeloro, *Storia dell'-Italia moderna* (Milan: Feltrinelli, 1956), 1: 49-50, traces the beginnings of this "social involution" all the way back to about 1300; S. F. Romano, *Le classi sociali in Italia dal Medioevo all'età contemporanea* (Turin: Einaudi, 1965), pp. 37-39, 124, sees the late fifteenth century as the starting point of the process; and Pasquale Villani, *Feudalità, riforme, capitalismo agrario* (Bari: Laterza, 1968), pp. 114-115, claims that the shift occurred toward the end of the sixteenth century.

42. Hans Baron, "The Social Background of Political Liberty in the Early Renaissance," *Comparative Studies in Society and History*, 2 (1960): 449. Renato Zangheri, "Agricoltura e sviluppo del capitalismo. Problemi storiografici," *Studi Storici*, 9 (1968): 536-538, has sounded another welcome note of caution on the use of the expression "return to the land" as synonymous with "social involution" and has stressed how much agriculture in northern and central Italy actually benefited from the investment of bourgeois wealth from at least the fourteenth century. Ruggiero Romano has pointed out that the "return to the land" of the sixteenth century was "sound business" and in no way a form of "bucolic" escapism and that it was accompanied by the vigorous expansion of agriculture; see his essay "La storia economica: dal

secolo XIV al Settecento" in *Storia d'Italia*, (Turin: Einaudi, 1974), 2: 1904. See also R. A. Goldthwaite, *Private Wealth in Renaissance Florence* (Princeton: Princeton University Press, 1968), p. 247, for some judicious comments on this issue.

43. A late fourteenth-century example in Giuseppe Aleati, "Una dinastia di magnati medievali: gli Eustachi di Pavia," in *Storia della economia italiana*, ed. C. M. Cipolla (Turin: Einaudi, 1959), 1: 313-323. The transformation of great merchants into landowners, of course, was a common phenomenon even at an earlier date (Jones, "Medieval Agrarian Society," pp. 348-351).

44. For England see W. T. MacCaffrey, *Exeter 1540-1640: The Growth of an English Country Town* (Cambridge, Mass.: Harvard University Press, 1958), p. 260: "the ambition of every successful merchant," he writes, "was to become a landed gentleman. To quote Hooker, the merchants 'do attain to great wealth and riches, which for the most part they do employ to buy land and little by little they do creep and seek to be gentlemen'." See also Barry E. Supple, "Class and Social Tension: The Case of the Merchant," in *The English Revolution, 1600-1660*, ed. E. W. Ives (London: Arnold, 1968), pp. 133-135, for a similar view. Henry Kamen, *The Iron Century: Social Change in Europe, 1550-1660* (New York-Washington: Praeger, 1972), ch. 5 and especially pp. 169, 171, 184, 185, discusses the same pattern from a Western European perspective.

45. H. J. Habakkuk, "The English Land Market in the Eighteenth Century" in *Britain and the Netherlands*, ed. J. S. Bromley and E. H. Kossman (London: Chatto and Windus, 1960), pp. 167-170. The "methodical purchase of land" was commonplace among fourteenth-century Florentine merchants, according to Armando Sapori, "I mutui dei mercanti fiorentini del Trecento e l'incremento della proprietà fondiaria," in his *Studi di storia economica*, 2nd ed. (Florence: Sansoni, 1946), p. 63. The landholdings of a prominent Milanese silk merchant and manufacturer of the sixteenth century are discussed in Aldo De Maddalena, "Excolere vitam per artem: Giovanni Antonio Orombelli mercante auroserico milanese del Cinquecento," *RSI*, 88 (1976): 38. Lesser merchants apparently followed a similar pattern in the management of their wealth: in 1645 one Carlo Landriano, seller of gloves, shoes, and notions in Milan, could boast, in addition to his shops and stocks of goods, a small country estate near Busto Arsizio (ASM, *Finanza p. a.*, 530, doc. of 4 Nov. 1645).

46. In the plain south of Milan around 1560, 58.7 percent of the land belonged to the urban aristocracy and another 7.6 to non-noble townsmen (Coppola, "L'agricoltura di alcune pievi," p. 218). At that time, in the *contado* of Cremona, 66 percent of all farmland was owned by city residents (Meroni, *Cremona*, pp. 28-29).

47. See Cipolla, "Per la storia delle terre," especially pp. 668, 672.

48. The possibility that capital may have flowed from agriculture into the urban economies has not been seriously investigated by students of late

medieval and early modern Italy. One known example of such flow is provided by Guiseppe Mira, *Vicende economiche di una famiglia italiana dal XIV
al XVII secolo* (Milan: Vita e Pensiero, 1940), pp. 34-36: in the first half of the
fifteenth century most of the wealth of the Odescalchi family was tied up in
land, while in the second half much of it was invested in the Como wool industry.

49. On the Borromeo, see Giorgio Chittolini in *Dizionario Biografico
degli Italiani*, vol. 13 (Rome: Istituto dell'Enciclopedia Italiana, 1971), s.v.
"Borromeo, Filippo, Giovanni, Vitaliano." The story of Pagano d'Adda, merchant and manufacturer, head of the Milan merchants' guild, financier, and
landowner, is vividly sketched in Chabod, *Lo Stato*, pp. 197-198. On the Litta
and their rise from the spice and cloth trades to landownership and gentility in
the course of the sixteenth century, see Zanoli, "Il patrimonio della famiglia
Litta," pp. 284-297.

50. The comment made by Gino Luzzatto about the view that the decline
of the Venetian economy resulted from merchants withdrawing from trade
and turning to landownership is worth quoting as it seems equally valid for
Milan: "Even if it were true that most established merchants chose to become
rentiers, this would not necessarily imply the decay of trade. Even in our own
day we witness a continuous turnover of families and individuals engaged in
trade, industry, and banking. It seldom happens that the same business firm
remains in one same family for more than three generations; as a rule, new
faces emerge to replace those who quit" ("La decadenza di Venezia dopo le
scoperte geografiche nella tradizione e nella realtà," *Archivio Veneto*, 54-55
[1954]: 164).

51. In the words of Francesco Guicciardini, "to buy land is one of the
objectives for which merchants are accustomed to labor" (quoted in Jones,
"Medieval Agrarian Society," p. 350). Referring to the middle class in Tudor
England, J. H. Hexter has pointedly remarked that its most successful mem-
bers' overriding ambition was to move up "to the place where the sun was and
long was to remain, among the landed gentlemen and noblemen of England"
("The Myth of the Middle Class in Tudor England," in his *Reappraisals in
History: New Views on History and Society in Early Modern Europe* [New
York: Harper, 1961], p. 114). Kamen, *The Iron Century*, p. 197, draws similar
conclusions for the European middle class in general.

52. The best discussion of this process from its inception at mid-four-
teenth century to its final codification in 1593 is that of Vismara, "Le istituzioni del patriziato," pp. 229-264. See also Barni, "Mutamenti di ideali sociali," pp. 776-782, and Petronio, *Il Senato*, pp. 198-201.

53. The belligerency of the guilds and their ability, in some instances, to
win the Spanish government over to their cause against the patriciate have
recently been brought out by Politi, *Aristocrazia e potere politico*, pp. 34-36,
40, 153-159, 167: although merchants had been excluded from the city council
in 1542 and legislation was enacted in subsequent years which favored the

landed interests, a compromise was reached in 1570 after the protests of the merchants' guild found partial support in Madrid.

54. G. B. Luca, *Il Dottor volgare* (Rome, 1673), 5: 29, quoted in Da Silva, *Banque et crédit*, 1: 242.

55. José Gentil Da Silva and Ruggiero Romano, "L'histoire des changes: Les foires de Bisenzone de 1600 à 1650," *Annales. E. S. C.*, 17 (1962): 721; Da Silva, *Banque et crédit*, 1: 245. According to Savary, "there are no merchants [*négocians*] in Europe as skilled and astute as the Italians . . . They manage their affairs so well that their money does not lie idle even for one day and constantly brings them some profit" (*Le Parfait Négociant*, pp. 65-66). Examples of patricians, provincial noblemen, and wealthy bourgeois investing in tax farming, rent charges, government loans, and the exchange are in Caizzi, *Il Comasco*, pp. 34, 81, 153; Meroni, *Cremona*, pp. 42 n., 61. The case of Marquess Omodei, a Milanese patrician and landowner who invested in government loans on a prodigious scale, is discussed below.

56. See Bruno Caizzi, "Le classi sociali nella vita milanese," in *SdM*, 11: 338.

57. ASM, *Deroghe giudiziarie del Senato*, 42 (Lodi), doc. of 17 Nov. 1682.

58. The whole story is in *Fd.* 122/2 and covers the years 1682-1685.

59. Ambrogio Oppizzone, *Informatione per modo di discorso in materia delle Equalanze Terrere, Provinciali et Generali* (Milan, 1643), pp. 1, 88-90.

60. Ibid., p. 110. The shift of part of the tax burden onto the cities in the seventeenth century is discussed by Caizzi, "Economia e finanza," p. 372, in the case of the city of Vigevano. For the quite different situation obtaining in the preceding century, see Olivero Colombo, "Mercanti e popolari," p. 136.

61. ASM, *Commercio p. a.*, 25/4, "Dimostratione dell'avvantaggio che hanno li Mercanti di Canzo nella fabrica de loro drappi di più di quelli di Milano," undated but attached to an official report of 2 Aug. 1663. Similar conclusions can be drawn from a printed table in ASM, *Commercio p. a.*, 228, of 25 Apr. 1679, comparing the taxes and labor costs involved in the production and export to France of one pound of silk thread. If originating in Milan, the silk thread paid 7s. 6d. more in taxes than if produced in the countryside; the wage bill in the city exceeded by 15s. 6d. that paid to rural workers. Twenty years later a proposal to reduce taxes levied on silk spun in the city so as to make it competitive with that spun in the countryside was dismissed by the Treasury on grounds that it would do little good, since in the country "the women who turn silk into thread are willing to work for less than the women in Milan" (ibid., doc. of 4 July 1699).

62. On the plague see Chapter III. As for military service, it must have made heavy demands on the work force, especially after the introduction in 1615 of compulsory service in both the urban and rural militias (*milizia urbana* and *forense*) during emergencies (Bendiscioli, "Politica, amministrazione e religione," p. 36). When, for instance, the militia was called in 1636, the city

of Milan alone had to provide 6,000 men (ASM, *Militare p. a.*, 205, doc. of 28 Sept. 1636). To make things worse, it seems that the militia was recruited from among "merchants, money dealers, shopkeepers, and artisans of some standing in order that the poor be not unduly burdened and that public security be better ensured" (ibid., doc. of 1658). Some data on the rural militia in Arrigoni, *Notizie storiche*, p. 271, and Ferrario, *Busto Arsizio*, pp. 83, 102.

63. The fact that rural craftsmen combined farming and handicraft industry is occasionally mentioned in our sources. A late seventeenth century petition speaks of the weavers of the village of Lissone as "poor peasants who engage in farming most of the time" (ACM, *Materie*, 575, doc. "L'Arte della Lana che negli anni passati . . . "). A 1669 petition refers to the hat makers of Monza as "all having to tend their fields" (quoted in Riva, *L'Arte del cappello*, p. 275).

64. According to Slicher van Bath, *Agrarian History*, p. 218, "the development of a rural textile industry was a phenomenon characteristic of the seventeenth-century agricultural depression" throughout Europe. On this point, see also the remarks in E. L. Jones, "Agricultural Origins of Industry," *Past and Present*, 40 (1968): 64-66.

65. High labor costs as a cause of the decline of urban industries in seventeenth-century Italy were first emphasized in Cipolla, "The Economic Decline of Italy," p. 139.

66. The "selective character" of industrial decline resulting from differences in labor intensity has been discussed, with reference to Holland, by Charles Wilson, "Taxation and the Decline of Empires, an Unfashionable Theme," in his *Economic History and the Historian: Collected Essays* (New York: Praeger, 1969), pp. 122-123.

67. If I interpret correctly a 1554 document published in Santoro, *La Matricola*, p. 191, and listing individual cost items that went into the making of a cloth in Milan, the wage bill accounted for 46 percent of total costs. For the "Milan gold thread" see the figures quoted in Cole, *Colbert*, 2: 197. On jewelry: seven gold necklaces presented by the governor of Milan to a Swiss diplomatic mission in 1633 cost the Lombard taxpayer L.9,819 11s. 6d., of which only L.239 10s. went to pay for the goldsmith's labor (ASM, *Potenze estere*, 145, doc. of 19 Sept. 1633). Information on velvet and damask, as well as on thrown silk, in ASM, *Commercio p. a.*, 228, doc. of 15 Mar. 1647.

68. ASM, *Commercio p. a.*, 1, "consulta Arese" of 4 July 1641.

69. ACM, *Materie*, 572, memorandum attached to "consulta" of 2 July 1680.

70. ACM, *Materie*, 269, "Ricordi del Sr Daniele de Capitani" of 1 Apr. 1658.

71. ASM, *Commercio p. a.*, 228, printed memorandum of 29 Nov. 1678.

72. ACM, *Materie*, 572, memorandum of 2 July 1680, quoted earlier.

73. Verga, "Le corporazioni tessili," p. 102. The Milan craft guilds also opposed the concentration of looms into fewer and larger shops, alleging that

these would be run by "overbearing and uncharitable merchants" (Catalano, "La fine del dominio spagnolo," p. 191). Such hostile attitudes were not, of course, to be found in Milan only. For similar attitudes in other Italian cities see Cipolla, "The Economic Decline of Italy," p. 137; and in other European nations, Hermann Kellenbenz, "Technology in the Age of the Scientific Revolution, 1500-1700," in *FEHE*, 2 (London-Glasgow: Collins, 1974): 243-244.

74. A telling example is that of the celebrated gold thread of Milan; this was one of the city's manufactures that best weathered the crisis of the seventeenth century; it was also one in which imitation proved hardest to achieve.

75. A. G. B. Paolini, *Della legittima libertà del commercio* (Florence, 1785), 1: 230.

76. ASM, *Uffici regii p. a.*, 654, reg. 1640-42, "consulta di Baldassar Grasso."

VI. RESILIENCE IN THE COUNTRYSIDE

1. This contrast has recently been underlined by Aldo De Maddalena in an important interpretive essay, "A Milano nei secoli XVI e XVII: da ricchezza 'reale' a ricchezza 'nominale'?", *RSI*, 89 (1977): 559-560. See also Domenico Sella, "The Two Faces of the Lombard Economy in the Seventeenth Century", in *Failed Transitions to Modern Industrial Society: Renaissance Italy and Seventeenth-Century Holland*, ed. F. Krantz and P. M. Hohenberg (Montreal: I.C.E.S., 1975), pp. 12-13; and for Italy as a whole, Fernand Braudel, "L'Italia fuori d'Italia: Due secoli e tre Italie", in *Storia d'Italia* (Turin: Einaudi, 1974), 2: 2229-2230.

2. Further evidence for the late seventeenth century is in Galantino, *Storia di Soncino*, 3: 419 (continuous rotation involving wheat or rye, flax or millet, oats, and grass); Zaninelli, *Una grande azienda agricola*, pp. 87-91 (3 to 5 years under grass followed by one year each of maize, flax, and wheat or rice). See also De Maddalena, "Contributo," p. 168, for data showing a pattern involving cereals and artificial grasses in the Pavia province.

3. Arthur Young, "Notes on the Agriculture of Lombardy," in his *Travels during the years 1787, 1788, and 1789*, 2nd ed. (London, 1794), 2: 146 ("Lombardy is one of the richest plains in the world"), 178 (irrigation), 203 ("the arable lands never repose").

4. *Fd.* 630/12 (Vernate), 1 June 1640; 635/9 (Vidigulfo), 22 Feb. 1642; 288/2 (Landriano), 1652; 516/6 (Salerano), 9 Mar. 1654; 158/20 (Casalpusterlengo), 25 Feb. 1655; 360/1 (Mirabello), 20 May 1655; 87/7 (Bertonico), 24 May 1656; 437/11 (Paullo), 15 May 1673; 213/6 (Codogno), 1678; 264/4 (Mulazzana), 7 Aug. 1678; 264/7 (Gattera), 11 Nov. 1686.

5. *Fd.* 578/11 (Soncino), 26 June 1640; 430/1 (Gombito), 23 Feb. 1649 and (Paderno), 6 Aug. 1649; 226 (Corte Madama), 19 Feb. 1643; 157/3 (Casalmaggiore), 10 May 1717; 496/1 (Vinzaglio), 31 Jan. 1654; 415/11 (Olevano Lomellina), 12 July 1677.

6. *Fd.* 487/3e (Rivolta), 30 June 1640: annual silk production was esti-

mated at 2,000 pounds; 149/2 (Caronno), 24 June 1646; 562/4 (Castelletto Ticino), 25 Jan. 1640; 536/1 (Sesto Calende), 7 May 1656 and "Descriptio bonorum" of 29 Oct. 1656; 129/11 (Busto Arsizio), 12 Dec. 1652; 258/5 (Gallarate), 28 Feb. 1656. South of Pavia the cultivation of maize rose dramatically in the second half of the century, according to Giuseppe Aleati, "Tre secoli all'interno di una *possessio* ecclesiastica: Portalbera, sec. XVI-XVIII," *Bollettino della Società Pavese di Storia patria*, new ser., 2 (1948): 33.

7. *Fd.* 414 (Oggiono), 14 Jan. 1652; 354/12 (Missaglia), 9 Sept. 1648; 293/11 (Leggiuno), 3 Mar. 1642; 217/6 (Isola), 1 Dec. 1637; 487/8a (Robbiate near Merate), 23 Oct. 1645.

8. *Fd.* 217/6 (Ossuccio), 15 Oct. 1637; 25 ("notificazione di Bognanco"), 3 May 1655; 616/3 (Valsassina), 4 May 1647.

9. *Fd.* 618/13 (Luino), 6 July 1642; 578 bis/11 (Soncino), 27 June 1640; 140/15 (Caravaggio), 5 Feb. 1643.

10. *Fd.* 258/5 (Gallarate), 28 Feb. 1656; 129/11 (Busto Arsizio), 12 Dec. 1652; 157/3 (Casalmaggiore), 10 May 1717; 544/5 (San Fiorano), 3 Feb. 1617; 545/1 (San Fiorano), 4 Dec. 1644.

11. *Fd.* 160/5 (Casalpusterlengo), 11 Oct. 1693; 87/7 (Bertonico), 24 May 1656; 213/6 (Codogno), 2 Aug. 1678.

12. *Fd.* 193/3 (Castelponzone), 20 Oct. 1696.

13. Giovanni Bonanome, *La Riviera del Lario descritta* (Como, 1668), p. 135.

14. *Fd.* 422/9 (Osteno), 21 July 1676. My estimate of the population of the valley is very rough and is based on the fact that 464 households were counted in 1647 (*Fd.* 28, "Notifica della Valle d'Intelvi, 23 Mar. 1647); with an average of five people per household, this would mean a total of 2,320 people; thirty years later the total may have been somewhat higher.

15. ACM, *Materie*, 139, "Nota delle folle," 24 Feb. 1666. From the context is is clear that the *folle* (literally "fulling mills") referred to in the document are *folle da carta* (paper mills).

16. See Sella, "Industrial Production," p. 242, and the bibliography cited there.

17. Galantino, *Storia di Soncino*, 2: 200.

18. Arrigoni, *Notizie storiche*, pp. 189-190.

19. On Francesco Zignone, the ironmaster from Bergamo who came to the Valsassina in 1641, see Frumento, *Imprese lombarde*, 2: 107-108. Actually, Zignone seems to have secured large contracts from the Spanish government as early as 1636, and these probably involved hardware produced in the Venetian province of Bergamo. In that year he supplied the Spanish forces stationed in Lombardy with some 17,000 artillery shells and grenades, 6,050 axes, 7,028 shovels, and nearly 50 metric tons of nails and "sundry hardware" (*diversa herramienta*). Similar contracts he secured in subsequent years (ASM, *Apprensioni*, 577, 18 Nov. 1648). By 1641, at any rate, iron production was well under way in the Valsassina itself: in that year the Venetian government was informed that in the valley thirty-six iron mills were in oper-

ation and in one of them "run by Zignone, bombs, grenades, and ammunition are manufactured and there are molds for casting ordnance." (Archivio di Stato, Venice, *Senato rettori, dispacci Brescia*, filza 43, 2 July 1641).

20. Fd. 616/4, petition of the *sindici* of Valsassina, 1647.

21. Fanfani, "L'industria mineraria," p. 175.

22. The data are from Frumento, *Imprese lombarde*, 2: 63 and 434. It is well to remember that a blast furnance in Valsassina could produce between 100 and 200 metric tons of pig iron a year, depending on the duration of the smelting campaign (Sella, "The Iron Industry," p. 104).

23. Pio Bondioli, *Un'azienda cotoni a Busto Arsizio tra il Seicento e il Settecento* (Busto Arsizio: Almanacco della Famiglia bustocca, 1958), p. 1. The shortage of firewood in the area is mentioned as early as 1628 and was ascribed to the recent depletion of local woodlands in *Fd.* 244/2 (Caiello), 2 July 1628.

24. Gualdo Priorato, *Relatione*, p. 162.

25. *Fd.* 220/4 (Concorezzo), 23 Sept. 1696. For sixteenth-century evidence, see Chapter I; for the eighteenth century see Caizzi, *Industria, commercio e banca*, p. 126.

26. According to a 1647 official inquiry, "it is to be feared that, unless great care is taken to revive their manufacture, the output of short cloths [*panni bassi*] of inferior quality and moderate price intended for the poor such as used to be produced in Monza, Como, Brianza, and Incino, will fall short of our needs." The inquiry goes on to list the surviving cloth firms: one each in Longone, Erba, Boffalora near Erba, Canzo, Magreglio, and Tegone, and three in Asso (ASM, *Commercio p.a.*, 199/1, report of 16 May 1647).

27. Verga, "Le corporazioni," p. 88.

28. According to a 1663 document, the cloth makers of Canzo "have caused great harm to those of Milan" (ASM, *Commercio p.a.*, 199/6, 16 Apr. 1663). The competition of Canzo continued to be felt and denounced in subsequent years (ACM, *Materie*, 572, 2 July 1680).

29. ASM, *Commercio p.a.*, 199/6, "Processo per il Lanificio . . . di Gorgonzola," 15 May 1662. The district around Erba was another source of concern to the Milan cloth makers (ACM, *Materie*, 269, 1 Apr. 1658).

30. ACM, *Materie*, 572, petition of 9 July 1698 filed by the villages of Valassina against the demand of the Milan weavers guild that all wool yarn spun by them be shipped exclusively to Milan. Such obligation, it was argued, would bring ruin to the district, because "this being a very populous and barren valley surrounded by mountains and unable to grow more than one sixth of the grain it needs . . . it has no way of earning its livelihood were it not for the fact that an infinite number of women spin wool . . . this being their sole and continuous occupation." The petitioners asked to be allowed to sell their yarn to the then-prosperous cloth industry of Bergamo. A similar argument in ACM, *Materie*, 270, 21 Feb. 1710, indicates that wool spinning was then widespread in the whole piedmont region between Lecco and the

Valassina, and that Bergamo continued to be the chief outlet for their yarn. Data showing the flourishing conditions of the Bergamo cloth industry in the late seventeenth and early eighteenth centuries are in Rapp, *Industry and Economic Decline*, p. 162.

31. Quoted in Ferrario, *Busto Arsizio*, p. 54.

32. Bondioli, *Un'azienda cotoni*, p. 1.

33. *Fd.* 129/11 (Busto Arsizio), 12 Dec. 1652.

34. Caizzi, *Industrie, Commercio e Banca*, pp. 33, 89.

35. A vivid description of the processing of flax by peasant women in the Lombard plain is reproduced in Zaninelli, *Una grande azienda agricola*, p. 142 n.

36. Verri, *Considerazioni*, pp. 93, 99, and table III.

37. See Table 5.

38. "Visite del Consigliere Pietro de la Tour" (1767), in Carlo Antonio Vianello, ed., *Relazioni sull'industria, il commercio e l'agricoltura lombardi del '700* (Milan: Giuffré, 1941), pp. 47-97.

39. *Fd.* 360/1, "Summa inventarij bonorum relictorum per Ill. quondam Com. Franciscum Somaliam," 3 June 1586.

40. ACM, *Materie*, 901, petition of 23 Dec. 1597.

41. ASM, *Censo p.a.*, 311, "Relazione de danni patiti . . ."

42. See Appendix D.

43. See Mira, *Vicende economiche*, p. 135.

44. General progress in the countryside in the second half of the seventeenth century is mentioned by Catalano, "La fine del dominio spagnolo," p. 180; Aldo De Maddalena, "L'immobilizzazione della ricchezza nella Milano spagnola: moventi, esperienze, interpretazioni," *Annali di storia economica e sociale*, 6 (1965): 28-29.

45. De Maddalena, "Il mondo rurale," p. 386.

46. See Appendix B.

47. De Maddalena, "Contributo," p. 174.

48. Aleati, "Tre secoli," pp. 32-35.

49. The two contracts for the estate of Castelnuovo Bocca d'Adda are in ASM, *Fondo di Religione p.a.*, 4222, and are dated 29 Sept. 1658 and 30 Sept. 1681 respectively.

50. De Maddalena, *Prezzi*, p. 86. For the whole State of Milan, see Pugliese, *Condizioni economiche*, p. 34: 85,512 *pertiche* at mid-sixteenth century and 591,316 two centuries later.

51. Pieraldo Bullio, "Problemi e geografia della risicoltura in Piemonte nei secoli XVII e XVIII," *Annali della Fondazione Luigi Einaudi*, 3 (1969): 49, 51-53.

52. *Fd.* 415/11 (Olevano Lomellina), 12 July 1677.

53. Caizzi, *Il Comasco*, p. 164. Somewhat surprisingly, Caizzi seems to ascribe the change to "the persecution of an inexorable fiscal machine" rather than to the decline of cereal prices, which made arable farming increasingly

224 *Notes to Pages 120-126*

unprofitable on the marginal soils of the hill zone.

54. The village of Montaldeo has been investigated by Doria, *Uomini e terre.*

55. Ibid., pp. 6-9, 24, 25, 28, 31, 32, 33, 37, 39, 42, 63-67, 103-108.

56. The decline of viticulture in the lowlands is briefly discussed by De Maddalena, "Contributo," pp. 178-179. Some information also in Galantino, *Storia di Soncino,* 3: 419.

57. Bullio, "Problemi e geografia," p. 49.

58. *Fd.* 415/11 (Olevano Lomellina), 12 July 1677.

59. Riva, *L'arte del cappello,* pp. 88, 92, 93, 108, 109, 123, 125, 275.

60. On the decline of the wool industry in Vigevano, see Caizzi, "Economia e finanza," pp. 357-376.

61. ASM, *Commercio p.a.,* 228, document of 4 July 1699.

62. Piero Landini, *La Lomellina: Profilo geografico* (Rome: Signorelli, 1950), p. 197.

63. Carlo Poni, "All'origine del sistema di fabbrica: tecnologia e organizzazione produttiva dei mulini da seta nell'Italia settentrionale (secoli XVII-XVIII)," *RSI,* 88 (1976): 472-473.

64. Ibid., p. 472, and ASM, *Commercio p.a.,* 228, report of 14 July 1654.

65. ACM, *Materie,* 269, "Ricordo del Sr. Daniele de Capitani" of 1 Apr. 1658.

66. ASM, *Commercio p.a.,* 228, printed report of 19 Aug. 1676.

67. ACM, *Materie,* 269, printed report of 29 Nov. 1678.

68. Report of 20 June 1679, quoted in Catalano, "La fine del dominio spagnolo," p. 183. See also ACM, *Materia,* 875, "Nota dei molini di seta . . . in data 24 giugno 1679."

69. Bognetti, "La seta in Lombardia," p. 40; Caizzi, *Industria, commercio e banca,* p. 99, for the figure on Milan; Verri, *Considerazioni,* p. 90, for the statewide total.

70. The growth of the imports of raw and thrown silk to Lyons provides a telling example of this: 100 bales imported in 1522, 2,000 in 1569, 6,000 in 1697, and 14,000 in 1714 (Gascon, *Grand commerce,* 1: 61).

71. See Chapter IV, note 19.

72. Caizzi, "Le classi sociali," p. 363.

73. Caizzi, *Il Comasco,* pp. 118-139 and ch. 2, especially pp. 61, 73, 81.

74. On the *fedecommesso* see Enrico Besta, *Le successioni nella storia del diritto italiano* (Padua: Cedam, 1935), pp. 159-163. The fedecommesso was normally associated with primogeniture: while the latter determined who should inherit the entire estate, the former was meant to prevent the heir from selling or donating any portion of the estate and to ensure that he would hand on his inheritance intact to the next generation.

75. The point did not escape contemporaries and one of them argued that without primogeniture and some form of entail "within three generations

families would fall into poverty as a result of the breakup of their estates" (quoted in Caizzi, "Le classi sociali," p. 349). Even some eighteenth-century critics of the fedecommesso conceded that it contributed to the preservation of noble families. See Luigi Tria, *Il fedecommesso nella legislazione e nella dottrina dal secola XVI ai nostri giorni* (Milan: Giuffrè, 1945), p. 63. For Europe as a whole see Kamen, *The Iron Century*, pp. 164-165.

76. *Fd.* 217/6, "relatione pro infeudatione" of 1 Dec. 1637.

77. *Fd.* 449/5 (Piovera), 13 Oct. 1650; 449/6, "relatione" of 22 Mar. 1651.

78. On Balbi see Pugliese, *Condizioni economiche*, p. 349.

79. Aldo De Maddalena, "Formazione, impiego e rendimento della ricchezza nella Milano spagnola: Il caso di Gottardo Frisiani (1575-1608)," in *Studi in onore di Epicarmo Corbino* (Milan: Giuffrè, 1961), pp. 156, 165, 170, 173.

80. *Fd.* 122/1 (Brignano), 15 Mar. 1680; 122/2, "Processus" of 1685; 122/3, report of 27 Mar. 1685.

81. Postan's remarks about medieval land sales are certainly applicable to seventeenth-century Lombardy: "they were mere transfer payments—a way in which the savings of some men compensated for the dis-savings of others, leaving the fixed capital resources of agriculture more or less unaffected. The most important economic consequence they had was to sustain the land market and to raise the cost of saleable land." M. M. Postan, "Investment in Medieval Agriculture," *JEH*, 27 (1967): 584.

82. ASM, *Finanza p.a.*, 746, "Memoriale di Prospero Rho" of 12 Jan. 1639. The estate was located at Ca' del Prato, ten kilometers south of Lodi.

83. *Fd.* 449/5 (Piovera), "Relatione dell'Ingegnere Bigorolo" of 30 Dec. 1650.

84. Caizzi, *Il Comasco*, p. 118.

85. A case in point in *Fd.* 557/11 (Sartirana), 23 Sept. 1631.

86. *Fd.* 47 (Annicco Cremonese), "1640: Notizie intorno ai beni delle famiglie Lampugnani e Stanga." The information contained therein refers to the year 1639, as shown by the mention on p. 136 of "Martinmas 1639."

87. *Fd.* 122/1 (Brignano), 15 Mar. 1680; 422/9 (Osteno), 21 July 1676.

88. ACM, *Materie*, 139, "Nota delle folle," 24 Feb. 1666.

89. Fanfani, "L'industria mineraria," p. 175; Frumento, *Imprese lombarde*, 2: 86n. Noble participation in business such as mining has led L. Bulferetti to speak of "feudal capitalism," in the sense of commercial, capitalistic enterprises being handled by aristocrats who enjoyed feudal privileges and revenues and increasingly replaced old merchant class ("L'oro, la terra e la societa," pp. 30, 38, 45, 47). Although useful in that it calls attention to the generally neglected role played by noblemen in business, the expression "feudal capitalism" may be misleading if it should convey the impression that feudal revenues were an important source of risk capital. So far as I have been able to determine, in Spanish Lombardy feudal revenue de-

rived from the administration of justice, monopoly rights, and levies did not loom large in the total income of fief holders and was overshadowed by the income accruing to them as landowners. See Chapter VIII.

90. Frumento, *Imprese lombarde*, 2: 122.

91. For some illustrations of this, see Domenico Sella, "European Industries, 1500-1700," in *FEHE*, 2: 407.

92. This system is well illustrated in the case of Zignone, already discussed. The documents referred to there make it quite clear that he received large cash advances from the Spanish government.

93. For one such negative judgment, see Caizzi, "Le classi sociali," pp. 343-344.

VII. THE LEGACY

1. The large body of literature on the subject has been discussed by Bulferetti in two articles: "L'oro, la terra, la società," pp. 6-66, and "Il problema della decadenza italiana," in *Nuove questioni di storia moderna* (Milan: Marzorati, 1964), 2: 803-845. For a more recent discussion see Guido Quazza, *La decadenza italiana nella storia europea: Saggi sul Sei-Settecento* (Turin: Einaudi, 1971), ch. 1, especially pp. 52-62. Although the blanket condemnation of the "Seicento" as a century of unrelieved gloom has, in recent years, been considerably softened and qualified, only a few writers have emphasized the positive, progressive aspects of the period. Among them: Nicolini, *Aspetti della vita italo spagnola*, pp. 183-184 (credits Spanish rule with "uprooting from its Italian possessions the evil of feudal anarchy and with establishing absolutism in them"); Visconti, *La pubblica amministrazione*, pp. 33-40 (calls attention to the "seeds of the modern state" planted by the Spaniards); H. G. Koenigsberger, "Decadence or Shift? Changes in the Civilization of Italy and Europe in the Sixteenth and Seventeenth Centuries," *Transactions of the Royal Historical Society*, 10 (1960): 1-18 (stresses Italian creativity in architecture and music during the Baroque age); and Delumeau, *L'Italie*, pp. 238-246 (stresses the "slow recovery," especially in northern Italy after 1630).

2. On this point see Max Barkhausen, "Government Control and Free Enterprise in Western Germany and the Low Countries in the Eighteenth Century," in *Essays in European Economic History*, ed. P. Earle (Oxford: Clarendon Press, 1974), pp. 224, 227, 245, 247-248; Braudel, *Capitalism*, pp. 439-440; and Bairoch, "Agriculture and the Industrial Revolution," p. 494.

3. Young, "Notes on the Agriculture of Lombardy," pp. 146, 203. Similar comments in J. J. Lalande, *Voyage d'un François en Italie fait dans les années 1765 et 1766* (Yverdon, 1769), 1: 338; and Abbé Richard, *Description historique et critique*, 1: 212-213. On the progress of land reclamation and irrigation in the second half of the eighteenth century, see Vianello, *Il Settecento*, p. 256.

4. G. C. Zimolo, "Canali e navigazione interna nell'età moderna," in *SdM*, 14: 862.

5. Vianello, *Il Settecento*, p. 258; Greenfield, *Economics and Liberalism*, p. 44.

6. On this point see Luciano Cafagna, "The Industrial Revolution in Italy, 1830-1914," in *FEHE*, 4, pt. 1 (London and Glasgow: Collins, 1973): 281.

7. Ibid., p. 282.

8. Piero Dagradi, "Il complesso industriale Legnano-Busto Arsizio-Gallarate," in *Panorama storico dell'Alto Milanese*, (Busto-Gallarate-Legnano: Rotary Club, 1971): 2: 5, 7-8, 25, 27.

9. Frumento, *Imprese lombarde*, vol. 1, ch. 4.

10. These two basic conditions for an early start of industrialization are stressed by Cafagna, "The Industrial Revolution," p. 284.

11. See Jones, "Agricultural Origins," pp. 64, 70.

12. Dagradi, "Il complesso industriale," pp. 19, 21, 47. Although the rise of modern industry in nineteenth-century Lombardy clearly lies outside the scope of this book, I am under the impression that the case of Lombardy conforms quite closely to the northern European pattern analyzed by Franklin F. Mendels in his article "Proto-industrialization: The First Phase of the Industrialization Process," *JEC*, 32 (1972): 241-261.

13. Dagradi, "Il complesso industriale," p. 9.

14. The role of rural entrepreneurs in the process of industrialization has been discussed, for the Zurich district, by Rudolph Braun, "The Rise of a Rural Class of Industrial Entrepreneurs," *Journal of World History*, 10 (1967): 551-556. See also Bairoch, "Agriculture and the Industrial Revolution," pp. 492-496.

15. Antonio Anzilotti, "Il tramonto dello Stato cittadino," *ASI*, 82 (1924): 72-105, is still an invaluable introduction to the economic policies of the enlightened rulers of Lombardy and Tuscany in the eighteenth century. For a later and fuller account see Luzzatto, *Storia economica*, 2: 148-192.

16. Verga, "Le corporazioni," p. 96.

17. Verga, "Il Comune di Milano," p. xliv.

18. Tridi, *Informatione*, p. 19.

19. *Gridario Caracena*, pp. 121, 161, 314; *Gridario Ponze de Leon*, p. 121.

20. *Gridario Ossuna*, p. 92, for an edict of the Magistrato Ordinario of 7 June 1673, duly approved by Governor Ossuna, which voided the decree issued on 8 July 1670 by Ossuna himself banning the export of raw silk.

21. *Gridario Ligne*, p. 124.

22. ASM, *Commercio p. a.*, 1, printed memorandum of 19 Aug. 1676.

23. One example: in 1662 the Senate ordered a cloth maker who had moved out of Milan "to dismantle the workshop he has built in Gorgonzola and to deliver here [in Milan] all wool yarn and any other material" (ASM,

Commercio p. a., 199/6, "15 maggio 1662. Processo per il lanificio disfatto in Milano e posto nella terra di Gorgonzola"). We do not know whether the injunction was complied with.

24. ASM, *Commercio p. a.*, 228, printed memorandum of 5 June 1679: "in search of such remedies as may help restore the processing of silk in this city, we have deemed that the proposed law forcing the owners of silk mills in the countryside to move to the city would be not only exceedingly harsh, but also impractical; for it seems to us that no one ought to be deprived of his natural liberty to earn a living in whatever place he can best do so." The Vicario went on to recommend changes in the excise system that would encourage production in the city.

25. The whole incident has been dramatized and given literary fame by Alessandro Manzoni in his celebrated novel *I Promessi Sposi* (1825-1827), chs. 12 and 13. For a modern, exhaustive analysis of the incident see Nicolini, "Il tumulto di San Martino," pp. 127-242.

26. De Maddalena, *Prezzi*, pp. 56-58, 100-101.

27. Tridi, *Informatione*.

28. See Catalano, "La fine del dominio spagnolo," p. 39, on the tensions between urban and landed interests at this point.

29. ACM, *Materie*, 268, "consulta" of 23 Dec. 1641. References to this document in Verga, "Le leggi suntuarie," pp. 90-91, and Catalano, "La fine del dominio spagnolo," p. 39.

30. See document quoted in note 24 of this chapter.

31. Luzzatto, *Storia economica*, 2: 151-152.

VIII. A POSTSCRIPT ON FEUDALISM

1. Rosario Villari, "Il riformismo e l'evoluzione delle campagne italiane nel Settecento, attraverso studi recenti," *Studi Storici*, 5 (1964): 164.

2. Romano, *Le classi sociali*, p. 29.

3. Candeloro, *Storia dell'Italia moderna*, 1: 19. It should be noted that Candeloro's concept of feudalism is very broadly construed to include, for instance, such forms of land tenure as share-tenancy. The dangers of too broad a construction of the terms "feudalism" and "feudal economy" are discussed in Jacques Heers, "The Feudal Economy and Capitalism: Words, Ideas, and Reality," *Journal of European Economic History*, 3 (Winter 1974): 609-653.

4. Ruggiero Romano, "L'Italia nella crisi del secolo XVIII," *Studi Storici*, 9 (1968): 736. Romano provides no documentation for his statements and neither do Candeloro, *Storia dell'Italia moderna*, 1: 50, and Catalano "La fine del dominio spagnolo," p. 176, when asserting that feudal lords increased seignorial obligations in order to compensate for their dwindling income from agriculture.

5. See Cesare Magni, *Il tramonto del feudo lombardo* (Milan: Giuffrè, 1937), pp. 92, 93, 104; Romano, "L'Italia nella crisi," p. 736; Catalano, "La

fine del dominio spagnolo," pp. 113, 115, 116; and Caizzi, "Le classi sociali," p. 341.

6. See Magni, *Il tramonto*, pp. 91-104.

7. Caizzi, "Le classi sociali," p. 341.

8. Romano, "L'Italia nella crisi," p. 737.

9. The whole question is thoroughly discussed in Magni, *Il tramonto*, pp. 225-231; his conclusion is that "out of 1600 communities under feudal rule at the opening of the eighteenth century only one-fourth can be regarded as having been newly enfeoffed by Spain: three-fourths of them had already been subject to the feudal bond before the coming of the Spaniards." See also Vismara, "Le istituzioni del patriziato," pp. 260-261.

10. Giorgio Chittolini, "Infeudazioni e politica feudale nel ducato visconteo-sforzesco," *Quaderni Storici* (1972), pp. 57-130.

11. See Magni, *Il tramonto*, p. 219 (on the general practice adopted by the Spanish government of selling, rather than freely granting, fiefs); p. 130 (on the obligation of all titles of nobility to be backed by investiture of an actual fief); p. 137 (on the introduction of the rule of primogeniture); see also Vismara, "Le istituzioni del patriziato," p. 260, for a discussion of the financial advantages which the Spanish government could expect from primogeniture.

12. The proclamation (*grida*) of 12 Feb. 1647 is quoted in Catalano, "La fine del dominio spagnolo," p. 115. The frankly venal (and fiscal) character of feudalism in Spanish Lombardy was noticed and explained by a jurist, Giuseppe Benaglio, in his *Relazione istorica del Magistrato delle Ducali Entrate Straordinarie* (Milan, 1711), p. 157: "Although fiefs are nothing but the conditional possession of immovable goods bestowed by the Sovereign out of sheer liberality . . . nevertheless the necessity of keeping fortifications in a state of readiness and of protecting the State against foreign powers has forced our Princes to grant for a price that which was formerly meant as a reward."

13. See the Note on Sources.

14. *Fd.* 430/3 (Polengo), 28 Aug. 1651; (Vinzasca), 27 May 1651; 487/8a (Robbiate), 23 Oct. 1643; 264/1, "Sommario" on Rovedario, Sigola, etc. of 28 Sept. 1640; 481/5 (Regina Fittarezza), 7 Mar. 1640.

15. *Fd.* 430/1 (Paderno), 6 Aug. 1649; (Oscasale), 6 Feb. 1649; (San Bassano), 16 Feb. 1649.

16. *Fd.* 258/5 (Gallarate), 28 Feb. 1656. On the transfer from Altemps to Visconti see Enrico Casanova, *Dizionario feudale delle province componenti l'antico Stato di Milano all'epoca della cessazione del sistema feudale*, 2nd ed. (Milan: Biblioteca Ambrosiana, 1930), p. 46; also G. D. Oltrona Visconti, "Il feudo e i feudatari di Gallarate," *Rassegna gallaratese di storia e d'arte*, 11 (1952): 32-46; and on the financial difficulties that forced Altemps to sell, Ludwig Welti, "Relazioni dei Conti di Hohemens con la città di Gallarate," ibid., 27 (1968): 165-175.

17. The expression *giogo dell'infeudazione* is found in a petition submit-

ted by two landowners of Inzago in 1692 requesting that the village be "redeemed" (ASM, *Comuni p.a.*, 38). Magni, *Il tramonto*, p. 93, asserts that redemptions were never numerous as only a few villages could afford the required ransom.

18. *Fd.* 248/1 (Fino), 6 Mar. 1656; 81/7 (Bellagio), "1601 al 1625. Causa tra la città di Como et il Conte della Rivera."

19. *Fd.* 155/5 (Casalmaggiore), 13 and 17 Mar. 1679; *Fd.* 156/3 (Casalmaggiore) where the whole incident is reported by the local magistrate (*podestà*) in two long reports dated 13 July and 28 July 1693.

20. Alessandro Giulini, *Vicende feudali del Borgo di Parabiago* (Bari: Giornale Araldico, 1902), pp. 3-7.

21. *Fd.* 593/1 (Tradate): the offer to purchase was made by Marquess Visconti on 6 Jan. 1648; it was opposed in a memorandum of 23 Jan. 1648; redemption was granted on 9 Jan. 1653.

22. *Fd.* 41/5 (Albairate): the petition against enfeoffment of 28 Nov. 1650 was filed by some "noble subjects . . . who own land in the community and district of Albairate"; among them was Alessandro Tadino, a physician who played a prominent role in framing emergency measures during the plague of 1630 and left a written account of it. See also Magni, *Il tramonto*, p. 96.

23. See Catalano, "La fine del dominio spagnolo," p. 116 n. *Fd.* 89/1: Besana was granted its freedom on 14 Jan. 1649; a brief of 7 Oct. 1659 charged that in 1649 "the poor had been deceived . . . into granting power of attorney to a few individuals who controlled the community." *Fd.* 654/9, memorandum of 26 Jan. 1649 reflecting peasant opposition to the redemption of Zelo Surigone, and memorandum of 28 Jan. 1649 expressing the opposite view of the landowners.

24. *Fd.* 593/1 (Tradate), memorandum of 23 Jan. 1648.

25. Catalano, "La fine del dominio spagnolo," p. 116 n.

26. The whole incident is narrated in detail in the minutes of an official investigation (*informazione*) conducted in Albese from 31 Dec. 1656 to 11 Jan. 1657; the minutes and the final resolution of the case on 22 Dec. 1657 are in *Fd.* 43.

27. I was unable to determine whether the priest belonged to the powerful Odescalchi family of Como, although I suspect he did. Pallavicini was one of four bankers called upon in 1660 to submit a plan for the reorganization of the Banco di S. Ambrogio (see Cova, *Il Banco*, p. 86 n).

28. As reported by the magistrate on 16 July 1693 in *Fd.* 156/3.

29. *Fd.* 81/7 (Bellagio), "1601 al 1625. Causa tra la Città di Como et il Conte della Rivera."

30. Magni, *Il tramonto*, p. 93.

31. *Fd.* 414 (Oggiono), memorandum of 20 Sept. 1658 and memorandum of 3 Dec. 1658.

32. Catalano, "La fine del dominio spagnolo," p. 116 n.

33. *Fd.* 89/lb (Besana), memorandum of 7 Oct. 1659; it appears that in 1648 the peasants had been "deceived" by some noblemen into disbursing the price of redemption and had gone heavily into debt to do so; now the new lord, Marquess Tiberio Crivelli, in purchasing Besana in fief, committed himself "to pay the community's entire debt"; the sale was made final on 28 Jan. 1660. *Fd.* 234/1 (Cuggiono), report of 16 Sept. 1672: redemption had been secured in 1652; in 1671 the Piantanida brothers had offered to buy Cuggiono in fief and to assume any such debt as the community might have incurred in the past; opposition to the proposed purchase was staged by eleven landowners, some of them of noble rank. *Fd.* 552/1 and 6 (S.Martino alla Strada): the village had redeemed itself on 1 Mar. 1651; on 10 June 1689 it asked to be allowed, "on account of the burdens it has to bear," to be re-en-feoffed to Marquess Alessandro Villani "owner of more than two-thirds of the land in the community." Petition granted in June 1689; petitioners were illiterate.

34. *Fd.* 144/3: Caravaggio had purchased its freedom on 13 July 1700 and the pertinent request had been filed, allegedly on behalf of the entire community, by two noblemen. *Fd.* 144/7 and 8: renunciation of the royal demesne occurred on 24 Sept. 1713 "the opposition of some landowners (*estimati*) notwithstanding," and 277 heads of family swore allegiance to the new lord. Opposition to the latter was voiced by the three largest landowners (*primi estimati*).

35. *Fd.* 350/1: Melzo had purchased its freedom on 9 May 1691. *Fd.* 350/5: brief of 2 Sept. 1702 opposing a new enfeoffment and reflecting the views of the larger owners (*maggiori estimi*); brief of 21 Jan. 1703 favoring enfeoffment on grounds that Melzo is "in great need of the protection of a feudal lord and must avoid any additional expense." Other briefs dated 27 Jan. 1703 (opposed) and 5 Mar. 1703 (in favor) in the same file; the quotation in the text is from this last document.

36. See Casanova, *Dizionario feudale*, p. 14; *Fd.* 81/14 (Bellagio), 20 Apr. 1647.

37. *Fd.* 81/7: a 1601 report states that three-fifths of the land around Bellagio "belongs to churchmen and burghers (*cittadini*) of Como who are subject to the higher [city] magistrate and recognize no feudal lord."

38. *Fd.* 200 (Cernusco Lombardone), 20 May 1647. Signor Cernuschio's influence in the village is suggested by a list of heads of family compiled on 29 Mar. 1647: out of a total of eighty-eight names, twenty-seven are listed as either tenants (*massari*) or day laborers (*pigionanti*) working for him; the next largest employer was the Milan Hospital with eighteen employees; Marquess Corio came fourth with two tenants and three laborers.

39. Caizzi, "Le classi sociali," p. 341, interprets the case of Codogno as an example of the "sacrifices" any community was willing to make in order to avert "the danger of falling under an authority possibly more exacting and certainly more arbitrary than that of the central government."

40. *Fd.* 215/4 (Codogno), 14 June 1680.

41. *Fd.* 616/4 (Valsassina), printed petition (undated, but clearly pertinent to the sale in fief effected on 7 May 1647).

42. See Frumento, *Imprese lombarde*, 2: 122.

43. *Fd.* 616/4, printed petition: "hanno il libero arbitrio di disponer di tal mercantia a suo compiacimento."

44. *Fd.* 627/1 (Vedeseta), briefs of 6 July 1647, 9 Feb. and 28 Feb. 1649; 627/4, 11 Sept. 1652. Eventually, Vedeseta was allowed to remain "free," but the government strictly limited its right to choose its own magistrate. See Casanova, *Dizionario feudale*, p. 106.

45. *Fd.* 38 (Abbiategrasso), petition of 25 Oct. 1651.

46. See Magni, *Il tramonto*, pp. 115-117. Vismara, "Le istituzioni del patriziato," p. 258, summarizes the situation in these words: "A feudal grant, no matter how comprehensive, gave the feudatory no property rights over the territory (of the fief) . . . It is thus possible to come across one fief in which the lord owned no freehold property (alod) at all and another in which the lord owned a great deal of land—land which he had purchased either before or after he had acquired the fief." Examples of the first kind are the fief of Magenta (*Fd.* 307/7, 11 Jan. 1617) and that of Codogno (*Fd.* 213/6, 2 Aug. 1678). Localities where the feudal lord owned virtually all the land include Corte Madama (*Fd.* 226/4, 21 Apr. 1607), Cusago (*Fd.* 233 bis, 20 Oct. 1610), Zorlesco (*Fd.* 657/1, 22 Nov. 1611), Riozzo (*Fd.* 482/5b, 13 Jan. 1616), Mirabello (*Fd.* 360/1, 20 May 1655), and Varano (*Fd.* 621/8, 29 July 1661). In a majority of cases, however, the feudal lord was but one (and not necessarily the largest) among several landowners. In no case did ownership of land depend on feudal investiture.

47. See Magni, *Il tramonto*, pp. 105-173, for a detailed discussion of feudal rights and perquisites. While the levies on meat, wine, and grain (*regalie ordinarie*) were normally part of a feudal investiture, the salt tax and the excise (*dazio della mercanzia*) never were, for they were regarded as the sovereign's prerogatives. Nor could a feudal lord raise additional taxes or duties besides those specifically indicated in his grant. I have found only one instance in which a lord was apparently entitled to tributes other than *regalie ordinarie:* in Caravaggio (*Fd.* 144/3, 30 Aug. 1698) he was entitled to an "annual recognition" of L.120 "for his sword and dagger," as well as to "donations in the event of the birth of a son and the wedding of a daughter." As for compulsory labor services, I have found no mention of them except in the case of Mariano (*Fd.* 338, 6 Feb. 1651) where the villagers were expected to dredge the moat around the lord's residence once a year. Another case is less clear: in Ierago (*Fd.* 244/2, 5 Oct. 1637) a tenant testified that "we owe nothing to our lord and yet we render him services such as carting and make him small gifts of eggs and chickens." But he added: "The lord, too, renders occasional services to our community, particularly in the matter of military billets."

48. Vacant fiefs were "sold at auction in the Piazza dei Mercanti" (Benaglio, *Relazione istorica*, p. 157). Bids had to be based on an official tariff

reflecting the number of hearths and the capitalized value of feudal revenue, if any. See Magni, *Il tramonto*, p. 128.

49. On the other hand, it was pointed out that "to the Treasury it is more advantageous to enfeoff than to grant redemption, both because (in the latter case) there is no prospect of a later devolution to the Crown and because redemption nets one-third less in cash than a sale in fief" (*Fd.* 215/4, memorandum on Codogno, 1679). By law, a community that chose to redeem itself had to pay two-thirds of the price offered by a prospective buyer.

50. See Magni, *Il tramonto*, p. 93.

51. On the meaning of *merum ac mixtum imperium* see Myron P. Gilmore, *Argument from Roman Law in Political Thought, 1200-1600* (Cambridge, Mass.: Harvard University Press, 1941), pp. 20-25. I am indebted to Professor Richard A. Jackson for this reference.

52. What follows is based on Magni, *Il tramonto*, pp. 152-173. His detailed analysis of the subject is fully confirmed by two seventeenth-century memoranda, one in *Fd.* 1 ("Si desidera sapere") and another in *Fd.* 16/1 ("Avertimenti circa l'Auttorità de Feudatari").

53. Doria, *Uomini e terre*, part 3, ch. 3.

54. On the so-called imperial fiefs, see Magni, *Il tramonto*, pp. 174-183.

55. *Fd.* 505/6 (Rocca Grimalda), "Apprensione del feudo e beni del Conte Andrea Grimaldi," 1621.

56. ASM, *Uffici regii p.a.*, 658, 25 Aug. 1661.

57. *Fd.* 307/7 (Magenta), 11 Jan 1617: the enfeoffment to Marquess Cusani was said to have taken place "about thirty-five years ago."

58. *Fd.* 413/8 (Oleggio), report of 27 Jan. 1640; Fd. 437/3 (Paullo), 21 May 1608; 94/7 (Binasco), 8 Feb. 1632; 415/11 (Olevano Lomellina), 12 July 1677; 654/14 (Zelo Surigone), 7 Dec. 1681. To feudal lords the exercise of judicial functions and the upkeep of the local jail could represent a heavy burden which many of them tended to shun (Magni, *Il tramonto*, p. 173).

59. See notes 29, 31, 32, and 35 in this chapter for Bellagio, Oggiono, Castelrozzone, and Melzo. In ASM, *Comuni p. a.*, 38, report of 1 Oct. 1692, there is a statement to the effect that the lord of Inzago, Prince Trivulzio, had somehow managed to prevent royal magistrates "from harassing his subjects."

60. This point is vividly illustrated by the attempt made by a group of Milanese landowners to bring the village of Oggiono under the jurisdiction of the Milan royal courts in the 1650s. The incident is discussed in detail in my article "Le redenzioni dei feudi nello Stato di Milano a metà del secolo XVII," in *Fatti e idee di storia economica nei secoli XII-XX. Studi dedicati a Franco Borlandi* (Bologna: Il Mulino, 1976), p. 486.

61. An interesting parallel is provided by Burgundy, where the feudal lords "gave protection to their men" and were even "a rampart against the state and against the soldiery," according to Roland Mousnier, *Peasant Uprisings: Seventeenth-Century France, Russia and China* (New York-Evanston: Harper, 1970), p. 30.

62. ASM, *Uffici regii p. a.*, 658, 25 Aug. 1661.

63. *Fd.* 350/1 (Melzo), 22 Apr. 1690. Attached to this document is a list of "the houses found vacant in the course of a survey of all the hearths of Melzo," showing 46 vacant houses out of a total of 180. The petition for a return to feudal rule is in *Fd.* 350/5, "1702-1703. Atti . . . "

64. ASM, *Comuni p. a.*, 38, folder "Inzago," 29 Feb. 1692. Attached is a list of local notables who had peasant houses razed to make room for new mansions.

65. See Giuliano Procacci, *History of the Italian People* (New York-Evanston: Harper, 1970), p. 124; also Franco Arese and Gian Piero Bognetti, "Introduzione all'età patrizia," in *SdM*, 11: 22.

66. Here are some examples: L.72 per hearth and revenues capitalized at 2 percent in *Fd.* 582/3 (Spino), 18 Feb. 1632, 293/11 (Leggiuno) 3 Mar. 1642, 381/10 (Mirasole Novarese), 21 Dec. 1663; L.40 per hearth and revenues capitalized at 3 percent in *Fd.* 451 (Pizzighettone), 3 Apr. 1647 and 231/10 (Crespiatica), 25 Sep. 1652; L.55 per hearth and revenues capitalized at 3.5 percent in *Fd.* 458/1 (Pontecurone), 20 Dec. 1668.

67. Pierre Goubert, *Louis XIV et vingt millions de Français* (Paris: Fayard, 1966), p. 160, aptly characterizes the sales of letters of ennoblement in France as "speculation on bourgeois vanity."

68. In the absence of a complete roster of Lombard communities sold in fief, which would also indicate whether or not the price paid for each included the capitalized value of future tax revenue, a rough estimate of the proportion of feudal tenures carrying no revenue at all can be formed from a close analysis of Casanova, *Dizionario feudale.* In it I have counted 168 localities for which it is recorded whether or not the incumbent enjoyed feudal revenues (*rendite feudali*): of these as many as 107 (or 64 percent) are listed as being "without revenues"; they were purchased, in other words, for the sake of prestige with no expectation of income other than occasional judicial fines.

69. The tendency toward income equalization was reinforced by the imposition, in times of financial stringency, of extraordinary taxes on such fiefs as enjoyed a revenue. These taxes were known as *annate* and they were equal to a fief's annual revenue. In the course of the seventeenth century *annate* were levied roughly every ten years; the yield thereof declined from L.800,000 to L.400,000 in the course of the century, apparently as a result of both administrative inefficiency and of the increasing number of exemptions. See Pugliese, *Condizioni economiche*, pp. 221-225.

70. See Magni, *Il tramonto*, pp. 253, 255. Vianello, *Il Settecento*, p. 66, goes too far when he writes that by the eighteenth century Lombard feudalism "had been reduced to a merely honorific relic." Its fiscal aspect continued to be important until all revenues previously alienated to feudal lords had been fully recovered by the Treasury during the reign of Joseph II.

BIBLIOGRAPHY

CONTEMPORARY SOURCES (WORKS PUBLISHED IN THE SIXTEENTH TO EIGHTEENTH CENTURIES)

Alberi, Eugenio, ed. *Relazioni degli ambasciatori veneti al Senato*, 2nd ser. *Relazioni d'Italia*, vol. 5. Florence, 1841.

Annali della Fabbrica del Duomo di Milano dall'origine fino al presente pubblicati dalla sua Amministrazione. 6 vols. Milan, 1877-1885.

Barozzi, Nicolò, and Berchet, Guglielmo, eds. *Le Relazioni degli Stati europei lette al Senato dagli ambasciatori veneziani nel secolo decimosettimo*, 1st ser. *Spagna*, vol. 1. Venice, 1856.

Benaglio, Giuseppe. *Relazione istorica del Magistrato delle Ducali Entrate Straordinarie nello Stato di Milano.* Milan, 1711.

Bonanome, Giovanni. *La Riviera del Lario descritta.* Como, 1668.

Botero, Giovanni. *Le Relationi universali.* Brescia, 1595.

————. *The Reason of State*, trans. P. J. Waley and D. P. Waley; and *The Greatness of Cities*, trans. Robert Peterson in 1606. In one volume. London: Routledge and Kegan Paul, 1956.

Boulainvilliers, Henri de. *Etat de la France: Extraits des mémoires dressés par les intendants du Royaume par ordre de Louis XIV.* 6 vols. London, 1737.

Bourdin, Charles. *Voyage d'Italie et de quelques endroits d'Allemagne fait ès années 1695 et 1696.* Paderborn, 1699.

Cavazzi della Somaglia, Carlo Girolamo. *Alleggiamento dello Stato di Milano.* Milan, 1653.

Coronelli, Vincenzo. *Città e fortezze dello Stato di Milano e confinanti.* Venice, 1683.

Coryate, Thomas. *Crudities.* 1611. Reprint. 2 vols. Glasgow: MacLehose, 1905.

Crespi Castoldi, Antonio. *La Storia di Busto Arsizio e le Relazioni.* Trans. and ed. L. Belotti. Busto Arsizio: Tipografia Orfanotrofio Civico, 1927.

Daverio, M. "Saggio storico sulle sete e setifici nello Stato di Milano," in *Economisti minori del Settecento lombardo*, ed. C. A. Vianello. Milan: Giuffrè, 1942.

Evelyn, John. *The Diary.* Ed. E. S. DeBeer. 2 vols. Oxford: Clarendon Press, 1955.

Galli, Demetrio. "Informazione della Città di Lodi compilata da Gian Francesco Medici e Defendente Lodi negli anni 1609, 1635 e 1647," *Archivio Storico di Lodi* (1943), pp. 58-91, and ibid. (1944), pp. 41-54.

Giampaolo, Leopoldo, ed. *La cronaca varesina di Giulio Tatto (1540-1620).* Varese: Società storica varesina, 1954.

Gridario dell'Eccellentissimo Signor Luigi de Benavides, Marchese di Caracena. Milan, n.d. (Caracena was governor from 1648 to 1656).

Gridario dell'Eccellentissimo Signor Conte di Fuensaldagna. Milan, n.d. (Fuensaldagna was governor from 1656 to 1660).

Gridario dell'Eccellentissimo Signor Don Luigi de Guzman Ponze de Leon. Milan, n.d. (Ponze de Leon was governor from 1662 to 1665).

Gridario dell'Eccellentissimo Signor Don Gaspar Tellez Giron Duca di Ossuna. Milan, n.d. (Ossuna was governor from 1670 to 1674.

Gridario dell'Eccellentissimo Signor Claudio Lamoraldo Principe di Ligne. Milan, n.d. (Ligne was governor from 1674 to 1678).

Gualdo Priorato, Galeazzo. *Relatione della Città e Stato di Milano.* Milan, 1675.

Hughes, Charles, ed. *Shakespeare's Europe: Unpublished Chapters of Fynes Moryson's Itinerary.* London: Sheratt and Hughes, 1903.

Johnsson, J. W. S., ed. *Storia della peste avvenuta nel borgo di Busto Arsizio nel 1630.* Copenhagen: Koppel, 1924.

Lalande, Joseph Jérôme. *Voyage d'un François en Italie fait dans les années 1765 et 1766.* 8 vols. Yverdon, 1769.

Lassels, Richard. *The Voyage of Italy or a Compleat Journey through Italy.* Paris, 1670.

Montaigne, Michel de. *Journal de voyage en Italie en 1580 et 1581.* Ed. M. Rat. Paris: Garnier, 1942.

Moryson, Fynes. *An Itinerary.* 4 vols. Glasgow: MacLehose, 1907-1908.

Noto, Antonio, ed. *Liber Datii Mercantie Communis Mediolani: Registro del secolo XV.* Milan: Università Bocconi, 1950.

Oppizzone, Ambrogio. *Informatione per modo di discorso in materia delle Equalanze Terrere, Provinciali et Generali.* Milan, 1643.

Paolini, Aldobrando G. B. *Della legittima libertà del commercio.* 2 vols. Florence, 1785.

Pavesi, Angelo. *Memorie per servire alla storia del commercio dello Stato di Milano e di quello della città e provincia di Como in particolare.* Como, 1778.

Reina, Carlo Giuseppe Maria. *Decrizione corografica e storica di Lombardia.* Milan, 1714.

Richard, Abbe Jerome. *Description historique et critique de l'Italie. Nouveaux Mémoires sur l'Etat actuel de son Gouvernement, des Sciences, des Arts, du Commerce, de la Population et de l'Histoire naturelle.* 2 vols. Dijon-Paris, 1766.

Ripamonti, Giuseppe. *Historiae patriae libri VIII.* Milan, 1641.

Rossi, Ottavio. *Le Memorie bresciane.* Brescia, 1616.

Salomoni, Angelo. *Memorie storico-diplomatiche degli Ambasciatori, Incaricati d'affari, Corrispondenti e Delegati che la Città di Milanò invio a diversi suoi Principi dal 1500 al 1796.* Milan, 1806.

Savary, Jacques. *Le Parfait Négociant.* Paris, 1675.

Savary des Bruslons, Jacques. *Dictionnaire Universel de Commerce.* 3 vols. Paris, 1723.

Scoto, Francesco. *Itinerario overo nova descrittione de viaggi principali d'Italia.* Venice, 1672 (1st Latin ed., 1600).

Sherley, Sir Thomas. "Discours of the Turkes." Ed. E. Denison Ross. *Camden Miscellany,* 16 (1936): 1-45.

Tabarrini, M. "Relazione inedita dello Stato di Milano di G. B. Guarini," *ASI,* 3rd ser., 5 (1867): 3-34.

Tarello, Camillo. *Ricordo d'Agricoltura.* Mantua, 1585.

Thomas, Williams. *The History of Italy.* Ed. G. B. Parks. Ithaca, N.Y.: Cornell University Press, 1963.

Torre, Carlo. *Ritratto di Milano.* Milan, 1674.

Tridi, Giovanni Maria. *Informatione del danno proceduto a Sua Maestà & alle Città dello Stato dall'imposizione dell'estimo della Mercantia & dall'accrescimento del terzo del Datio & dall'introduttione delli panni di lana & altre merci forastiere; Et all' incontro dell'utile che ne risulterebbe a levarli.* (No date or place of publication, but actually printed in 1641.)

Verri, Pietro. *Considerazioni sul commercio dello Stato di Milano.* Ed. C. A. Vianello. Milan: Università Bocconi, 1939.

———. *Memorie storiche sulla economia pubblica dello Stato di Milano* in *Scrittori classici italiani di economia politica: Parte moderna,* vol. 17. Milan, 1814.

Vianello, Carlo Antonio, ed. *Considerazioni sull'annona dello Stato di Milano nel XVIII secolo.* Milan: Giuffrè, 1940.

———. *Relazioni sull'industria, il commercio e l'agricoltura lombardi del '700.* Milan: Giuffrè, 1941.

Visconti, Filippo. "Commentarius de peste quae anno Domini MDCXXX Mediolani saevit," *ASI,* Appendix 1 (1842-43), pp. 486-514.

Young, Arthur. "Notes on the Agriculture of Lombardy," in his *Travels during the Years 1787, 1788, and 1789.* 2nd ed., 2: 145-301. London, 1794.

MODERN SOURCES

On Lombardy

Agnelli, Giuseppe. "Lodi e territorio nel Seicento," *ASL,* 3rd ser., 6 (1896): 81-137.

Aleati, Giuseppe. "Tre secoli all'interno di una *possessio* ecclesiastica (Portalbera sec. XVI-XVIII)," *Bollettino della Società Pavese di Storia Patria,* new ser., 2 (1948): 1-36.

————. *La popolazione di Pavia durante il dominio spagnolo*. Milan: Giuffrè, 1957.

————. "Una dinastia di magnati medievali: Gli Eustachi di Pavia," in *Storia dell'economia italiana* ed. C. M. Cipolla, pp. 313-323. Turin: Einaudi, 1959.

————, and Cipolla, Carlo M. "Il trend economico nello Stato di Milano durante i secoli XVI e XVII: Il caso di Pavia," *Bollettino della Società Pavese di Storia Patria*, 49-50 (1950): 1-16.

————, and Cipolla, Carlo M. "Contributo alla storia dei consumi e del costo della vita in Lombardia agli inizi dell'età moderna," in *Eventail de l'histoire vivante: Hommage à Lucien Febvre*, 2:317-341. Paris: Colin, 1953.

————, and Cipolla, Carlo M. "Aspetti e problemi dell'economia milanese e lombarda nei secoli XVI e XVII," in *SdM*, 11:377-399.

Arrigoni, Giuseppe. *Notizie storiche della Valsassina e delle terre limitrofe dalla più remota fino alla presente età*. Milan, 1840.

Barbieri, Gino. *Economia e politica nel Ducato di Milano, 1386-1535*. Milan: Vita e Pensiero, 1938.

Barili, Antonio. *Notizie storico-patrie di Casalmaggiore*. Parma, 1812.

Barni, Gianluigi. "Mutamenti di ideali sociali dal secolo XVI al secolo XVIII: Giuristi, nobiltà e mercatura," *Rivista internazionale di filosofia del diritto*, 34 (1957): 766-787.

Baroni, Costantino. "La maiolica antica a Lodi," *ASL*, 6th ser., 8 (1931): 443-462.

Basini, G. L., and Spaggiari, P. L. "Proprietà, redditi e spese del Collegio: Profilo storico," in *I quattro secoli del Collegio Borromeo di Pavia*, pp. 163-184. Milan: Alfieri e Lacroix, 1961.

Bendiscioli, Mario. "Politica, amministrazione e religione nell'età dei Borromei," in *SdM*, 10: 69-118.

Besta, Beatrice. "La popolazione di Milano nel periodo della dominazione spagnola," in *Proceedings of the International Congress for the Studies of Population (Rome, 1931)* 1:593-610. Rome: Istituto Poligrafico dello Stato, 1933.

Bognetti, Gian Piero. "La seta in Lombardia," *Problemi italiani*, 1 (1922): 22-48.

————, and Arese Lucini, Franco. "Introduzione all'età patrizia," in *SdM*, 11: 3-26.

Bondioli, Pio. *Origini dell'industria cotoniera a Busto Arsizio*. Varese: Tipografica Varese, 1936.

————. *Un'azienda cotoni a Busto Arsizio tra il Seicento e il Settecento*. Busto Arsizio: Almanacco per la Famiglia Bustocca, 1958.

Caizzi, Bruno. "La ville et la campagne dans le système fiscal de la Lombardie sous la domination espagnole," in *Eventail de l'histoire vivante: Hommage à Lucien Febvre*, 2: 363-369. Paris: Colin, 1953.

————. *Il Comasco sotto il dominio spagnolo: Saggio di storia economica e sociale.* Como: Centro Lariano per gli Studi economici, 1955.

————. "Economia e finanza a Vigevano nel Cinque e Seicento," *NRS,* 39 (1955): 357-376.

————. "I tempi della decadenza economica di Cremona," in *Studi in onore di Armando Sapori,* pp. 1009-1019. Milan: Cisalpino, 1957.

————. "Le classi sociali nella vita milanese," in *SdM,* 11: 337-373.

————. *Industria, commercio e banca in Lombardia nel XVIII secolo.* Milan: Banca Commerciale Italiana, 1968.

Cantù, Cesare. *La Lombardia nel secolo XVII: Ragionamenti.* Milan, 1854.

Casanova, Enrico. *Dizionario feudale delle province componenti l'antico Stato di Milano all'epoca della cessazione del sistema feudale.* 2nd ed. Milan: Biblioteca Ambrosiana, 1930.

Catalano, Franco. "La fine del dominio spagnolo," in *SdM,* 11: 29-224.

Cattaneo, Carlo. *Notizie naturali e civili su la Lombardia.* Milan, 1844.

Chabod, Federico. *Lo Stato e la vita religiosa a Milano nell'epoca di Carlo V.* Turin: Einaudi, 1971 (revised edition of a work first published in 1934).

————. "L'età di Carlo V," in *SdM,* 9: 3-506.

Cherubini, Francesco. *Vocabolario milanese-italiano.* Milan, 1839.

Chittolini, Giorgio. "Borromeo: Filippo, Giovanni, Vitaliano," in *Dizionario Biografico degli Italiani,* vol. 13. Rome: Istituto dell'Enciclopedia Italiana, 1971.

————. "Infeudazioni e politica feudale nel ducato visconteo-sforzesco," *Quaderni storici,* 19 (1972): 57-130.

Cipolla, Carlo M. "Condizioni economiche e gruppi sociali a Pavia secondo un estimo del '500," *Rivista internazionale di scienze sociali,* 51 (1943): 264-287.

————. "Per la storia della popolazione lombarda nel secolo XVI," in *Studi in onore di Gino Luzzatto,* 2:144-155. Milan: Giuffrè, 1950.

————. "Ripartizione delle colture nel Pavese secondo le 'misure territoriali' della metà del '500," *Studi di economia e statistica dell'Università di Catania,* 1 (1950-51): 251-261.

————. *Mouvements monétaires dans l'Etat de Milan, 1580-1700.* Paris: Colin, 1952.

————. *Prezzi, salari e teoria dei salari in Lombardia alla fine del Cinquecento.* Rome: Edizioni di Storia e Letteratura, 1956.

————. "I precedenti economici," in *SdM,* 8: 337-385.

————. "Per la storia delle terre della 'bassa' lombarda," in *Studi in onore di Armando Sapori,* pp. 665-672. Milan: Cisalpino, 1957.

Coppola, Gauro. "L'agricoltura di alcune pievi della pianura irrigua milanese nei dati catastali della metà del secolo XVI," in *Contributi dell'Istituto di storia economica e sociale dell'Università Cattolica del S. Cuore,* 1 (1973): 185-286.

Cotta Morandini, Natale. *Il censimento milanese.* 3 vols. Milan, 1832.

Cova, Alberto. *Il Banco di S. Ambrogio nell'economia milanese dei secoli XVII e XVIII.* Milan: Giuffrè, 1972.

Dagradi, Piero. "Il complesso industriale Legnano-Busto Arsizio-Gallarate," in *Panorama storico dell'Alto Milanese,* 2:1-120. Busto-Gallarate-Legnano: Rotary Club, 1971.

De Maddalena, Aldo. *Prezzi e aspetti di mercato in Milano durante il secolo XVII.* Milan: Malfasi, 1949.

――――. "I bilanci dal 1600 al 1647 di un'azienda fondiaria lombardia: Testimonianza di una crisi economica," *Rivista internazionale di scienze economiche e commerciali,* 2 (1955): 1-45.

――――. "Contributo alla storia dell'agricoltura della bassa lombarda: Appunti sulla possessione di Belgiojoso (secoli XVI-XVIII)," *ASL,* 8th ser., 8 (1958): 162-193.

――――. "Formazione, impiego e rendimento della ricchezza nella Milano spagnola: Il caso di Gottardo Frisiani (1575-1608)," in *Studi in onore di Epicarmo Corbino,* pp. 149-182. Milan: Giuffrè, 1961.

――――. "Affaires et gens d'affaires lombards sur les foires de Bisenzone: L'exemple des Lucini (1579-1619)," *Annales E. S. C.,* 5 (1961): 939-990.

――――. "Malcostume e disordine amministrativo nello Stato di Milano alla fine del '500," *ASL,* 9th ser., 3 (1963): 261-272.

――――. "L'immobilizzazione della ricchezza nella Milano spagnola: Moventi, esperienze, interpretazioni," *Annali di storia economica e sociale,* 6 (1965): 1-34.

――――. "Excolere vitam per artes: Giovanni Antonio Orombelli mercante auroserico milanese del Cinquecento," *RSI,* 88 (1976): 10-39.

Doria, Giorgio. *Uomini e terre di un borgo collinare dal XVI al XVIII secolo.* Milan: Giuffrè, 1968.

Dowd, Douglas F. "The Economic Expansion of Lombardy, 1300-1500: A Study in Political Stimuli to Economic Change," *JEH,* 21 (1961): 143-160.

Fanfani, Amintore. "L'industria mineraria lombarda durante il dominio spagnolo," in *Saggi di storia economica italiana,* pp. 159-254. Milan: Vita e Pensiero, 1936.

Ferrario, Luigi. *Busto Arsizio: Notizie storico-statistiche.* Busto Arsizio, 1864.

Fondazione Italiana per la Storia Amministrativa. *Acta Italica. Stato di Milano.* Milan: Giuffrè, 1966.

Frattini, G. *Storia e statistica dell'industria manifatturiera in Lombardia.* Milan, 1856.

Frumento, Armando. *Imprese lombarde nella storia della siderurgia italiana.* 2 vols. Milan: Società Acciaierie Falck, 1958.

Gaibi, Agostino. "Le armi da fuoco," in *Storia di Brescia,* ed. G. Treccani degli Alfieri, 3:819-885. Brescia: Morcelliana, 1961.

Galantino, Francesco. *Storia di Soncino con documenti,* 3 vols. Milan, 1869.

Gargantini, G. *Cronologia di Milano.* Milan, 1874.

Gelli, Jacopo. *Gli archibugiari milanesi: Industria, commercio, uso delle armi da fuoco in Lombardia.* Milan: Hoepli, 1905.

Giulini, Alessandro. *Vicende feudali del Borgo di Parabiago.* Bari: Giornale Araldico, 1902.

Greenfield, Kent R. *Economics and Liberalism in the Risorgimento: A Study of Nationalism in Lombardy, 1814-1848.* Rev. ed. Baltimore: Johns Hopkins University Press, 1965.

Istruzione su le Misure e su i Pesi che si usano nel Regno d'Italia. 2nd. ed. Milan, 1806.

Jacini, Cesare. *Il viaggio del Po.* Vol. 5, pt. 2. Milan: Hoepli, 1950.

Jacopetti, Ircas. *Le finanze del Comune di Cremona durante la dominazione spagnola.* Vol. 14 of *Annali della Biblioteca Governativa e Libreria Civica di Cremona.* Cremona: Atheneum Cremonese, 1962.

Landini, Piero. *La Lomellina: Profilo geografico.* Rome: Signorelli, 1950.

Levi Pisetzky, Rosita. "Le nuove fogge e l'influsso della moda francese a Milano," in *SdM*, 11: 549-593.

Lodovici, Corrado. "Alessandria sotto la dominazione spagnola (1537-1707)," *Rivista di Storia, Arte, Archeologia per le Province di Alessandria e Asti,* 66-67 (1957-58): 5-140.

Magni, Cesare. *Il tramonto del feudo lombardo.* Milan: Giuffrè, 1937.

Meroni, Ugo. *Cremona fedelissima: Popolazione, industria, commercio, imposte camerali, commercio dei grani, moneta e prezzi a Cremona durante la dominazione spagnola.* Vol. 10 of *Annali della Biblioteca Governativa e Libreria Civica di Cremona.* Cremona: Atheneum Cremonese, 1957.

Meuvret, Jean. "Conjoncture et crise au XVIIe siècle: L'exemple des prix milanais," *Annales E. S. C.,* 8 (1953): 215-219.

Mezzanotte, Paolo. "L'architettura milanese dalla fine della Signoria sforzesca alla metà del Seicento," in *SdM*, 10: 561-645.

————. "L'architettura da F. M. Ricchino al Ruggeri," in *SdM*, 11: 441-478.

Mira, Giuseppe. "Provvedimenti viscontei e sforzeschi sull'arte della lana a Como, 1335-1535," *ASL*, 7th ser., 4 (1937): 345-402.

————. *Aspetti dell'economia comasca all'inizio dell'età moderna.* Como: Cavalleri, 1939.

————. *Vicende economiche di una famiglia italiana dal XIV al XVII secolo.* Milan: Vita e Pensiero, 1940.

————. *Le fiere lombarde nei secoli XIV-XVI: Prime indagini.* Como: Centro Lariano per gli Studi economici, 1955.

Morandi, Carlo. "La fine del dominio spagnolo in Lombardia e le premesse storiche delle riforme settecentesche," *ASI*, 94 (1936): 181-200.

Nicolini, Fausto. "La peste del 1629-1632," in *SdM*, 10: 499-560.

Novasconi, Armando, et al. *La ceramica lodigiana.* Lodi: Banca Mutua Popolare Agricola, 1964.

Olivero Colombo, Diana. "Mercanti e popolari nella Vigevano del primo Cinquecento (1536-1550)," *RSI*, 85 (1973): 114-166.

Olivieri, Dante. *Dizionario di toponomastica lombarda.* Milan: Ceschina, 1961.

Oltrona Visconti, Gian Domenico. "Il feudo e i feudatari di Gallarate," *Rassegna Gallaratese di Storia e d'Arte,* 11 (1952): 27-54.

Palestra, Ambrogio. *Storia di Abbiategrasso.* Milan: Banca Popolare, 1956.

Petronio, Ugo. *Il Senato di Milano: Istituzioni giuridiche ed esercizio del potere nel Ducato di Milano da Carlo V a Giuseppe II.* Milan: Giuffrè, 1972.

Politi, Giorgio. *Aristocrazia e potere politico nella Cremona di Filippo II.* Milan: SugarCo, 1976.

Pugliese, Salvatore. *Le condizioni economiche e finanziarie della Lombardia nella prima metà del secolo XVIII.* Turin: Bocca, 1924.

Reggiori, Ferdinando, "L'architettura militare durante il periodo dell'occupazione spagnola," in *SdM,* 10: 649-670.

Riva, Giuseppe. *L'arte del cappello e della berretta a Monza e a Milano nei secoli XVI-XVIIT: Contributo alla storia delle corporazioni artigiane.* Monza: Tipografia Sociale Monzese, 1909.

Romani, Mario. *L'agricoltura in Lombardia dal periodo delle riforme al 1859: Struttura, organizzazione sociale e tecnica.* Milan: Vita e Pensiero, 1957.

————. "I rendimenti dei terreni in Lombardia dal periodo delle riforme al 1859," in *Studi in onore di Amintore Fanfani,* 5 (1962): 549-572. Milan: Giuffrè, 1962.

Saba, Franco. "Una parrocchia milanese agli inizi del secolo XVII: S. Lorenzo maggiore. Materiali per una storia demografica," *NRS,* 59 (1975): 407-457.

Santoro, Caterina. *La Matricola dei Mercanti di lana sottile di Milano.* Milan: Giuffrè, 1940.

Sella, Domenico. "Premesse demografiche ai censimenti austriaci," in *SdM,* 12: 459-478.

————. *Salari e lavoro nell'edilizia lombarda durante il secolo XVII.* Pavia: Fusi, 1968.

————. "Au dossier des migrations montagnardes: L'exemple de la Lombardie au XVIIe siècle," in *Mélanges en l'honneur de Fernand Braudel,* 1: 547-554. Toulouse: Privat, 1973.

————. "Le redenzioni dei feudi nello Stato di Milano a metà del secolo XVII," in *Fatti e idee di storia economica nei secoli XII-XX. Studi dedicati a Franco Borlandi,* pp. 481-492. Bologna: Mulino, 1976.

Thomas, Bruno, and Gamber, Ortwin. "L'arte milanese dell'armatura," in *SdM,* 11: 699-829.

Toubert, Pierre. "Les statuts communaux et l'histoire des campagnes lombardes au XIVe siècle," *Mélanges d'archéologie et d'histoire de l'Ecole française de Rome,* 72 (1960): 397-508.

Verga, Ettore. "La Congregazione del Ducato e l'amministrazione dell'antica provincia di Milano (1561-1759)," *ASL,* 3rd ser., 8 (1895): 382-407.

———. "Le leggi suntuarie e la decadenza dell'industria tessile in Milano, 1565-1750," *ASL*, 3rd ser., 13 (1900): 49-116.

———. "Le corporazioni delle industrie tessili in Milano: Loro rapporti e conflitti nei secoli XVI e XVII," *ASL*, 3rd ser., 19 (1903): 64-125.

———. "Il Comune di Milano e l'arte della seta dal secolo XV al XVII," *Annuario storico-statistico del Comune di Milano* (1915), pp. vii-lix.

Vianello, Carlo Antonio. *Il Settecento milanese*. Milan: Baldini Castoldi, 1934.

Vigo, Giovanni. "Manovre monetarie e crisi economica nello Stato di Milano (1619-1622)," *Studi Storici*, 17 (1976): 101-126.

Visconti, Alessandro. *La pubblica amministrazione nello Stato milanese durante il predominio straniero (1541-1796)*. Rome: Athenaeum, 1913.

Vismara, Giulio. "Le istituzioni del patriziato," in *SdM*, 11: 226-286.

Welti, Ludwig. "Relazioni dei Conti di Hohemens con la città di Gallarate," *Rassegna gallaratese di storia e d'arte*, 27 (1968): 165-175.

Zanetti, Dante. *Problemi alimentari di una economia preindustriale. Cereali a Pavia dal 1398 al 1700*. Turin: Boringhieri, 1964.

———. *La demografia del patriziato milanese nei secoli XVII, XVIII, XIX: Con una appendice genealogica di Franco Arese Lucini*. Pavia: Università, 1972.

Zaninelli, Sergio. *Una grande azienda agricola della pianura irrigua lombarda nei secoli XVIII e XIX*. Milan: Giuffrè, 1964.

———. *Vita economica e sociale*. Vol. 3 of *Storia di Monza e della Brianza*, ed. A. Bosisio and G. Vismara. Milan: Polifilo, 1969.

Zanoli, Paola. "Il patrimonio della famiglia Litta sino alla fine del Settecento," *ASL*, 9th ser., 10 (1971-73): 284-346.

Zimolo, Giulio Cesare. "Canali e navigazione interna nell'età moderna," in *SdM*, 14: 833-864.

General

Abel, Wilhelm. *Crises agraires en Europe (XIIIe-XXe siècles)*. Trans. from 2nd German ed. Paris: Flammarion, 1973.

Anzilotti, Antonio. "Il tramonto dello Stato cittadino," *ASI*, 82 (1924): 72-105.

Aymard, Maurice. "Bilancio d'una lunga crisi finanziaria," *RSI*, 84 (1972): 988-1017.

Bairoch, Paul. "Agriculture and the Industrial Revolution, 1700-1914," in *FEHR*, 3: 452-506.

Barkhausen, Max. "Government Control and Free Enterprise in Western Germany and the Low Countries in the 18th Century," in *Essays in European Economic History, 1500-1800*, ed. P. Earle, pp. 212-273. Oxford: Clarendon Press, 1974.

Baron, Hans. "The Social Background of Political Liberty in the Early Italian

Renaissance," *Comparative Studies in Society and History*, 2 (1960): 440-451.

Basini, Gian Luigi. *L'uomo e il pane: Risorse, comsumi e carenze alimentari della popolazione modenese nel Cinque e Seicento*. Milan: Giuffrè, 1970.

————. *Sul mercato di Modena fra Cinque e Seicento: Prezzi e salari*. Milan: Giuffrè, 1974.

Bauer, Peter T., and Yamey, Basil S. *The Economics of Under-developed Countries*. 4th ed. Chicago: University of Chicago Press, 1963.

Beloch, Karl J. *Bevölkerungsgeschichte Italiens*. Vol. 3: *Die Bevölkerung der Republik Venedig, des Herzogtums Mailand, Piemonts, Genuas, Corsicas und Sardiniens*. Berlin: De Gruyter, 1961.

Besta, Enrico. *Le successioni nella storia del diritto italiano*. Padua: Cedam, 1935.

Blanchard, Raoul. *Les Alpes occidentales*. 5 vols. Grenoble: Arthaud, 1941-1952.

Borlandi, Franco. "Futainiers et futaines dans l'Italie du Moyen Age," in *Eventail de l'histoire vivante: Hommage à Lucien Febvre*, 2: 133-140. Paris: Colin, 1953.

Boserup, Ester. *The Conditions of Agricultural Growth: The Economics of Agrarian Change under Population Pressure*. Chicago: Aldine, 1965.

Braudel, Fernand. *The Mediterranean and the Mediterranean World in the Age of Philip II*. Trans. Sian Reynolds. 2 vols. New York: Harper, 1972-73.

————. *Capitalism and Material Life*. Trans. M. Kochan. London: Weidenfeld and Nicholson, 1973.

————. "L'Italia fuori d'Italia: Due secoli e tre Italie," in *Storia d'Italia*, 2: 2092-2248. Turin: Einaudi, 1974.

Braun, Rudolf. "The Rise of a Rural Class of Industrial Entrepreneurs," *Journal of World History*, 10 (1967): 551-556.

Bulferetti, Luigi. "L'oro, la terra e la società: Un'interpretazione del nostro Seicento," *ASL*, 8th ser., 4 (1953): 5-66.

————. "Il problema della decadenza italiana," in *Nuove questioni di storia moderna*, 2: 803-845. Milan: Marzorati, 1964.

Bullio, Pieraldo. "Problemi e geografia della risicoltura in Piemonte nei secoli XVII e XVIII," *Annali della Fondazione Luigi Einaudi*, 3 (1969): 37-93.

Bustico, G. "Sulla industria e il commercio del refe nella Riviera Benacense," *Commentari dell'Ateneo di Scienze, Lettere ed Arti in Brescia* (1913), pp. 81-90.

Cafagna, Luciano. "The Industrial Revolution in Italy, 1830-1914," in *FEHE*, 4 (pt. 1): 279-328.

Candeloro, Giorgio. *Storia dell'Italia moderna*. Vol. 1: *Le origini del Risorgimento*. Milan: Feltrinelli, 1956.

Cattini, Mario. "Produzione, autoconsumo e mercato dei grani a S. Felice sul Panaro, 1590-1637," *RSI*, 85 (1973): 698-753.

Cipolla, Carlo M. "Four Centuries of Italian Demographic Development," in *Population in History*, ed. D. V. Glass and D. E. C. Eversley, pp. 570-587. London: Arnold, 1965.

———. "The Economic Decline of Italy," in *Crisis and Change in the Venetian Economy in the 16th and 17th Centuries*, ed. Brian Pullan, pp. 127-145. London: Methuen, 1968.

———. *Cristofano and the Plague: A Study in the History of Public Health in the Age of Galileo*. London: Collins, 1973.

———, and Zanetti, Dante. "Peste et mortalité différentielle," *Annales de démographie historique* (1972), pp. 197-202.

Cole, Charles W. *Colbert and a Century of French Mercantilism*. 2 vols. New York: Columbia University Press, 1939.

Coleman, D. C. "Labour in the English Economy of the Seventeenth Century," *EcHR*, 2nd ser., 8 (1956): 280-295.

———. "An Innovation and Its Diffusion: The New Draperies," *EcHR*, 2nd ser., 22 (1969): 417-429.

Coniglio, Giuseppe. *Il Viceregno di Napoli nel secolo XVII. Notizie sulla vita commerciale e finanziaria secondo nuove ricerche negli archivi italiani e spagnoli*. Rome: Edizioni di storia e letteratura, 1955.

Coornaert, Emile. "Draperies rurales, draperies urbaines," *Revue Belge de Philologie et d'Histoire*, 28 (1950): 59-96.

Crossley, D. W. "The English Iron Industry, 1500-1650: The Problem of New Techniques," in *Schwerpunkte der Eisengewinnung und Eisenverarbeitung in Europa 1500-1650* ed. H. Kellenbenz, pp. 17-34. Cologne-Vienna: Boehlau, 1974.

Da Silva, José-Gentil. *Banque et crédit en Italie au XVIIe siècle*. 2 vols. Paris: Klincksieck, 1969.

———, and Romano, Ruggiero. "L'histoire des changes: Les foires de Bisenzone de 1600 à 1650," *Annales E. S. C.*, 17 (1962): 715-721.

Delumeau, Jean. *L'Italie de Botticelli à Bonaparte*. Paris: Colin, 1974.

De Maddalena, Aldo. "Il mondo rurale italiano nel Cinque e nel Seicento," *RSI*, 76 (1964): 349-426.

———. "Rural Europe, 1500-1700," in *FEHE*, 2: 273-353.

Deyon, Pierre. "Variations de la production textile aux XVIe et XVIIe siècles: Sources et premiers résultats," *Annales E. S. C.*, 18 (1963): 939-955.

——— and Lottin, Alain. "Evolution de la production textile à Lille aux XVIe et XVIIe siècles," *Revue du Nord*, 49 (1967): 23-28.

Duby, George. *Rural Economy and Country Life in the Medieval West*. Trans. Cynthia Postan. Columbia, S.C.: University of South Carolina Press, 1968.

Fanfani, Amintore. *Storia del lavoro in Italia dalla fine del secolo XV agli inizi del XVIII*. 2nd ed. Milan: Giuffrè, 1959.

Felloni, Giuseppe. *Gli investimenti finanziari genovesi in Europa tra il Seicento e la Restaurazione*. Milan: Giuffrè, 1971.

Gascon, Richard. *Grand commerce et vie urbaine au XVIe siècle: Lyon et ses marchands (1520-1580)*. 2 vols. Paris-The Hague: Mouton, 1971.

Gilmore, Myron P. *Argument from Roman Law in Political Thought, 1200-1600*. Cambridge, Mass.: Harvard University Press, 1941.

Giorgetti, Giorgio. *Contadini e proprietari nell'Italia moderna: Rapporti di produzione e contratti agrari dal secolo XVI a oggi*. Turin: Einaudi, 1974.

Goldthwaite, Richard A. *Private Wealth in Renaissance Florence: A Study of Four Families*. Princeton: Princeton University Press, 1968.

Goubert, Pierre. *Beauvais et le Beauvaisis de 1600 à 1730*. Paris: SEVPEN, 1960.

————. *Louis XIV et vingt millions de Français*. Paris: Fayard, 1966.

Habakkuk, H. J. "The English Land Market in the Eighteenth Century," in *Britain and the Netherlands*, ed. J. S. Bromley and E. H. Kossman, pp. 154-173. London: Chatto and Windus, 1960.

Heers, Jacques. "The 'Feudal' Economy and Capitalism: Words, Ideas, and Reality," *Journal of European Economic History*, 3 (Winter 1974): 609-653.

Helleiner, Karl F. "The Population of Europe from the Black Death to the Eve of the Vital Revolution," in *Cambridge Economic History of Europe*, vol. 4, ed. E. E. Rich and C. H. Wilson, pp. 1-95. Cambridge: Cambridge University Press, 1967.

Hexter, J. H. "The Myth of the Middle Class in Tudor England," in his *Reappraisals in History. New Views on History and Society in Early Modern Europe*, pp. 71-116. New York: Harper, 1961.

Hinton, R. W. K. *The Eastland Trade and the Commonwealth in the Seventeenth Century*. Cambridge: Cambridge University Press, 1959.

Hobsbawn, E. J. "The Crisis of the Seventeenth Century," in *Crisis in Europe, 1560-1660*, ed. T. Aston, pp. 5-58. London: Routledge and Kegan Paul, 1965.

Houston, J. M. *The Western Mediterranean World: An Introduction to its Regional Landscapes*. New York: Praeger, 1967.

Jacquart, Jean. "French Agriculture in the Seventeenth Century," in *Essays in European Economic History, 1500-1800*, ed. P. Earle, pp. 165-182. Oxford: Clarendon Press, 1974.

Jones, E. L. "Agricultural Origins of Industry," *Past and Present*, 40 (July 1968): 58-71.

Jones, Philip J. "Medieval Agrarian Society in Its Prime: Italy," in *Cambridge Economic History of Europe*, vol. 1, ed. M. M. Postan, pp. 340-431. Cambridge: Cambridge University Press, 1966.

Kamen, Henry. *The Iron Century: Social Change in Europe, 1550-1660*. New York-Washington: Praeger, 1972.

Kellenbenz, Hermann. "Industries rurales en Occident de la fin du Moyen Age au XVIIIe siècle," *Annales E. S. C.*, 18 (1963): 833-882.

————. "Technology in the Age of the Scientific Revolution, 1500-1700," in *FEHE*, 2: 177-272.

Koenigsberger, H. G. "Decadence or Shift? Changes in the Civilization of Italy and Europe in the 16th and 17th Centuries," *Transactions of the Royal Historical Society*, 10 (1960): 1-18.

Krantz, Frederick, and Hohenberg, Paul M., eds. *Failed Transitions to Modern Industrial Society: Renaissance Italy and Seventeenth-Century Holland.* Montreal: Interuniversity Center for European Studies, 1975.

Le Roy Ladurie, Emmanuel. *Le territoire de l'historien.* Paris: Gallimard, 1973.

Lombardini, Gabriele. *Pane e denaro a Bassano: Prezzi del grano e politica dell'approvvigionamento dei cereali tra il 1501 e il 1799.* Venice: Neri Pozza, 1963.

Luzzatto, Gino. "La decadenza di Venezia dopo le scoperte geografiche nella tradizione e nella realtà," *Archivio Veneto*, 54-55 (1954): 162-181.

———. *Storia economica dell'età moderna e contemporanea.* 2 vols. 4th ed. Padua: Cedam, 1955.

MacCaffrey, Wallace T. *Exeter 1540-1640: The Growth of an English Country Town.* Cambridge, Mass.: Harvard University Press, 1958.

Mazzaoui, Maureen F. "L'organizzazione delle industrie tessili nei secoli XIII e XIV: I cotonieri veronesi," *Studi storici veronesi Luigi Simeoni*, 18-19 (1968-69): 97-151.

———. "The Cotton Industry of Northern Italy in the Late Middle Ages, 1150-1450," *JEH*, 32 (1972): 262-286.

Mendels, Franklin F. "Proto-industrialization: The First Phase of the Industrialization Process," *JEH*, 32 (1972): 241-261.

Meuvret, Jean. "Demographic Crisis in France from the Sixteenth to the Eighteenth Century," in *Population in History*, ed. D. V. Glass and D. E. C. Eversley, pp. 507-522. London: Arnold, 1965.

———. "Les crises de subsistance et la démographie de la France d'Ancien Régime," in *Etudes d'histoire économique*, pp. 271-278. Paris: Colin, 1971.

Mols, Roger. "Population in Europe, 1500-1700," in *FEHE*, 2: 15-82.

Mousnier, Roland. *Peasant Uprisings: Seventeenth-Century France, Russia and China.* Trans. B. Pierce. New York-Evanston: Harper, 1970.

Nicolini, Fausto. *Aspetti della vita italo-spagnola nel Cinque e Seicento.* Naples: Guida, 1934.

Parker, Geoffrey. *The Army of Flanders and the Spanish Road, 1567-1659: The Logistics of Spanish Victory and Defeat in the Low Countries' War.* Cambridge: Cambridge University Press, 1972.

Piuz, Anne-Marie. *Recherches sur le commerce de Genève au XVIIe siècle.* Geneva: Jullien, 1964.

Poni, Carlo. "All'origine del sistema di fabbrica: tecnologia e organizzazione produttiva dei mulini da seta nell'Italia settentrionale (secoli XVII-XVIII)," *RSI*, 88 (1976): 444-497.

Postan, M. M. "Investment in Medieval Agriculture," *JEH*, 27 (1967): 576-587.

Priestley, Margaret. "Anglo-French Trade and the 'Unfavorable Balance' Controversy, 1660-1685," *EcHR*, 2nd ser., 4 (1951-52): 37-52.

Procacci, Giuliano. *History of the Italian People.* Trans. A. Paul. New York-Evanston: Harper, 1970.

Quazza, Guido. *La decadenza italiana nella storia europea: Saggi sul Sei-Settecento.* Turin: Einaudi, 1971.

Quazza, Romolo. *Preponderanza Spagnola (1559-1700).* 2nd ed. Milan: Vallardi, 1950.

Rapp, Richard T. "The Unmaking of the Mediterranean Trade Hegemony: International Trade Rivalry and the Commercial Revolution," *JEH*, 35 (1975): 499-525.

————. *Industry and Economic Decline in Seventeenth-Century Venice.* Cambridge, Mass.: Harvard University Press, 1976.

Romano, Ruggiero. "A Florence au XVIIe siecle: Industries textiles et conjoncture," *Annales E. S. C.*, 9 (1952): 508-511.

————. "Tra XVI e XVII secolo: Una crisi economica: 1619-1622," *RSI*, 74 (1962): 480-531.

————. "L'Italia nella crisi del secolo XVII," *Studi storici*, 9 (1968): 723-741.

————. "Una tipologia economica," in *Storia d'Italia*, 1:256-304. Turin: Einaudi, 1972.

————. "La storia economica: Dal secolo XIV al Settecento," in *Storia d'Italia*, 2: 1813-1933. Turin: Einaudi, 1974.

Romano, Salvatore F. *Le classi sociali in Italia dal Medioevo all'età contemporanea.* Turin: Einaudi, 1965.

Sapori, Armando. "I mutui dei mercanti fiorentini del Trecento e l'incremento della proprietà fondiaria," in *Studi di storia economica.* 2nd ed., pp. 43-73. Florence: Sansoni, 1946.

Sella, Domenico. *Commerci e industrie a Venezia nel secolo XVII.* Venice-Rome: Istituto per la collaborazione culturale, 1961.

————. "Contributo alla storia delle fonti di energia: I filatoi idraulici nella Valle Padana durante il secolo XVII," in *Studi in onore di Amintore Fanfani*, 5:621-631. Milan: Giuffrè, 1962.

————. "The Rise and Fall of the Venetian Woollen Industry," in *Crisis and Change in the Venetian Economy in the 16th and 17th Centuries*, ed. B. Pullan, pp. 106-126. London: Methuen, 1968.

————. "Industrial Production in Seventeenth-Century Italy: A Reappraisal," *Explorations in Entrepreneurial History*, new ser., 6 (1969): 235-253.

————. "The Iron Industry in Italy, 1500-1650," in *Schwerpunkte des Eisengewinnung und Eisenverarbeitung in Europa 1500-1650*, ed. H. Kellenbenz, pp. 91-105. Cologne-Vienna: Boehlau, 1974.

————. "European Industries, 1500-1700," in *FEHE*, 2: 354-426.

Sereni, Emilio. *Storia del paesaggio agrario italiano.* 3rd ed. Bari: Laterza, 1972.

Sivori, Gabriella. "Il tramonto dell'industria serica genovese," *RSI*, 84 (1972): 893-943.

Slicher van Bath, B. H. *The Agrarian History of Western Europe, A.D. 800-1850.* Tráns. O. Ordish. London: Arnold, 1963.

Smith, C. T. *An Historical Geography of Europe Before 1800.* New York: Praeger, 1967.

Supple, Barry E. *Commercial Crisis and Change in England, 1600-1642.* Cambridge: Cambridge University Press, 1959.

————. "Class and Social Tension: The Case of the Merchant," in *The English Revolution, 1600-1660,* ed. E. W. Ives, pp. 131-143. London: Arnold, 1968.

Trasselli, Carmelo. "Finanza genovese e pagamenti esteri (1629-1643)," *RSI,* 84 (1972): 978-987.

Tria, Luigi. *Il fedecommesso nella legislazione e nella dottrina dal secolo XVI ai nostri giorni.* Milan: Giuffrè, 1945.

Tucci, Ugo. "L'industria del ferro nel Settecento: La Val Trompia," in *Ricerche storiche ed economiche in memoria di Corrado Barbagallo,* 2:419-462. Naples: Edizioni Scientifiche Italiane, 1970.

Vigo, Giovanni. "Real Wages of the Working Class in Italy: Building Workers' Wages (14th to 18th Century)," *Journal of European Economic History,* 3 (1974): 378-399.

Villani, Pasquale. *Feudalità, riforme, capitalismo agrario.* Bari: Laterza, 1968.

————. "La società italiana nei secoli XVI e XVII: Studi recenti e orientamenti storiografici," *Ricerche storiche ed economiche in memoria di Corrado Barbagallo,* 1:251-291. Naples: Edizioni Scientifiche Italiane, 1970.

Villari, Rosario. "Il riformismo e l'evoluzione delle campagne italiane nel Settecento, attraverso studi recenti," *Studi Storici,* 5 (1964): 609-632.

————. *La rivolta antispagnola a Napoli: Le origini (1585-1647).* Bari: Laterza, 1967.

Wilson, Charles. "Cloth Production and International Competition in the Seventeenth Century," *EcHR,* 2nd ser., 13 (1960-61): 209-221.

————. "Taxation and the Decline of Empires, an Unfashionable Theme," in *Economic History and the Historian: Collected Essays,* pp. 114-127. New York: Praeger, 1969.

Zangheri, Renato. "Agricoltura e sviluppo del capitalismo: Problemi storiografici," *Studi Storici,* 9 (1968): 531-563.

INDEX